ONLY CONNECT

ONLY CONNECT

THE WAY TO SAVE OUR SCHOOLS

DR. RUDY CREW

WITH THOMAS DYJA

SARAH CRICHTON BOOKS · FARRAR, STRAUS AND GIROUX · NEW YORK

SARAH CRICHTON BOOKS
Farrar, Straus and Giroux
19 Union Square West, New York 10003

Distributed in Canada by Douglas & McIntyre Ltd.
Printed in the United States of America
First edition, 2007

Library of Congress Cataloging-in-Publication Data
Crew, Rudy.
    Only connect : the way to save our schools / by Rudy Crew.
      p.   cm.
    "Sarah Crichton Books."
    ISBN-13: 978-0-374-29401-4 (hardcover : alk. paper)
    ISBN-10: 0-374-29401-1 (hardcover: alk. paper)
    1. Public schools—United States.   2. School improvement programs—
United States.   3. School management and organization—United States.
4. Educational change—United States.   I. Title.

LA217.2.C747 2007
371.010973—dc22

                                                                2007008772

Designed by Gretchen Achilles

www.fsgbooks.com

10   9   8   7   6   5   4   3   2   1

TO MY DAD, EUGENE CREW

CONTENTS

ONLY CONNECT

WHERE WE ARE, AND WHERE WE HAVE TO GO

When I was young, my father used to give me a hard shake to wake me up. Then he'd stick his head right up next to my ear and say, "Rudy," in his deep voice. "Rudy, time to get up. Sun's coming up and something *good* is gonna happen today."

My father, Eugene, worked hard. My mother died when I was two, so he raised me and my two sisters on his own, paid the bills as a night watchman at the IBM plant in Poughkeepsie after years of playing jazz in New York City. He had a lot of reasons to stay in bed every morning, but for as long as I lived under his roof, he didn't just get himself up and out; he launched all of us out into the world full of expectations for ourselves and for the day.

Today I'm the superintendent of the Miami-Dade County public school system, the fourth largest in the country, with some 356,000 children in my care. Before that I was chancellor of the nation's largest school system, New York City, which enrolls more than 1.1 million kids. I've been superintendent or deputy superintendent in Tacoma, Sacramento, and Boston. One part of my job has been to help millions of children, parents, teachers, and principals all wake up and believe the same thing that my father used to tell me every morning—that something good was going to happen today, that some light would go on in a child's head that would let him see the way into the future and maybe even someday lead others there, too. For more than thirty years I've been doing that. But six years after the passage of the No Child Left Behind Act I'm faced with facts like these:

- One-third of American eighth graders cannot perform basic math. That means more than a million thirteen-year-olds can't do the simplest calculations needed to buy a candy bar or ride a bus.

- One-third of all teachers leave the profession in their first three years; by five years, half of them have left.

- A black child in Washington, D.C., has less than a 30 percent chance of learning how to read before he turns ten.

- The odds that *any* given ten-year-old in a large American city can read are about fifty-fifty, and six in ten for the nation as a whole.

- Only one in five students entering college are prepared for college-level work in math, reading, writing, and biology.

Besides running school systems, I've been a principal, a teacher, a father who put all four of his kids through public schools, and I even went to some of them myself back in the day. So let me tell you: if those statistics don't make you feel angry or ashamed or sad as an American, then at the very least they should make you scared because, beyond the disappointing things those numbers say about our national character and values, they put our future in peril.

For all the laws being passed and tests being handed out, America's public schools continue to struggle. Every year millions of teenagers graduate from high school with no tools, no skills, and no sense whatsoever of what they're going to do with their lives. That's easy to sniff at as if it were someone else's problem. But the fact is, those kids aren't just living in the nation's inner cities; they live in corn-fed towns in Iowa and under the shadows of the Rocky

Mountains, too. And what they're missing in their lives goes deeper than test scores.

The first question is, What will they do for a living? Unemployment for Americans between the ages of twenty and twenty-four runs around 8 percent; 16 percent for eighteen- and nineteen-year-olds. Our usual response to those numbers is a vague clamor for more jobs and better jobs and job training, and then some screaming about all the jobs outsourced to India and China. Well, in my experience American businesses *want* to hire American workers. The first meeting I went to as superintendent in Miami was with the Chamber of Commerce to discuss the fact that the city's business community wanted to hire more local workers. The problem was—and remains throughout America—that we're not providing enough workers with the skills to compete. Major companies look at our cities and ask whether the public school system can produce the quality of people they need to operate their machinery, program their computers, even simply answer their phones. Ken Chenault, CEO of American Express, and Richard Parsons, CEO of Time Warner, and countless other business leaders I've met have all told me that more and more the answer is no. The young people they're seeing out of American public schools are unable to perform even the most routine, elementary business functions. This, at a time when jobs that involve "complex interactions requiring a high level of judgment," according to *The Economist*, "make up some 40% of the American labour market and account for 70 percent of the jobs created since 1998." By not producing adequately skilled, adaptable workers, we're all but pointing businesses toward India and other nations where labor's cheaper and worker loyalty is easier to rely on. The research firm Gartner has calculated that information technology outsourcing will go from $193 billion in 2004 to $260 billion by the end of the decade.

Outsourcing is only the tip of the iceberg, though. The real problem lies under the surface, and it's big and dangerous. Not only are our children not able to keep up with the better-equipped competition coming from India and China, but if things don't change very soon, all these tens of millions of our sons and daughters will grow up to be adults unable to even *function* in our economy, let alone compete. As demand for unskilled labor continues to shrink and even the lowest-level jobs require skills beyond what most eighteen-year-olds graduate with, most of them will enter the labor market completely unprepared and essentially clueless as to how to interact with the marketplace. Who will hire them when they don't even know *how* to get a job? What will tens of millions of young adults barely able to read or multiply do with their lives? Who will pay for Social Security and health care? Even the military will be out of reach for them because they won't be able to pass the entrance exams. There'll be nothing left for them but to take their meaningless diplomas and plunge into the enormous gap that has opened in this country between those who have and those who don't. No matter where you're from—rural Appalachia, suburban Wellesley, or the Ninth Ward of New Orleans—a lack of skills is a tragic life sentence. For millions more, the issue is not that they can't get a job; it's that the connection between effort and earning is gone. They don't want the jobs that are available. I hear it all the time: Who wants to flip burgers or type letters for a few years? I oughta be rich right *now*!

Letting a generation slip through our fingers hurts more than just our economy. It cuts to the essence of who we are as a nation. Every so often Jay Leno on *The Tonight Show* takes a camera out to some mall and asks young people easy questions such as "What's the vice president's name?" "Who was the first president?" "What's the capital of the United States?" The joke, of course, is that no one knows the answers. Everybody in the studio laughs away, but if Leno asked the same questions in his own theater, chances are he wouldn't find answers there, either, because the truth is, the audience is laughing *with* them, not at them. I mean, who could be expected to know anything as obscure as the name of the first president, right?

Well, I've spent my life teaching America's children. My father was a World War II veteran. Dr. King and the Civil Rights martyrs gave their lives so we could all have our full share of America's promise. I am devoted to this country, and over the years I've sent too many of my students off in uniforms to Vietnam and the Middle East to find that kind of blithe ignorance funny. Why are politics in this nation so polarized right now? It's simple: a vast and growing segment of our electorate has no knowledge or interest in the history and workings of our nation. The few issues they care about they see in black and white. Nuanced thought, bridging gaps, creating consensus, finding equitable resolutions—those things are all but gone.

More than any other country, this nation depends on the thoughtful participation of its citizens. Sometimes I give speeches to newly sworn citizens in Miami, and when I see thousands of people ecstatic to be a part of this remarkable, albeit imperfect, nation, I still believe it can all work, but we need true citizens who comprehend the rights and responsibilities that title entails, who understand how they got here and why. That's a job for our schools, but right now our children don't learn the words of "The Star-Spangled Banner," let alone how a bill becomes a law.

Our schools aren't just struggling to teach academics and civics; they're also failing to produce young men and women of substance. And before you shrug your shoulders and say, "That's not a problem in my neighborhood, no gangstas in my gated community," you should know that in 2006 the Josephson Institute of Ethics reported that 60 percent of students surveyed said they had cheated on a test in the past year; 35 percent admitted to doing so at least twice. One-third had plagiarized from the Internet, and 62 percent said they had "lied to a teacher about something significant." Plagiarism and cheating, you see, are nothing but upper-class versions of Fast, Quick, and in a Hurry. I don't care where you are—some big-lawn suburb, Compton, or a small town in the Midwest—we're all doing a terrible job of teaching our children how to define their principles and live them out every day, how to define success in terms other than dollar signs.

When I was coming up, my father built in me a bone-deep sense that life owed you nothing. You had to work hard, and your effort would determine how far you'd go. Anything worth having was worth working for. I got all this early on, from selling bottles and scrap iron and cleaning yards, taking out big old heavy garbage cans. A lot of it I didn't even do for the money. Some of it I did because my father would drive by and see Miss McMurry's garbage, and he'd say, "You gotta go down the street to help Miss McMurry with her garbage every Monday . . ."

I'd think, *Am I Miss McMurry's son?*

". . . 'cause somebody got to do it. Lady was good to you, took care of you when you was a little boy, wiped your behind, cleaned your diapers, washed your clothes when I couldn't get to it. This is your payback. Pick this woman's stuff up. Father Time got hold ta her and she just can't do it. No tellin' when in this life you're gonna need help someday."

So I did it. It was just the right thing to do. I did it for the same reason my father would bring her bouquets of peonies from our yard, or go over and open her venetian blinds when she was bedridden, just so she could see the sun. It wasn't just about God liking you more. It was simply your job to be an ethical, honest person, work your ass off, do some good for somebody else, and be happy you got to do it.

By and large, our children have only the slightest grasp as to what constitutes ethical behavior. More and more of them believe that if they haven't made their bling-bling by a certain time, it's pretty much over, and who cares if they die. So die they do, horrible, tragic deaths caused first by their emptiness, then by drugs and bullets. And the folks who have theirs just keep walking.

It's no surprise that our children are so lost when their schools are starved for purpose. A classroom should be a place where we help children enter the world beyond themselves, where they build confidence, maximize effort, and are obligated to perform. But right now, instead of clarifying things for our kids, schools confuse them. Should they care about truly learning things, or is nailing the test the only point? Will any of it even matter in real life? Our classrooms are losing their pulse. Teaching and learning have become hollow, desperate acts punctuated by recess, lunch, and homecoming. That moment in the development of a child's mind when the challenge of the task goes head-to-head with the motivation to get it right, where a furrowed brow and shifting eyes mean *Be quiet! I'm gonna figure this out*, is disappearing. Parents and society keep hoping a patch here and there will hold things together until at least *our* kids are out of the system.

It's a dismal situation. Now add something else. The National Center for Education Statistics, or NCES, which is part of the Department of Education, reports that between 1993 and 2003 "the population growth rate for youth ages 5 to 19 was higher in the United States than in any other G8 country." That means we're in the midst of the greatest wave of immigration to the United States since the turn of the twentieth century. In those ten years 4.7 million more children entered the public school system. Sixty-four percent of those children, about 3 million, were Hispanic, while at the same time white enrollment dropped by 1.2 million. The Department of Education estimates that 200,000 more children, largely minority, will enter our public schools every year, and unless we want *MTV Cribs*, MySpace, and YouTube to be their primary instructors about life in America, we will need schools that accept the responsibility for bringing not just them but their families into our society. Millions of new Americans must understand that this nation is based on more than just buying and selling.

Don't get me wrong—I'm not anti-immigration. I believe this is a great opportunity for this country. Regular infusions of new energy, new ideas, and new dreams have let America grow and change and continue to lead throughout its history; immigration confirms that there's something universal about what our Constitution offers. But if we don't capitalize on the opportunity our public schools offer to manage this huge influx, if America walks away from its public schools because they're no longer full of white faces, then you can simply multiply all the problems I've laid out by a factor of five.

On those cold mornings way back when, what my father was really saying to me was, If you don't get up, if you don't expect anything out of this day, you gonna miss. I don't know what exactly. But you'll miss something *good*. So even on the coldest, snowiest mornings in Poughkeepsie, when I wasn't even sure the sun existed, I'd still get out of bed with a sense of anticipation. It wasn't Christmas—that was for sure—but maybe despite the snow and the cold, maybe my father was right. Maybe something good *was* out there today. And so every day I walked into school right on the edge of expectation.

I came to like that feeling of expecting something good. And I have that feeling now. I believe the crisis in American public education can be solved. But this book isn't about patching up public education. We're long past the point of plaster and paint. The global economy is reshaping the way we live; like it or not, it's our future. In our hearts we know we need a change in our educational system that goes deeper than new reading programs or smaller class sizes, but we can't imagine what that should look like or how it should work, and frankly, we're scared. How can schools connect us to our best selves as individuals, communities, and cultures so we can meet the future with strength and creativity?

We don't need reform; we need reenvisioning. *Only Connect* is about just that—preparing our educational system for the future, with a practical strategy that's already showing results. I believe the battle against ignorance and illiteracy and despair is eminently winnable. This nation does mighty things when it listens to its better angels.

So what have we, as a nation, done so far?

The No Child Left Behind Act was passed in 2001. It has made us focus on standards, which is good. And there have even been some improved scores. According to the Council of the Great City Schools, students in sixty-six major city school systems in thirty-eight states showed gains in fourth- and eighth-grade math and reading in 2005.

So No Child Left Behind is better than nothing. But "better than nothing" is saying a newspaper over your head is "better than nothing" when you're running through a hurricane. Here's a reality check. Here's where we stand internationally.

The Condition of Education 2006, a report published by the NCES, had our fourth graders scoring twelfth in the world in math skills, after such nations as Singapore, Latvia, and Hungary. Our eighth graders were fifteenth, below Malaysia and Slovakia. And by the time they reached tenth grade, they had slipped off the map—twenty-fourth place internationally. Our 2005 science scores, released by the National Assessment of Educational Progress (NAEP), were even more shocking. Just as an example, 78 percent of eighth graders in Los Angeles public schools have a "below basic" understanding of science.

The reality is that our "improving scores" are often watered-down. Since No Child Left Behind, or NCLB, is nothing but a patchwork of state standards, many states have begun to lower their standards to make it look as if they've actually succeeded at educating their children. As Diane Ravitch of the Brookings Institution wrote in *The New York Times*, "Basically, the states have embraced low standards and grade inflation." And the former education secretaries Bill Bennett and Rod Paige pointed out in a recent article in *The Washington Post* that "most states have deployed mediocre standards, and there's increasing evidence that some are playing games with their tests and accountability systems."

Something does look funny. Tennessee claims an 87 percent "proficient" level among its fourth graders; the NAEP puts the number closer to 27 percent. Idaho says 90 percent, but a federal test says 41 percent. New York boasts 85 percent; the national assessment is 36 percent. On and on it goes. Oklahoma's list of schools that "need improvement" shrank by 85 percent in a year. How? The state simply lowered its standards. Beyond whether or not the numbers are real is the question of what those numbers would actually prove even if they were. NCLB gave educators across America the task of creating numbers, not functional citizens.

The future will swallow us if we keep on with this game.

By this point in my career, I've heard just about every educational and business theory that you can find, but when I want to get things done, when I want to make a difference, I go back to what my father taught me, basic things about expectations and will and commitment, things that we all seemed to know once upon a time. Eugene Crew wasn't a wealthy, sophisticated man, or a man who spouted Bible verses. He had standards and believed in knowledge and in a future. He loved FDR and Paul Robeson, Marian Anderson and Adam Clayton Powell. He put his faith in hard work and social justice. His thinking is the kind we need right now in education—generous but exacting.

He had another ability, too—the ability to look at situations from many angles. When I was in high school, I struggled with both math and reading, but algebra was particularly hard for me, so my father picked up some extra jobs around the neighborhood. Every time he did that, went and cleaned the high school gyms on weekends or did some handyman work, I knew something was going to happen to me, and this time it turned out he was sending me to a tutor, a wonderful man named Mr. Bock. I would go to Mr. Bock's home, and we'd talk about algebra over a big piece of butcher paper. Every week I'd meet with him for an hour or two of fabulous one-on-one time, and little by little I felt more and more confident of my ability to tackle the math. Pretty soon I wanted to please him, show him I was getting algebra, and that made me push myself that much harder. My math teacher, Mrs. Fox, helped, too, by keeping me for a few minutes after class and giving me extra assignments. When my grade finally came, I'd turned an F into a B and I was on top of the world.

"So, son," my father said to me when he saw the grade, "what did you do to get the B?"

I said, "Well, I studied more, I did all the homework, took all of Mr. Bock's quizzes. I took all that extra time with Mrs. Fox, did the extra work she gave. You saw me do all this stuff, Pop."

"Yeah, yeah," he said. "And what did you learn?"

"I learned this equation and that equation and x plus y . . ." And on and on. I figured he wanted details.

"Right. But what *else* did you learn?"

By now I was lost. What exactly did he want from me? I'd gotten the gentleman's B. My father looked at me hard. "I'm glad you got all these equations now," he said, "but really what you got is, you got you a chance to get an A."

My father was all about fresh angles like that, and more than anything else, fresh angles are the purpose of *Only Connect*. I started thinking about this book by asking myself what exactly it would look like if we truly left no child behind. And behind *what*, exactly? Are the standards we have the *right* standards? Is leaving no one behind the same as helping everyone to fly as far and as high as they can? When I asked these questions, I meant them not in some pie-in-the-sky, philosophical way but in the context of the real world. I wanted to figure out, straight up, what every child would need to make it here while China and India ramp up their economies and our deficits balloon and good long-term employment gets harder to find. What do we need as a nation to move forward with any kind of confidence in our future? What would the students look like? What would the schools have to look like to make them? What would we need from the teachers and the parents and the community? Would mayors be in charge, turning the schools into virtual branches of the government? What roles would school boards play, and local businesses? How would we pay teachers and deal with unions? And what became immediately clear to me was that before we move any deeper into a century that poses opportunities and challenges and ways of doing business we never imagined ten years ago, let alone fifty, when most of our schools were built, we need to talk straight and unpack some of our basic assumptions about public education in America.

Let's start with some good news. Despite the persistent dumbing down of our culture, as a nation we do value education. You may not have liked your fourth-grade math teacher, but you can't show me one person who regrets learning how to read and write. We don't ask ourselves whether or not to educate our children or even whether or not we want public schools. Beyond any question of policy, people move to be near good schools; they change jobs and save and sacrifice so their children can attend them. Since the first common schools opened in the 1830s, America has shown that it understands education's value by making it free and universal.

And we do know *how* to educate kids. Every year children across America do indeed learn how to read and write and multiply and divide. Unfortunately, there are too few of them, and most of those live within a few particular social strata.

So what *exactly* are we talking about when we talk about education in America? Mostly navel-gazing and catfights, I'd say. We talk about the bits and pieces affecting our children at that moment: hypercompetitive high-stakes testing, SATs, coed versus single sex, whole language versus basal, bilingual, small schools and charters and vouchers, and on and on. The media covers "issues" such as: Do our children have too much homework? Are our children overscheduled? Is first grade too hard now? Of course these topics affect only a blessed fraction of the children in American schools, public and private, but they make for sexier news stories than the crumbling facilities and tragic dropout rates that affect millions more. Look at the supposed crisis over college admissions. Stanford received 14,522 applications in 2006—most of them from the same kids who applied to Harvard, Yale, and Princeton— and only around 10 percent were accepted. Meanwhile, there are more than sixteen million students attending postsecondary institutions across America. In 2006, 70 percent of college applications were accepted, which makes me ask: *What* crisis in college admissions? Yes, America loves to talk about education, but the one conversation it's loath to have, despite the enormous impact it has on *all* of us, is a national one about giving a quality public school education to *every single* child in America.

It seems obvious that the goal of American public education should be to deliver a quality education to every child in the nation. Not just an adequate one—a *quality* one. That's my goal when I walk into the office every morning. That's the goal of millions of parents who pay thousands of dollars in tuition to private schools, the goal of parents in Scarsdale and Mission Hills and Highland Park and Shaker Heights. It's what parents in Bed-Stuy and Watts and the West Side of Chicago dream of for their children. It should be the goal for all of America. After all, if we want a nation of quality, we have to equip our people with quality educations.

But listen closely to all the conversations we have about education, and you'll hear something else behind the chatter about test scores and homework, something we don't like to admit. Not so deep down, a lot of us are not interested in delivering quality education to all our fellow citizens. Yes, Americans do value education, but they value it for *their* child. *Your* child is another story. The underlying tone of every discussion on TV and in the schoolyard at pickup is that education is a matter of Us against Them. Define "Us" and "Them" however you like, but right now American education is not a cooperative venture or even a competitive one, with all the collegiality and rigor that word implies. It's out-and-out adversarial. We

define our children's educations not in terms of quality but in terms
of winners and losers and whatever it takes to get ours.

That's because knowledge is power. And increasingly, what
matters even more than our actual knowledge is where we got it.
Not so much *what* you learn but *where* you learn it has become the
object of education for many, twisting education from the process
of creating rounded humans into a set of assumptions and exclusive credentials that the owners wave around like any other brand
name. Or let me say it more clearly: My kid's diploma from a plush
suburban high school is more valuable because one from an inner-
city high school is worthless. Our charter school is better because
it doesn't take just anyone off the street. Your diploma from Yale is
worth more because of all the thousands who didn't get in and the
millions more who didn't even dream of applying.

Now, I have nothing against elite schools and private education. I went to Catholic schools for many years. I attended Babson
College and have lectured at Harvard, Columbia, and Stanford. By
no means am I looking to tear down or minimize success and hard
work. I want more of both. I admit and even support the idea that
enlightened self-interest is crucial to securing your children a good
education, but unfortunately too many of us have lost the "enlightened" part of that. Elite and exclusive schools are not the sum of
our educational system. If you find the value of your education is
in its exclusivity, if you tell me where you went before you tell me
what you learned, then you are missing the point. That attitude
and its effects have not just gutted public education; over time
they've made those who have been kept away from knowledge dis-
trustful of education.

We express this self-interested, fragmented vision in the way
we approach education on a national level. By making schools a local issue, with no direct accountability to the federal government,
we've made it impossible to have any sort of true national educational policy beyond cheerleading. Everything we do, we do piecemeal, but the crisis is national in scope and rooted in one inescapable

fact: We've never given *all* our schools the mandate and the resources to properly educate our children. Fifty-plus years of moral imperatives, constitutional and legislative mandates, *Brown v. Board of Education*, words like "fairness" and "justice"—all of these have failed to create an equitable educational system in America. While too many of us have been making sure our own kids get what they need, we've let the system as a whole collapse. It's time to confront the reality, an uncomfortable one for many, that if we don't provide equitable educational services to minority children in this country, we'll all be doomed.

Any vision of what our schools need to become so that children can succeed in the new economy must be based firmly on a foundation that affirms that we are once and for all sincere about giving *every* American child a quality education.

That's fine, you might say, but *your* kids are in a good school. Why should *you* worry?

Because no matter who you are—retiree, businessman, bodega owner, single mother, *Mayflower* descendant, salesman—you pay taxes not just to finance your child's access to public education, but so you can enjoy the benefits of living among an educated populace. Morality and justice aside, even if the only thing you care about is your own bank account, you should support an efficient, effective, and entirely equitable educational system in this country. An educated populace benefits you as creators, consumers, innovators, investors, and voters, and the success of others increases the opportunities for yourself and for your children. (Unless, of course, you're counting on sliding by with the minimum of work and relying on your class or color to get you through life, in which case you are deeply vested in the failure of others.)

For decades, widely accepted models created by economists such as Edward Denison, Robert Solow, and most recently Paul Romer— the sort of people we expect to care only about the bottom line—

have named education and knowledge as the prime drivers of economic growth. Nor is this just a matter of theory; the statistics bear it out. According to the Brookings Institution, since the end of World War II, American output has grown around 3.5 percent a year, productivity around 2.4 percent a year, and studies give education up to 30 percent of the credit among the reasons for this constant upward trend. More than half the worth of America's public companies, and some estimate the number to be as high as 70 percent, is made up of "intangible assets," which include not just knowledge but all that knowledge creates and all those who create it.

Turn on your computer, log on to the Internet, and you'll see what I'm talking about. Here in the first decade of a new century with an economy based on information, in the flat world Thomas L. Friedman talks about, it's become apparent that the old laws of supply and demand don't apply to knowledge in the same way they do to oil or air conditioners in the summer. Knowledge is not a finite resource, and scarcity economics don't apply to it. We have enough knowledge for everyone. It is both *what* we trade and *how* we trade. In the terms of economics, knowledge is a non-rival good; it can be infinitely reproduced, and the more of it the better. If I teach you how to do algebra, we won't have any less algebra in the world, whereas if I give you a banana to eat, we have to grow another banana. Yes, knowledge is indeed power, but the view of education as a self-serving enclave—a "good" one helps you, and others' not having one as "good" as yours helps you even more— runs tragically counter to the evidence because it defines "power" in the old sense of control and domination. For America to charge ahead, its excellence in the face of globalization depends entirely on as many of us as possible setting smart goals and reaching them, putting more knowledge into more hands of those who will then create more opportunities. In the twenty-first century we must define knowledge as "power" in the other sense of the word: as a limitless fuel for the economy and our society.

This means we are all vested, financially if not morally, in helping every one of our fellow citizens to operate at the highest possible level, and public education is the key to that. If the poverty, ignorance, and illiteracy that occur now don't hurt your soul, then they hurt your pocketbook in a million little ways in both the private and the public sectors, and, worst of all, they hurt you through the opportunities lost. Keeping any segment of the population undereducated through selfishness and racism not only creates those painful, frightening statistics that I opened the book with but also prevents a more general prosperity for all of us. What if we were able to reduce the billions we pay out in unemployment benefits? What if millions more Americans didn't need publicly funded housing? We can no longer look at public education as if it were a "black problem" or a "Hispanic problem." Distributing knowledge equitably and efficiently throughout all levels of American society isn't a "problem"; it's the solution to a challenge we all face together. We can only go as far as our slowest member. Offering a global-ready education to every American is the only way to reclaim our excellence.

Struggling school systems, then, are not an educational side issue; they are a primary economic one, with an impact on every aspect of American life. To guarantee the future of this country— economic, military, and otherwise—we need to push aside all the prejudice and shortsighted greed and decide at last that we are going to provide this service of a quality education to everyone. Stoking America's educational fire is how we will contend with the upheavals of globalization, the massive transitions in our economy, and these uncertain times.

It's a tall order.

But I believe Americans truly do want to do the right thing. The 2006 annual poll conducted by the Phi Beta Kappa Society and Gallup showed that support for public education continues to rise.

Americans are concerned about the achievement gap between white students and minorities; they understand the challenges posed by low funding, and they don't want their children's educations based solely on passing NCLB-mandated tests. We know in our guts what's right for our kids, and it's what I see when I imagine what schools will look like when we finally decide to leave no child behind: a nation full of schools pumping the endless resource of knowledge into our economy in the form of rounded, fully functional graduates. That's what leaving no child behind really means.

You're going to see the word "strategy" a lot in this book. My father was big on strategy. To him, everything was a question of strategy. He wanted me to go further in this world than he did, so he created a strategy. The first step was to send me to Blueberry Cove Camp, at the time the first interracial coed camp in Maine, where I saw things I hadn't dreamed existed. I swam and sailed and painted watercolors and found a peace and civility that made me understand that the world was very large and that I had a place in it. My father made sure I had a safe place to take risks, to learn independence, and eventually to believe that poor for now did not mean poor forever. "Think past the present task to the next one," he would say, "past the present day into the next week and past this phase of your life into adulthood." It wasn't a question of whether or not I'd get into college; the question was, *How* was I going to do it? If I needed 1100 on the SATs, then by God, that's what I would get. "Now, tell me, boy," he'd ask, "how many hours do we need to get to our books to do that? What books do we have to get?" It wasn't about wishing or dreaming or luck; it was about knowing your goals, knowing what you had to do to reach them, and then doing it. When you have a strategy, you're in control. You haven't surrendered to the chaos.

But strategies are complicated. They're not the same as plans. Plans are linear and causal, which is fine if you're taking a trip or making a piece of furniture. But when you're faced with a situation that demands success on many fronts simultaneously, then you need a strategy. Strategies take into account all the variables in a situation and admit that many things have to happen at once. Generals use strategies. Chess players use strategies. When you're merging your car into another lane on the highway, *you* use a strategy: You need to gauge where the cars are in front of you, behind you, and all the way along the side you're moving to. You need to adjust your speed to those constantly changing positions, and you need those other cars to maintain their speeds and positions, or else you need to readjust, and what if it's raining or nighttime? What you don't do is just turn the wheel and hope for the best.

That's what we've been doing so far on education—turning the wheel in one or another direction and waiting to see what happens. But there's no one single thing that will transform public schools in America. Money alone won't do it. Laws such as NCLB, smaller class sizes, greater parental involvement, even valuable innovations such as national standards—none of these in and of themselves will solve the problem. If we're serious about change, all of them—and more—have to happen, and all at the same time, because education is a sum of many parts all relating to each other simultaneously. Anything less than that is passing the buck.

Any new vision of public education has to scrape away the old arguments and paradigms and replace them with something flexible and adaptable that mirrors the fact that learning is a lifelong process. The act of accumulating information and synthesizing it into knowledge isn't restricted to a few hours in a classroom or the topics covered in textbooks—it's one of the essential actions of our lives. The job of educators is to insist on habits and to develop minds that will be able to perform that work for a lifetime. And yet educational policy in this country, especially in light of the test-crazy NCLB, forces most educators to waste the best hours of their day dealing with unnecessary politics and inadequate funding rather than concentrating on the true task of preparing our students.

We have to get smart about how we make people smart. And in order to free educators to do that fine work of producing thinking, functional people—the people who will be our bank tellers and English professors and electricians and ballet dancers and Internet entrepreneurs, the people who will make informed choices in the voting booth—we must, as individuals and as a society, view education in a new way: a three-dimensional way. We'll have to pick up a saying near and dear to environmental activists back in the 1970s, one that takes on a new meaning in a world tied together by fiber-optic cables and multinational corporations: "Think globally, act locally."

Schools must be the common garden where we grow our future. Let's begin by seeing our schools as places of connection. We must put schools squarely in the center of all the things that make up our communities—families, teachers, businesses, government, the arts, and faith and service organizations. Once we've done that, schools will no longer be perceived as a social program or form of charity. Rather, the relationship between schools and various community entities will be transformed into an agreement to produce children who can compete anywhere on the globe. Schools must be places where we all plug in our best inputs and demand outcomes for ourselves and our society, where we align our homes and our communities, where every child is one of *our* children.

That means opening up the parameters and purpose of "school," building a bigger, wider concept of just what "school" is. The fact is that while schools are without question the chief educators of our children, they're not the only ones responsible for that work; from now on, every part of the community must teach what it knows, in a manner that's integrated into our educational system. We need to envision a society where schools *direct* education as much as they provide it, where they serve for each student as a point of connection to the greater world, using their expertise in child development to orchestrate the whole host of educational experiences in the arts, business, service, and beyond that the community must present to that student.

What would that look like? Here's a taste: Let's give all our children serious academic work and show them how it matters in the world directly around them. Let's create programs that introduce children to the workplace, that teach them the dignity and honor that come with a productive day. And let's have those programs overseen by men and women in the business community who can share what they've learned with the next generation. Let's not just offer our children a host of ways within the school structure to lead, follow, and serve as athletes, debaters, and artists, in clubs and in student government, but let's tie them to activities and organizations in the wider community around them. Let's equip our children with the character to make good choices by teaching the qualities that create character.

Here's what "connection" and "global" do not mean: They do not mean the Internet in every classroom. They do not mean laptops for every child. In many communities the idea of the global classroom is a reflection of how much hardware and software your district has, when the real question is whether or not your kids experience contact with skill sets that will be demanded of them when they go out into the world. Focusing on computers alone is like spending all your time and money on buying shovels when your job is to build a skyscraper. Addressing that mismatch of perception and effort between the global economy and the American classroom is at the center of this book.

Building a connective tissue between home, school, and community will demand serious expectations and serious commitments, financial and otherwise. Across the board, from every ghetto P.S. Something to every leafy hilltop academy, deep work will have to happen. An equitable distribution of money, personnel, facilities, and programming is the foundation of any true and lasting change to American public schools, and the federal government's role should

be to guarantee that. Putting Jim Crow behind us by finally creating genuine, tangible equity will do more than create justice; it will
create efficiency in the system.

But this new kind of school won't magically appear because the
government writes checks. From Capitol Hill we look to homes
across America. There are some seventy-five million public school
parents in this country, and too many of them for too long have
had the news kept from them that the public school system is not a
welfare program. That, in fact, it belongs to them. Schools provide
a service, and their function is not to assimilate, channel, educate,
or determine the futures of their clients; their function is to provide
their clients with what they need to do those things for themselves.
Our parents and children are those clients, and they need to learn
that for their schools to work, they must demand performance
from teachers, principals, and all the way up the ladder. They must
demand better classrooms and schools. They must demand choices
between a range of viable opportunities, not a choice between what
they're handed or nothing. And in return they have to demand of
themselves, at school, at home, and in the community. Parents in
the best and brightest schools have figured out that formula of
give-and-take, of sacrifice and demand, and I don't begrudge them
that. But it's time to share that knowledge. We need to call out millions of Demand Parents, people who can shout for action and
check the homework, too. This book will show people how to become Demand Parents—involved parents equipped and motivated
to guide the progress of their own children's education. And for
those not yet ready to answer the call, we have to systematically
build bridges so we can meet them halfway and teach the have-nots
how to have, how to get what they need for their children, how to
participate in the first and most fundamental building block of
American culture, the classroom.

Nations such as India and China have taken to heart the fact
that education drives economies, and the enormous national com-

mitments they have made to fueling their economies through education have had a remarkable impact on not just their nations but ours as well. Instead of inducing panic, though, this should be a spur to action. We know how to do this work; we know how to teach children. The world may be flat, but that doesn't mean that we've been rolled over.

When I walk into my office in downtown Miami, when I visit classrooms in Liberty City and Coconut Grove and Palmetto, in Homestead and Little Havana, I see children and parents and teachers looking for something good today. And they're finding it. The Miami-Dade County public school system has been called a model for the state of Florida; I think it's on its way to being a model for the nation as a whole. The system *can* change, and without vouchers and charter schools. Our parents will tell you that.

So I'm asking you to shake your head clear of studies and surveys and assessments and all those numbers and theories that somehow never mention the look on your daughter's face when she finally understands how to do long division. Imagine with me what our schools could be if we thought less about rescuing them, about making them "good enough" to meet watered-down state regulations, and decided instead to reach for that A of delivering a quality education to all. If we revitalize our public schools, we will revitalize not just our economy but what it means to be American as we step further into a new and already very challenging century.

Something good *can* happen today.

WHAT EACH CHILD NEEDS

CHAPTER TWO

Every June I spend a fair amount of time handing out diplomas. I love graduations. They keep me honest. When I see an auditorium full of excited kids in their gowns, their families beaming, that day's as much a reward for me as it is for them. By now I've been to hundreds of graduations, but the one I remember most was at my first principalship, at Monroe Junior High School in Inglewood, California.

Monroe was a small school, around twelve hundred kids, mostly Hispanic and African-American, and graduation for the eighth graders going on to ninth was a *big* deal there. Leading up to the day, I put them all through practice after practice so they'd understand the decorum around the ceremony, and I especially worked with the boys on shaking my hand and looking me in the eye—things my father had drilled into me *very* early—before taking the diploma. That morning the gymnasium was packed—parents, grandparents, aunts, uncles; this was a truly formal occasion for them. Today this place was *church*. All the students were there on time, sitting in their best, whatever best meant for them—a skirt or a shirt and a tie. Whatever it was it seemed to say, *I know it ain't much, but it is 100 percent of what I got and it's here.* Come the ceremony, the children walked up to me one by one, looked me in the eye, shook my hand, and in front of their families took the diploma. That was it. No band or banners or "Pomp and Circumstance." No one got up and gave a funny or moving speech. But in all its simplicity and pride, that graduation was as important and regal an event as any I have ever experienced. I walked out of that school feeling I'd been treated to something as powerful as religion.

These days my work as superintendent has me going at all hours, on the phone, reviewing budgets, attending six-hour board meetings, preparing for six-hour board meetings, but when a young man who has struggled for his diploma shakes my hand with respect and confidence and gratitude, I'm reminded that all the policies and politics aren't the point—*he* is.

And so let's begin with a basic question: What exactly do our children need to become mature and conscious contributors to society? If communities, governments, businesses, and families decide to put their schools at the center of their shared life, what should they expect these schools to produce? Surely it's more than just young men and women with the ability to read and write, or do well on a test.

I first started thinking about this question during college, when I took a job coaching at a small school called the Meadowbrook School outside of Boston in Weston. This was during the early days of desegregation in the 1960s, and Meadowbrook was one of the private schools that received children from inner-city Boston as part of something called the Metco Program. Every day from my freshman year straight through to my senior year I went to this suburban private school and coached classes made up of mostly very affluent kids with a couple of Metco kids thrown in.

The kids from Metco were incredibly afraid and shy, and they locked their knowledge away behind that shyness. They didn't want anybody to know what they knew, and the teachers had trouble unlocking that shyness. Yet they weren't the real challenge. Your average Metco kids had seen a lot growing up in Roxbury and Dorchester, so they were quite adaptable; if you found areas where they could excel, be it sports or art or whatever, you could get a warming effect. The real work was with the kids from around Meadowbrook, who came fortified with all the baseline abilities and content you'd expect and who in many ways assumed that their job was just to help the poor little ghetto kids. They were academically smart, and when I say that, I don't mean that they were all little geniuses; I mean they knew a lot of things. They knew facts and had a vocabulary; they'd seen things, been to Disneyland. But as someone who'd grown up from Poughkeepsie to Harlem, I could also tell that in a cultural sense, they were completely unaware of their surroundings. It was as if they were the only people on the planet.

At the time I had a huge Afro, and one day I was sitting on the ground waiting for the kids to come out for their gym class when a fourth-grade girl I knew very well named Rachel came up behind me and put her hands in my hair and just ruffled my Afro all up.

Wow, I thought, *she just doesn't know that you do not come up to a brother and mess with his hair.*

As I took a deep breath, I had to decide whether to scold her or to teach her. I was close with Rachel and her family, and I knew she hadn't meant any harm. She was like most of the local kids at Meadowbrook; they weren't bad kids—they'd just been raised devoid of this content. Much more than they wanted to believe, they had a lot to learn. At that moment I understood that Rachel's education wasn't just about whether she could read and write. It was about whether she could understand her world, and that was a much bigger tablet of commandments than how smart you are and how strong your vocabulary is.

So I told her that her hair was really beautiful and when she came to school it looked really gorgeous and that when I come to work I try to get my hair to look as nice as she does when she comes and I really don't want somebody to mess it up. It's okay if *I* mess it up, but I really don't want anybody else to mess it up. Simple things, obvious to many, but certainly not to her, and she was happy to learn them. What I taught her that day was a kind of literacy, a sense of how to be in the world with people who don't look like you, whose hair doesn't feel like yours, or who have different understandings of things as simple as running your fingers through your friend's hair. As the single vision of America as a white European nation was melting away, I saw that there was no longer just one cultural standard, and efforts such as Metco would in the future have to have a broader purpose than simply teaching black kids how to "be smart," because it wasn't just the black kids who were lacking knowledge.

Everyone, I was learning, had these great gaps in their understanding of the world—grown-ups, too, including me. After I had graduated from Babson College and had begun my doctoral work, Rachel's father died. Her mother now needed to go to work, so she came to me and offered me a deal: while I was going to school and working in Boston, I could live at their place in return for watching her four kids. And so I became the night crew while she worked at Beth Israel Hospital in Brookline. I spent time with the kids, got them out in the morning, and became in effect their big brother while the mother kept an eye on me.

I moved in with my own preconceptions about what living in an affluent area would be like, but as I watched this family unfold, I saw my own family. I saw a family dealing with the loss of a parent. Well, *I* grew up without a parent, and that loss had figured into every day for us. I saw them having a struggle about money. Well, *I* grew up struggling for money. I saw them trying to make sense out of a life that had suddenly become complicated in all possible ways, and I finally admitted to myself that on a human level we all, every one of us, have some serious baggage to carry. Rachel and her family taught me that pain is pain, hurt is hurt, a death in your family is a death in your family. Inadequacy in some area is an inadequacy no matter who you are, and it really doesn't matter but that we're all in it.

A few years later I began teaching at the Alternative School in Pasadena, California. Alternative was not your average school, though schools like it were not uncommon then, in that the relationship between the teacher and the students in many respects really *was* the curriculum. You'd go horseback riding with the kids, paint with them, see them in all different contexts, and at the same time they got to know you outside the boundaries of the traditional student-teacher relationship. It also had the most diverse school clientele that I've ever seen in all my years in education, much more so than the forced tokenism of Boston busing. Children of wealthy banking families and professors at Cal Poly walked the halls with kids from the 'hood; every kind of human experience was poured into these kids and turned into the content they brought into the school, and seeing the kids from the different angles afforded by the school structure let me understand where the content was coming from. Again, just like at Meadowbrook, some kids came with a lot of content that the school recognized—things like the ability to play the piano or debating skills or creative writing—while others had content the school didn't recognize, like survival skills, social delicacy, machismo; but they all came in with content, an enormous range of capacities, abilities, and interests.

Right away it was clear to me that these young people weren't all that different from the Meadowbrook kids. Each was adequate in some areas and not adequate in others, and it really had nothing to do with how rich or poor they were financially. It was all about the wealth of their experience. Where had they lived? What had they seen, and how did they make sense of it? How did they interact with their peers and their teachers? How aware were they of the world beyond their own noses? Did their universe stop outside the playground or did it go to the moon? Did they take risks? Stand up for others? No one in either school *lacked* all the skills you needed to manage and grow, and certainly no one *had* all of them.

Nor were they skipping about in blissful ignorance as to what they were missing. In fact, the kids in both schools were struggling with their inadequacies. Sam, the smart kid who got a kick out of showing up everyone else, may have had good grades, but he was troubled emotionally, and getting regularly pounded on by his classmates, too. Ricky, the inner-city boy who walked through the halls like he owned them, was struggling to read and struggling even harder to hide the fact that he couldn't. They all had some parts of themselves that were absolute genius, but at that moment in their lives they were filled with more questions than answers. School was where they were learning how to articulate their questions, to pull together facts and information from other sources, and to piece together answers for themselves. Inside each child was a very complex matrix of qualities that made up his or her singular presence on earth. Some qualities, largely the academic ones, we closely tended and measured. Many others we didn't even count, but the children were working on those as much as if not more than the academic subjects. These, I realized, were just as important for their development into mature and conscious contributors to society, and if I didn't take these other areas into account, I wouldn't be able to form them academically. The purpose of schooling, it seems to me, is far more than the accumulation of knowledge—it's the mental exercise of learning how to adapt and grow.

As a teacher, though, I found it hard to explain what diamonds in the rough these children were. There was no place to tell anybody that they had these qualities here but not those other important ones over there, that they had some skills over here that we needed to bridge across to another place. So my report cards evolved from simple reports of academic progress into ways of looking at each child as through a kaleidoscope where he or she had many attributes and many needs. The gaps in the picture were where the home had to provide input, and if the child didn't have a home, then I quickly accepted that it was on my shoulders as the teacher to do it. Test scores lost some of their luster, in my eyes. While I didn't necessarily think they were a bad thing, I thought they were incomplete. As I got older, working in other dimensions of my professional career as a principal and superintendent, I started saying: Well, yeah, that's great, I want to know that test score, I want to know that performance stanine, but does the kid come to class? Is the kid asking questions? Are the kids ultimately trying? Are you seeing effort in that class? Do the parents call you? Do you call the parents? Do the kids have a dream in their heads?

Those remain the things I look for. The education of each individual child has much more to it than letters and numbers. Whether in private school or public school, whether rich or poor, whether born to a twisted life at the outset or living a life twisted by virtue of things that happen along the way, your child will be confronted with the need to have some qualities that people won't ever teach him or talk to him about, and if they do, it'll probably be after he's made a mistake. But given that the United States needs a population of thinking, functioning people to meet the challenges of a global economy, we can't leave this work up to chance. We need to prepare each child *now*. The outcome, the product we need our schools to produce are children who come out of our public school system with all the qualities they need to compete. And we'll have to reframe and redesign schooling to do that.

The four qualities of a mature and conscious contributor to society are

1. **Personal Integrity**

2. **Workplace Literacy**

3. **Civic Awareness**

4. **Academic Proficiency**

When we talk about education right now, we still concentrate on the last one, the academics, just as we did at Meadowbrook almost forty years ago, and consider the other three as somehow outside of the discussion. *That* is our central educational mistake. Mature, conscious people are more than just book smart, and success in the real world depends on qualities beyond grades, qualities Dick Murnane of the Harvard Graduate School of Education calls "soft skills." Schools should play just as important a role in teaching the first three qualities as they do in academics, but since all we pay for now are high test scores, all we care about and all we measure is how well schools are teaching academics. And then nothing seems to improve. We miss Personal Integrity and Civic Awareness in our schools, but we've stopped expecting our schools to teach them, and we certainly don't measure them, because we're not paying for them as an outcome. We must make the production of these four qualities in our children the basic point of our public schools and focus everything, from curriculum and facilities to teacher training, leadership, and financial support, on that.

Don't assume you'll find all four qualities in your child. If Tiffany hops into your Escalade for her ride to school and doesn't know how the electoral system works and Max believes he's entitled to all the wonders of the world without having to lift a finger, then they're both lacking qualities whose absence will leave them as profoundly damaged as any teenage gangbanger out of the barrio. Does your son say "please," look grown-ups in the eye? Has your daughter ever written a thank-you note without being threatened? The four qualities are neither conservative nor liberal; they're not a behavior modification program meant to keep children in check. These qualities are commonsense ways of seeing the world and connecting to it.

As they're taught together, they reinforce one another and create the functional base of the child. One quality can't be taught alone, just as you wouldn't go to a gym and lift weights to only make your arms bigger. Learning to say "please" and "thank you," basic aspects of Personal Integrity, are the foundation of more complex skills learned in the worlds of Civic Awareness and Workplace Literacy. Even though I'm treating one skill set at a time in this chapter, in practice and within the child they intertwine in count-less ways that together form the structure of a whole person. Children show whether or not they have them by what they say and do, so while they may have everything to do with how a child feels and thinks, those feelings and thoughts will manifest themselves in behaviors that schools can observe, monitor, and measure.

As you read this chapter, you'll surely recognize the qualities. You might even think they're obvious; of course a kid *should* do those things. But I'm telling you that there's a reason *why* they have to have them that far outstrips any *should*. Mature and conscious contributors to society—black, white, or brown, rich or poor—must be able to display certain personal and social behaviors, and not so they'll be "good people" or be able to scramble to the top. They need these qualities to survive today, and even more so in the future. This chapter is not a discussion of theoretical values or philosophies of life. It's a survival guide for your sons and daughters, a list of the minimum working tools they'll need in the global economy. If we let our children graduate without these skills, if we keep telling ourselves that it's not our jobs, that it's too hard, that it's not as important as how well they score on a test, what happens to our sons and daughters will be on our heads.

PERSONAL INTEGRITY

When my daughter Lauren was ten, she put on one of those "I Need to Have" campaigns for a pair of sneakers she'd seen in a Janet Jackson video. So I dragged her down to Payless, and "dragged" is the right word since we weren't headed in the direction of Foot Locker. Lots of shoes at Payless, none of them the ones she wanted. I was pretty worn down by then, so I did what we parents do more often than we should, which was take the path of least resistance. Off to Foot Locker. Lauren cheered up, and she all but hit the clouds when some salesgirl handed her the "right" pair of sneakers. Why those shoes cost $89.95 I still don't understand, but I do know that I had the same kind of sticker shock I had the day I—for the heck of it—checked out what a Porsche cost. Once I caught my breath, I asked her why it had to be *those* sneakers, and she said the phrase that's driven millions of parents insane: "Everybody has them." Well, at the time I was superintendent of schools in Sacramento. I was in schools constantly, and I knew for a fact that not "everybody" was walking around with those shoes on their feet, so I called her on it. "But, Daddy," she said, "if I don't have *those* sneakers, kids'll make fun of me, like I'm poor."

I had some work to do, and it had nothing to do with making money.

Our children know something's not right about how they see the world. A survey taken in 1997 showed that 81 percent of black, 79 percent of Hispanic, and 73 percent of white students in public schools said their fellow students paid "too much attention to what they are wearing and what they look like." Fifty percent said too many of their classmates were allowed to be late and duck their work. Sixty-five percent of high school students admitted they could do better in school if they tried. Only 13 percent said their classmates were "very respectful" of teachers. Children *want* deeper reasons in their lives, but they don't know how to find them. Labels like Eckō and iPod and Timberland and Nike are what children substitute for Personal Integrity.

But labels aren't what you need to work well in a team or create a new business or raise a family. You need Personal Integrity for those things. Personal Integrity is about feeling good in your own skin. It means that you have a moral center, that you know that right and wrong exist, and that you must have a sense of ethics even when you're alone. It means that you know there is value in who you are, and that you impart value to your name and your word through your actions. With that confidence in yourself, you're able to believe others are of value, too, and you demonstrate that attitude through your deportment. You make choices based on your own needs and goals, not your peers', and define success as much on the planning and hard work as on any rewards. Personal Integrity is what gets a person out of bed every morning, helps him do his job all day and then come home and sleep well at night.

Back in the 1980s this nation embraced a culture of greed and it hasn't let go. The American Dream is no longer a lifetime of hard work at something you enjoy. Now it's Hitting It Big—on Wall Street, with the lottery, in Hollywood, whatever. Whether it's suburban white folks trading their way to a mansion and a private jet or ghetto kids trying to dunk their way there, the message is the same: I deserve *mine*, and I shouldn't have to work for it. People feel that way, companies feel that way, the government feels that way. These days what we own is who we are, and most of America's creativity goes toward coming up with reasons to be unhappy with what you have.

When I walk through my schools, I can see how this is affecting our children. Fast, Quick, and in a Hurry has supplanted progress and growth, so concepts such as paying your dues and learning hard skills—things that actually *will* count when they enter the adult world—skip off students' backs as they forge ahead without the fuss and clutter of developing into stand-up people. Then there's Bling-Bling, which means I need money—not paper route money; we're talking substantial money—in my hands right now, without my having to do anything. I've heard this phrase coming out of the mouths of first graders. And then there's Drop It Like It's Hot, which includes everything from relationships to babies to schooling, anything whose value isn't immediately consumable.

The problem is that just being greedy doesn't make you rich. We're a greedier nation than we've ever been, and it's China that has $700 billion in the bank. The reality is that the same few folks just keep getting richer and richer and everybody else, no matter how big the dollar signs are in their dreams, keeps losing ground.

Fast, Quick, and in a Hurry and Drop It Like It's Hot are not good strategies for staying alive, let alone reaching success. Success in life, whether we're talking in the marketplace or in your home, demands the ability to take the necessary time, to make commitments, follow through, keep your word, and exercise self-control. And that's just to start.

Yes, we still teach those things, but now we teach them in Sunday school. It's time to make school the place where we instill Personal Integrity in our children, from the moment they walk in the door in preschool to the day they graduate. Schools and families and communities must work together to teach respect, responsibility, and self-worth. You can't make choices for yourself in this world without the internal foundation of Personal Integrity and the box of tools it gives you, tools that let you solve problems and bring ideas to life. Later we'll talk about how our new vision of schools makes Personal Integrity a part of every student's life, but let's start on a very practical level by measuring student behavior. And let's do it not so much to punish as to give feedback about how each child is developing as a person. These are learned behaviors, and a child's actions prove whether or not he has them. Count how often he hands in his assignments on time, assess whether he always does his best work, whether he plans his work and then follows through with it. Is she respectful to her teachers and her fellow students? Is she organized? All day, every day, in every classroom in America, every child manifests his or her executive function, discipline, and self-control. The best schools monitor these behaviors; *all* public schools should make them part of a child's assessment and ongoing portfolio, along with Workplace Literacy and Civic Awareness. Students' development in these qualities should be guided and applauded as much as their math skills.

Another obvious measure of Personal Integrity is manners and deportment. Shaking hands, politely addressing elders, saying "hello," "please," and "thank you," looking people in the eyes—these are the bare minimum of polite behavior, and they should be taught. If your children don't do these things, they will have great trouble entering adult society, and especially the world of work. Baruch College in New York has begun teaching etiquette and other social skills to students looking to go into business careers. I think it's a great idea, but it shouldn't wait until college, and it most definitely shouldn't be seen as only for those going into the business world. Everyone's life is full of transactions, and manners are the signals we send to others to show we are willing and able to interact.

Personal Integrity can manifest itself in profound and even moving ways. One summer day when I was a principal at Hawthorne High School south of Los Angeles, I remember walking the campus—and it was a big campus, about thirty-five acres—preparing for the new school year when I saw a young man pushing another kid in a wheelchair. My first impulse was that they were goofing around, but as I got closer, I could see that they both had pretty serious looks on their faces.

"Where are you going?" I asked them.

The boy pushing the wheelchair didn't have the look of a football star or class president. He was thin and nondescript. He introduced himself as Donald and said, "Well, I got my schedule in the mail. I'm a ninth grader and I don't know the campus very well, but I'm afraid I'll be lost the first day."

"Is your mom or dad or anybody from your family gonna be here?" I asked. He was already showing a lot of energy by coming out early and trying to figure things out. "I'd be happy to take your whole family around and just show you the whole campus."

Donald shook his head. "No, it really isn't just for me. I have my friend . . ." He pointed to the kid in the wheelchair. "I have my friend here and he doesn't know the campus, either, and you can see that he's gonna have a little harder time than I am getting around on the first day and neither one of us really wants to be late for class. We're really trying to make sure we go to college and we don't want to be late."

I said to him, "Well, now, how were you going to do this?"

Donald pulled a piece of paper out of his pocket and said, "Here's my schedule." Silently, the other kid gave me his. "And here's his schedule, so we're just walking around campus finding our rooms, where's first period, where's second period . . ."

They were worried. There were a lot of kids in the school and the hallways were tight, so navigating the wheelchair around this spot where we were standing would be tough. They were figuring out how they would make the most efficient use of their five-minute passing period when they got here.

Donald wasn't sitting there waiting for somebody to help him; he didn't even seem to consider it. He was doing a fabulous job of standing up for himself. But as much as he was taking care of his own needs and problem solving, he was taking care of his friend, who in this case was wheelchair-bound. And he was doing it with grace, energy, and, best of all, no idea that he was doing a service. It was just who he was.

I looked at this kid and thought, *You know, I hope you get to be president someday.*

I want you to be able to look at your children and admire them as much as I admired that boy.

CHILDREN SHOW THEY HAVE PERSONAL INTEGRITY BY

- *Shaking hands.* If upper-crust schools really have a secret handshake, it comes when your child interviews for nursery school. An admissions person will extend her hand to your child, and if your child shakes it without prompting, he's cleared a hurdle. It may seem silly and forced, but it's a significant, visible sign of confidence and self-awareness. A simple handshake is the first step toward recognizing a higher level of personhood.

- *Addressing adults in an appropriate manner,* using terms such as "Mr.," "Mrs.," "Ms.," "Dr.," "sir," and "ma'am."

- *Saying "please" and "thank you" and being generally polite.*

- *Admitting mistakes.* This doesn't mean guilt and self-punishment; it's about correcting problems without losing one's sense of intrinsic worth. And saying "my bad" isn't enough; "I'm sorry" matters more.

- *Accepting and fulfilling tasks and responsibilities.*

- *Setting goals and following through on them to the best of their ability.*

- *Taking risks by weighing consequences for themselves and others.*

- *Creating good moments by recognizing behaviors that are respectful of time and circumstances.*

- *Making independent choices.* A "choice" isn't a choice if it's simply copying what others are doing.

- *Delaying gratification.*

- *Exercising self-control both in public and at home.*

- *Giving someone else credit.*

- *Winning and losing with equal grace.*

WORKPLACE LITERACY

Once, while I was chancellor in New York, I was washing my hands in the bathroom at the main office of the Board of Ed in Brooklyn when a high school junior who was working there for work-study credits came in. We talked and he said that he liked it there so much that he was actually about to interview for a summer job. I wished him good luck, and we walked out of the men's room, at which point he stopped, tugged his shirt out of his pants, dropped his pants down a few inches from his waist, and headed for the elevator.

I called him over and pulled him back into the men's room.

"Why did you do that?" I asked. "You're about to go to an interview."

The shock on his face matched the shock on mine.

"I was trying to look right for the interview," he said. "What's wrong?"

Somehow this bright, motivated kid had made it to his junior year of high school without being taught what was appropriate for the situation he was going into. I quickly invited him into my office and handed him one of the extra ties I kept on hand for evening events.

"I can tell you what I'm about to say as a father or as the chancellor, but either way it's going to come out the same: Pull up those pants, tuck that shirt in, put on this tie, and don't ever let me see you sag your pants while working in this building again."

From that day forward, all student interns and work-study students were asked to wear a uniform while working in the downtown office.

It is unacceptable for students not to know the rules of work: that there is a time and a place for everything and that a work environment, interview, or formal setting requires different attire from a mall, a ball game, or just hanging out. It is more than counterproductive; it is *insidious* to let our children become young adults, train them to think they are competitive, to think they are prepared, and then set them up for the rude awakening that they didn't get the job they were after because someone who knew how to present himself better got it.

The global marketplace is just that—a common realm where people exchange not just money but themselves, and to function in it, you need to know the currency in use. Just as your dollar bill won't work in England and the pound isn't valuable here until it's exchanged for dollars, our children need to understand that they must work in the personal currency of where they want to work, until the day they control their own workplace. The same people who may bristle at the idea of my telling a young black man to clean up his look—to make it a little less "real"—so he can get an office job would laugh at a white kid going into the offices of FUBU in a blue suit, a button-down shirt, and a rep tie. And they'd be right. But both examples speak to the same point. The working world has always rewarded desire and adaptability, but as work more and more includes interaction and competition on scales ranging from global corporations to a one-woman Web site out of an attic, these qualities become mandatory. The education of our children must include providing them with knowledge of themselves in the form of Personal Integrity, knowledge of the world around them through Civic Awareness, and the language and mores of work through Workplace Literacy.

Workplace Literacy means understanding how the world of work and money operates, having a sense of where you want to go in the working world, and then exhibiting the behaviors that will take you there. Our children must have the confidence in themselves to find interests, set goals, and learn how to develop and exchange their personal currency in the marketplace under the rules of engagement that, like it or not, exist there, without feeling that they'll lose who they are. They need to know that work is noble, that there's a time and a place for everything, and that there are dues to be paid.

You can call P. Diddy a lot of things, and "capitalist" is one of them. For all the flash and noise he might make, he has to interact and use a skill set that's already ordained as the language of business entrepreneurs. Every day he has to come and bring it. He has to trade off of the honor and dignity and respect he gives other people. He's learned there's a process by which the rules of the road get applied, and he follows them. You may not like how he does it, but this isn't a question of style. This is a question of knowledge, and P. Diddy has that knowledge. So do Russell Simmons and

Jay-Z. These guys have crossed over from time and place being insignificant to time and place being *very* significant. Unfortunately, too many children do not live in environments where they're rewarded for knowing the right time and place to wear their pants off their rear and when to wear a shirt and tie; the time and place for street language versus office decorum; the time and place for rolling a walk down the street versus workplace deportment. They're just going to stay off in this little world over here, getting poorer and poorer, having babies who are then going to have babies who, like their parents, will not know time and place.

Schools have to break that cycle. Teaching children about time and place is as important as teaching them about math and science. And if we don't teach them that, we're consigning them to a permanent place in the underclass of society. Every day I see children who are academically bright enough to rock this world, but they're failing because they have no idea how to take what's in their talented brains and connect it to a world that's asking them to come in and speak the King's English, stand up tall, speak without garbling their mouths and slumping their shoulders. Instead, they're being pointed back out the door because no one has said to them, "Look, brother, I love you dearly, man, but you can't come in here and talk in an interview that way. You just can't." That's why I told that boy to pull up his pants. I loved him enough to have the conversation with him. I wasn't willing to exempt him. Maybe I hurt his feelings, but that was better than his job or his pocketbook being hurt twenty years down the road.

The opposite side of this coin is a sense of entitlement. Rising up the ladder is what America sells the world about itself, but when families get up to the higher rungs, that taste for hard work and personal drive can be replaced in later generations with the belief that all things shall be handed to them because it's their due. The effects can be disastrous. While I was principal of a court-adjudicated high school in San Antonio for kids going in and out of detention centers, I met the single most challenging student of my educational career. He was an African-American boy from a very wealthy area of San Antonio, very well dressed and handsome, and all I could think when I met him was, What problem could this kid possibly have? Well, I found out soon enough. His parents had given him everything he wanted, but he didn't have boundaries or the belief that anyone else on the planet matters. The world was his oyster, and he was the only piece of sand in it. The education he needed had nothing to do with academics; we worked, and I do mean worked, with him on fitting into normal group constructs. He had to learn manners and basic respect for others. He had to learn not to challenge and demean others because they didn't have as much as he had. This boy was completely unfit for adult life in a community, and it was because he had too much, because the future for him was nothing more than a constant procession of satisfied desires.

Workplace Literacy starts by helping young people see a place for themselves in the future. Just as you can't build a staircase into the sky and hope it hits something, so you need to craft life toward a future. I'm not talking about picking colleges in first grade. I mean discussing the future with children, asking them what kind of life they want to have and talking about what they'll have to do to reach it.

During high school in Poughkeepsie, I wanted some pocket money, so I went out and found a job in the mailroom of a men's clothing store called M. Schwartz & Co., where I boxed up other people's suits for shipping. One day the owner, a very stern guy named Mr. Morris, very well dressed, very soft-spoken, came up to me. He never had much to do with the kids who worked there, but that afternoon he rattled off a whole list of days that he'd need me to work. At the time I was on the football team, and so I mumbled that I had practice on such and such days at such and such times, trying to figure out how to explain to him in my own naive way that I might not be able to make it every time he wanted me there.

Finally he looked at me and said, "Rudy, I need you to understand this as an opportunity for you to make a contribution to our company, and you have to make a choice. I'll leave it to you as to what that choice will be."

Mr. Morris didn't give me any more than that—no pat on the back, no "let me help you make your decision about this." He just left me to my own devices.

Something about the conversation felt odd, so I repeated everything to my father. "Well, son," he said, "tell me about what you do at the job."

"I box up people's suits," I said, and I explained my handful of other duties.

"What are you learning?"

"Well, you know, I can fold a suit."

"Show me."

So I went in his closet and pulled out a suit, and I showed him how you fold it and how you tuck the sleeves in and all the other steps that went into folding a suit.

"Why do you do that?" he asked.

"So it doesn't wrinkle, and when the customer gets it . . ." And again, on and on. I went through the whole process of sending out a suit, how the machinery and system worked, when the busiest times of the year were—all this knowledge that, to be honest, I had never really considered knowledge, but as I said it all to him, I realized that I had been learning things about the business, not just boxing up suits.

He said, "Well, let me ask you a question. You gonna play football? I mean, for your *life*? Do you honestly think you got a chance for a scholarship or to play professional football? I know you like to play and everything, but, you know, is that gonna be the way you try to make your *living*?"

I said, "I don't think so, Pop."

"I'm gonna tell you this. Here's how I would approach it." My father seldom told me what to do, but that day he gave me a serious hint. "I would ask myself where I'm gonna get the real payday.

Where's my real payday here? Do you see yourself as a football player, or do you see yourself as wearing those suits? 'Cause the place where you see yourself, that's where you oughta be."

I sat with that for a while. For sure I wasn't Jim Brown or Gale Sayers; no scholarships were coming to this noseguard. So the question was, Where *did* I see myself? For the first time, I took all the random dreams and inclinations I'd ever had about what would happen down the line and began to press them together into some kind of coherent picture. I didn't decide my career path that day, but I did start to create a vision of who I was. In the end, I handed in my pads and went to work. As much as I loved playing ball, M. Schwartz & Co. was the right place to be.

Something else dawned on me while I was imagining my future: I realized that no one was ever going to walk up to me and hand me a million dollars. Unfortunately, our culture of effortless greed has convinced a huge number of our children to think that's more than a possibility, that it's a reasonable plan. I can't count the kids who've said to me, I'm just not gonna flip burgers or park cars or bag groceries. Well, all right, I say to them. I understand you don't want to live your whole life flipping burgers, but there is nobility in work, whatever that work is. And it's more noble than waiting for your welfare check. Flipping burgers or running deliveries is called paying dues. To suggest there are only certain lines of acceptable work hurts the American pocketbook and the American psyche.

Schools must provide the counterargument, and home and community must support the effort to teach Workplace Literacy the way my father did. Kids need someone like Mr. Morris, a guy to push them right to the edge and leave them no choice but the choice they make. A lot of us absolve our kids from those kinds of decisions, and we let them couch-potato their way through. If that meeting with Mr. Morris had happened today with *your* child, ask yourself what you would have done. "Poor Rudy, let me see what I can do." Does that sound familiar? "I'll call him. I'll see if we can work something out. He doesn't understand how important football is to you." As parents, we are instinctively inclined to clear the vines out of the path, but children greatly benefit from having to make cold, hard decisions about their own lives, decisions that they get to make on their own. That kind of situation only comes from exposure to work and the notion of work, something that our new vision of schools must integrate into their structure. By instructing students on the basics, such as finding a job and balancing a checkbook, as well as more advanced subjects, such as macroeconomics, our schools will produce people who are productive and savvy, men and women who can keep our economy and our culture healthy and vibrant.

YOUNG PEOPLE WITH WORKPLACE LITERACY SHOULD GRADUATE KNOWING

- *Basic financial realities and budgeting.* We tend not to share the financial details of our families with our children, but you'd be surprised how little they comprehend what things cost. They may know what a pair of shoes costs, or a video game, but ask your daughter what a one-bedroom rents for in your area, or how much a month's electricity costs.

- *How to balance a checkbook.*

- *How interest and credit work.* Young people are the largest abusers of credit, often digging themselves holes that they can't get out of. We should be the ones teaching responsible credit use to our children, not the credit card companies or, worse, the repo man or collection agent.

- *What to wear and how to conduct themselves in an interview.* The adequacies build on each other; the walls between them are low. These skills build off the kind kids learn earlier as Personal Integrity.

- *How to write a proper and effective letter and e-mail.*

- *What general area of study or employment they want to head toward.*

- *The fundamentals of how money works in our economy and government.*

CIVIC AWARENESS

Isolationist mind-sets, from madrassas in the Middle East to American exceptionalism, have put the entire planet at risk. They're both counterproductive and unrealistic in a flat world where television and the Internet bathe our children in news and music and fashion and God knows what else from every corner of the planet. The children who understand today that they are citizens of the world, that international networks of economics, politics, and culture affect every aspect of their lives, will be the people who thrive in the coming decades. They'll be the ones able to read global conditions, and then prepare and profit. As soon as possible, our children must grasp that they are part of larger communities that involve various types of interactions and that their actions have an impact on others. If Personal Integrity is about our children feeling good in their own skin, Civic Awareness is about them finding roles for themselves in all the greater circles of community that surround them.

In order to make it in the global economy as mature and conscious contributors, children will have to become diplomats representing themselves, their communities, even their nation, and they must be taught with that in mind. When kids walk into kindergarten, they begin to make sense out of regular interaction with people who don't necessarily look like them, or have the same hair texture or voice or skin color. These are the first lessons in diplo-

macy. How children make sense out of and interpret each other's
actions may result in friendship, in further discussion, in a whole
host of things, but the health of our democracy depends on this
kind of interaction happening on larger and larger scales. To keep
us moving as a nation, our schools must bring the world into the
classroom in controlled ways that help children make sense of an
increasingly complicated planet and prepare them for interactions
that may take place across the street or across the globe. Acceptance and respect, the value of plurality—these, along with foreign
languages, geography, and familiarity with and interest in other
cultures, are the minimum equipment kids will need to survive.

This work is the province of social studies and, even more so,
the arts. In every community there's a cultural life made up of museums and music and festivals, and our young children should be in
the audience for all of them. While it's important for our children
to express themselves through the arts, as much if not more effort
must be put into their learning how to receive them. Learning how
to appreciate music, drama, dance, and the other arts means learning how to see the world through the eyes of others, whether that's
the girl sitting next to you or a fifteenth-century Florentine painter or
Louis Armstrong. The arts are how we speak to each other through
the ages and across borders. Through them we discover who we are
in the context of not just this moment but all the moments man has
known. In Miami we're planning a program wherein every child
will have gone to a museum or an opera or a theater before third
grade. Maybe some of them will see themselves up on that stage or
painting those paintings at some point later in their lives, but the
real thrust of the program is for them to participate in the building
of the cultural establishment of their own community. The benefits
of this go deep. As cultural literacy rises, society gets more just; a
2006 National Endowment for the Arts report showed that "half
of all performing arts attendees volunteer or do charity work."
Schools bear an incredible obligation to put people through a set of
experiences that chisel their characters out of the raw material God

stuck down on this planet. An awareness of the arts is one of the sharpest, finest tools we have.

Once they've begun to derive meaning out of all the raw color and noise and information around them, when they see how the world at large has an impact on their daily lives, then our children can in turn have an impact on the world, and by that I don't mean working for the UN. I'm thinking closer to home. We need our young people to participate in their communities, by both working through the systems that exist and, if necessary, fighting the powers that be. Institutions, like people, have a conscience, but like people, sometimes they get lazy, and every so often a new generation must reevaluate our ideas and sensibilities in relation to justice and the common good.

Who will do that work for us? In terms of the national community, I am continually shocked by how little most American children know about their own country, whether it's a failure to understand the three branches of the government or a complete lack of familiarity with basic historical facts. The development, design, building, and strengthening of the democracy are falling on the shoulders of fewer and fewer people. It is absurd that eighteen-year-olds, who can register to vote, serve on a jury, fight and die for this country, will graduate from high school without having to demonstrate their understanding of the Constitution. No matter where we stand politically, we must agree that Civic Awareness begins with our children knowing the common history and values that our Constitution stands for. Without political inculcation, our schools must teach the concepts this nation was built on and convey in clear and honest terms how we've succeeded and where we've failed.

If you want, you can take this knowledge and go march on Washington, which is fine by me because I came of age in the 1960s, but Civic Awareness in these terms isn't just a matter of protests and voting and political activism. It's about asking yourself every day if there's a way you can serve the people closest to you. Not long after I arrived at Hawthorne High, which was predominantly white, one of the other schools in the district closed, and most of its primarily Hispanic and black student body was now due to come to us that fall. For all kinds of reasons, both good and bad, many parents got worried, so I put together an outreach campaign for the incoming ninth-grade class. Guidance counselors and teachers would make home visits to eighth graders, visit the new students' old school, do registration there, and otherwise work to put a human face on both sides of the change.

As I was working on all this, I got a note in my office from a student named Kyra, requesting a meeting. Now, I was used to getting the occasional high five in the hallway, a nod or a sulk maybe when some cutup was sent to my office, but I was not accustomed to getting memos from my students, so this immediately caught my attention. We made an appointment, and in came this very outgoing, personable tenth grader.

"I think," she said, "that the students can do something to make these other kids feel welcome."

Until then, I thought I'd had the situation pretty well under control, but apparently not, so I asked her what she had in mind.

"I think we should host a barbecue and welcome those incoming ninth graders who weren't in our eighth-grade class. We have to do something."

Needless to say, I bought her suggestion. She organized the whole thing, and it went off perfectly. That fall the schools merged without incident. What was most remarkable about what Kyra did was that she wasn't in student government, she wasn't her class president or a debater or from any of the clubs that I'd have expected this idea to come from. She was just a kid who cared. When I asked her why this idea came to her, she said that when she was in ninth grade, she'd been scared, and she wanted to make things better for the new kids. It was that simple. A few years later a student at the school died and Kyra jumped in again, helping to create ways for all members of the school community to come together and deal with their grief.

If given an opportunity to lead, kids will lead. If given a chance to provide service, kids will provide service, and they'll be happy to do it. A 2006 study commissioned by the Carnegie Corporation of New York in five different states showed that a curriculum that integrated service into its academic program elevated not just the students' civic knowledge but their academic achievement as well. And the more engaged they felt they were in their service work and the longer they did it, the better their grades and what the study calls "prosocial behaviors"—what I would call the four qualities of a mature and conscious contributor to society. Kyra, my friend Donald, and the other kids whom I, as manager of a building, came to depend on as almost an extension of my own management team were surely mature and conscious contributors. They were thoughtful. They gave meaning and conscience to the institution; they made us think of things that we might not have thought of for ourselves. Kyra entered an unclaimed skill area and made herself an ambassador across racial lines. Even today, the students who have sat on our Miami school board continue to astound me with their insights and ethics.

Community service is a completely organic activity within the development of children—we need to give them ways to serve. What I have in mind here is not kids breaking their piggy banks for the penny harvest or running laps around the track to raise money for a cause. Those are certainly good actions; don't get me wrong. But let's not confuse philanthropy with service. Let's not put walking and chatting with our friends on the same plane as interacting with those who need our help. Buying a brightly colored rubber bracelet is not a bad thing, but it has required no draw from who you are. Service is something that molds character. It opens minds and hearts, neither of which is all that necessary for opening a wallet. "Caring-about is empty," writes the educator and philosopher

Nel Noddings, "if it does not culminate in caring relationships." The choices you make as an adult are yours, and donating money is almost always a good one, but as we raise our children, we should teach them how to give of themselves most of all. And as much as this goes toward those with deep pockets, those with less also have to remember that they, too, have things within themselves that we all need.

Beyond organized service in the school and community, students can provide perhaps their most important service through their innate ability to influence other students. Peer pressure is not necessarily a bad thing; we just don't harness it. As I've already made clear, I'm a stickler when it comes to personal appearance, and as the principal at Hawthorne High I insisted that all my students came to school dressed as if they were coming to school. No bedroom slippers, no curlers, none of that. I loved these kids, thought about them all day and night, and they knew I cared about them, but I was strict on this. So one day I was out in the halls during passing periods, and a girl was walking down a hallway, hair up in curlers. *Big* curlers.

Now, I did this quietly, but I pulled her off to the side and said, "Sweetie, where *are* you going in those?"

"All right, Dr. Crew," she said. "Well, you know we got a dance tonight and I'm not gonna be able to get home after school so I'm thinking I'm gonna put my hair up now and . . ."

"Honey, I understand you got a dance tonight, but the dance is *tonight*. Your hair's gonna have to come down, you're gonna have to go in the ladies' room and go comb your hair and go to class."

She didn't give me an inch. "I'm really gonna feel bad if I don't look right at the dance."

So I say, "But, sweetie, while you're worried about the dance being the arena where you have to worry about looking right, I'm worried about you in the hallway in the school in daylight with your hair in big curlers and bedroom shoes on. That's the place where you have to look right. You can look right at the dance tonight or not, as far as I'm concerned. That isn't really the issue. I presume you're gonna look fabulous at the dance."

Despite all I've said about Personal Integrity and the importance of knowing the right time and place for certain behaviors, this girl's appearance isn't the point of this story; it's what came next. One of her friends saw me having this conversation with her and came up to us. With enormous grace, which is really the word, she said to her, "You know, you are really such a beautiful girl but you don't look right out here and I'm your friend and I want you to know that Dr. Crew is right. Come on with me and we'll get you put together."

And they just left me standing there. It had taken me twenty minutes to try to coax her into doing what it took one of her peers three minutes to convince her was right. With respect to what they are learning in the day-to-day struggle to acquire maturity, youth can tutor youth.

CHILDREN DISPLAY THEIR CIVIC AWARENESS BY

- *Dressing appropriately for school.*

- *Understanding the basic tenets of American democracy and the structure of American government.*

- *Having some familiarity with—and opinions on—current affairs.*

- *Participating in the community.*

- *Participating in service activities and connecting them to someone else's benefit.*

- *Never engaging in bigoted behavior.*

In this nation we're free to pursue our happiness. It is not guaranteed. Happiness is something you work for by weaving your intrinsic character into the structure of society, and that weaving requires a range of knowledge that extends past the boundaries of the purely academic. It requires knowledge of yourself and the communities you belong to. It requires the ability to keep yourself and the world around you safe and healthy not just now but into the future, so that generations to come can pursue their happiness, too. The task of educators is not to create happy people—that's a fantasy. It's to raise the level of the four qualities of a mature and conscious contributor to society within all children to a place where they can go forth confidently into the world and pursue their happiness, each in his or her own way. It's what you want for your child, your grandchildren, the children of your friends. It's what we all want, so it's time we as a nation asked our schools to be organized around producing these four qualities. That will demand, though, schools, businesses, communities, and families working together to accept the challenge of producing young people well armed for their lives. It is a joint responsibility, not one we should expect our schools to shoulder on their own; elements of learning, and therefore schooling, must be reframed to fit into the global economy, and we must all participate in the effort. If we do that, India and China and a host of our other problems will take care of themselves.

As W. H. Auden once wrote, "America is what you do." It's in the doing that we'll find America again.

WHERE WE DO IT: THE CLASSROOM

The point of our schools, then, must be to produce young men and women with the four qualities of mature and conscious contributors to society: Personal Integrity, Workplace Literacy, Civic Awareness, and Academic Proficiency. It is not to produce test scores, make people happy, or advance political agendas. With that clearly stated, we can tackle how and where that work is done. If we were to look at the educational process in a cold, business sort of way, which is not always a bad thing, we would say that those young adults are the product, the outcome, of this new educational model we're putting in place.

The unit of production is the how and where a thing is made or a service performed: the pilot flying the 747; the writer composing a book; the farmer milking a cow; the team installing software at a GM plant. It's who is doing the work, how and where it's being done. In terms of education, the student-teacher relationship within the classroom is the unit of production. The classroom is the primary center where the four qualities are instilled.

Now, the classroom is a very scary place. When you visit on parent-teacher night, the crayon smell and piles of fresh drawing paper might stir up nostalgia, but there's a reason many of us still have nightmares about standing in front of the class in our underwear. Every day risks are taken here of a level that would put off mountain climbers. This is where your daughter has to publicly admit that she doesn't know certain things. It's where your son has to take enormous chances, in front of his friends and the class bully and the girl he has a crush on, in order to learn. If we had to go onto center court at halftime during a Miami Heat game and try to sink a three-pointer in front of twenty thousand people, most of us would be nervous, to say the very least. It's not a sure thing that you're going to make the basket; heck, it's not a sure thing that you're going to even hit the rim, and if you do indeed utterly fail and heave up an air ball, people will laugh. You might very well just run back to your seat and let someone else give it a try.

That's what performing in class feels like to millions of children, and what they do is exactly what you'd feel like doing: they hide; they simply never learn how to take the risks that are inherent in learning. That unit of production, that relationship between a teacher and a student, is predicated on building enough confidence in the child so he will take that risk to learn. Content and cognition come next, but confidence is the marker for me. If I can get a kid confident, I can teach that kid how to play the guitar. If I can get a kid confident, I can teach him to run track. If I can get an overweight child confident, I can get him to work out. But if I don't build that confidence, these children will remain exactly where they are—because the risk is *too* great.

Going to Blueberry Cove Camp had been such a life-changing experience for me that I wanted to share that. So when I was chancellor in New York, I worked with the American Camping Association to extend the school year for two or three weeks for ten thousand or so kids by sending them to some closed camps in the area. We hired teachers as counselors and trained them to work within a camp setting. It was a terrific program. One day a middle-grade boy in his bathing suit came up to me and grabbed my sleeve.

"Chancellor!" he said. "Chancellor! I can swim! Could you come watch me?"

How could I resist? We went down to the lake, which up near the shore had been cordoned off into three sections. The boy was fairly big for his age, a good five feet eight, and he led me to the intermediate section, where he tossed his towel on the side of the fence and then jumped in feetfirst. With the water up to about his waist, flailing his arms around, he walked to one end of the section and walked back.

Then he hopped out of the lake and wrapped his towel around his waist. I don't know if he even got his head wet, but he was glowing as if he'd just won a gold medal. "What do you think?" he asked me.

The one thing I did *not* want to do was break his confidence, but I had no clue what I'd just seen, and I was working hard to keep a straight face. "Son," I said, "now, I'm not sure I've ever seen . . . Can you tell me what stroke that is?"

He nodded eagerly. "It's the *pre*-swimmer's stroke. I'm not ready yet, but I'm *hopeful*."

If you taught your son how to swim by tossing him off the end of the dock, you probably wouldn't approve of this boy's gradual approach, but the odds of this boy's loving the water are a lot higher than your son's. This boy wasn't up for the risk yet, but he was close; he was making sense of the task. While I fairly doubt he's going to be swimming the English Channel, I'm sure that boy can swim now. Schools must be patient and safe environments where children get to try various ways to attack tough tasks. Kids might still laugh (people will always laugh), but the risk takers learn not to mind.

So how can we tell if that unit of production is functioning in a school? Is there a way beyond test scores to tell if children are truly risking and learning in a classroom?

At this point in my life, through all my different roles, I've been in more classrooms than I can count, and all the while I've kept my eyes open. For all the dozens of theories and programs and philosophies, many of which are complicated and brilliant, no matter where you are—in the Arctic Circle in Alaska; Milwaukee, Wisconsin; or Memphis, Tennessee—no matter what kinds of kids are being taught—public or private, kindergarten or AP French—or who the teacher is, I can tell you that every successful classroom has three things:

1. Caring

2. High expectations

3. Diverse approaches to learning and fidelity to those strategies

Simple stuff. Look at your own child's classroom. Scrape away all the talk, and you should see these three essential elements, just the way every good batter stays balanced, rotates his hips, and holds his hands back in the box. If caring, high expectations, and diverse approaches to learning are there, the unique relationship between student and teacher will be there and the classroom will work. As we go forward, the way our schools will instill the four qualities of a mature and conscious contributor to society in all children is by guaranteeing that the unit of production—the student-teacher relationship based on the three factors—exists in every one of our classrooms.

CARING

So there you are, on the three-point line at halftime, ball in your hand and twenty thousand Miami Heat fans waiting to see if you can hit a jumper.

What would make you willing to take that shot?

Some kind of reward would be good, a million dollars or a new car. You might heave it up just for the heck of it, just to see what would happen, but you'd be laughing even while you were doing it, so that really doesn't count as a shot.

But now let's say Shaquille O'Neal or Dwyane Wade spent some time with you in the gym that afternoon. And he told you that he really, actually believed that you could hit that thirty-footer as long as you listened and tried what he showed you. He *really* wanted you to hit that shot. It mattered to *him*, so he worked with you for hours, starting from a little five-footer and working all the way out, and then that night he went out there with you to the line, reminded you of what to do, gave you a pat on the rear, and handed you the ball. Whether the ball goes in or not doesn't matter as much as the fact that under those circumstances, you *would* try. You would take the risk because you had some small glimmer of confidence that came from the fact that *he* believed in you.

A teacher's job is not necessarily to build a child's love of, or acumen in, math or science or social studies. It's to get him or her confident enough to take the risk to go from one skill step to the next. Tiger Woods started off missing a lot of putts. And he was so devoted to his father because in the most intimate moments of his development, when he was taking risks, his father was there with him. When Tiger was afraid, when he hit a bad shot or blew a putt, his father was there. And instead of laughing or giving up, his father said, *Let's try it one more time.* He built Tiger's confidence within a safe place of development. Caring teachers make it possible for children to take risks. They create a protected zone amid all the hostility surrounding kids where they can develop on their own terms with constant feedback, encouragement, and adjustments. No matter what kind of school or learning situation, professional, conscious care on the part of the instructor will make smarter, better students who will be more willing to take risks the next day.

While I was at Hawthorne High in Los Angeles, I saw one of the most moving examples of what a caring teacher can do. A certain young man had a terrible attendance record; his older brother had dropped out just before graduation; his sister was pregnant; his mother was doing what she could with two jobs and an absent husband; and this boy, a senior, was in danger of just slipping away. So the special-ed teacher saw this and devoted herself to the cause of making sure the boy graduated. She didn't want to lower standards for him, which would, in effect, make his diploma little more than honorary, so she sat down with him, and together they created a document that listed everything he would say at his graduation, all his goals and everyone he wanted to thank, and then they framed it. Graduation was real to him now, not just a dream. Things were touch-and-go down to graduation day, but when I looked at the graduating list, this boy's name was there. When he came up to get his diploma, instead of heading straight to me, he stopped at the podium, pulled a piece of paper out from his cap, and read everything he'd listed on that original document. But for the caring of a single adult, that boy would have sunk under the waves.

"To care for another person," writes Milton Mayeroff, "in the most significant sense, is to help him grow and actualize himself."

This teacher performed some fine, fine work—day-to-day work—so that young man could go step-by-step to where he needed to go. But she was doing more than building confidence and skills; she was doing healing work, and that's another way that caring creates risk taking—it heals. In the early 1980s the philosopher and educator Nel Noddings developed a philosophy of caring that gave an otherwise vague concept true heft. She examined the interaction between the person being cared for and the person doing the caring, especially within the context of education. Her work has had a great influence by widening the role of the teacher from one who simply delivers facts to one who enters into a relationship with a child. That is the sort of relationship I believe every child needs in his or her schooling experience.

In hospitals, a recent study found, what keeps patients most hopeful is the regular presence of people who touched them, who extended caring moments to them, who talked with them and engaged them, who made them feel normal in spite of their illness. And the more normally patients are treated, the more they begin to feel better about their prospects of getting better. In other words, emotional and intellectual caring can be as healing as clinical care.

Now, around the time I read this study, I saw a survey that asked young people to describe their favorite teachers. The main reasons they gave for favoring one teacher over others were that the teacher knew their first names and at some point the students had felt they'd been the center of the teacher's attention. Somehow or other, the teacher had acknowledged their unique presence on the earth. Sometimes it had simply been that they'd been called on. And that helped them not just to feel good about themselves—it had helped them *learn*.

When I put these two ideas together in terms of the classroom, I could identify a caring classroom as a place where the people in it—and not just the teacher—see beyond your condition. They see you beyond your poverty or your wealth, beyond your clothing or color or the language you speak. They see you as normal, even though you sometimes—or all the time—feel completely abnormal, for whatever reasons. As Noddings puts it, "To the cared-for no act in his behalf is quite as important or influential as the attitude of the one-caring." The psychological value of caring is what makes results possible. Caring heals by making students feel normal.

Kids know when they're cared for—and they're dying to care for others. Once, while I was in New York, I visited a middle school in Brooklyn for a special morning assembly that included a breakfast the students had put together specially for the event. Now, in this school there was a young boy who everybody said looked just like me. He'd written me a letter and sent me a picture, and when one of my deputies introduced us, I had to admit the boy really did look like me. I gave him a big hug and told him as much, and he basked in all the attention.

As the assembly went on and the breakfast came closer, he began to watch me very carefully, almost as if he were concerned about something. Finally, during a break in the speeches, he scooted over to me. "Chancellor," he whispered in my ear, "I know you're a diabetic and we only have donuts and orange juice and bagels, so I found out what you could have and my mother made something special for you."

Where does a young child learn that kind of caring? At home, certainly, but creating the culture that results in such a caring child is also the teacher's job. The teacher does it not just in the way she interacts with the class as a whole but also, as that survey showed, by interacting with each individual child. And for that to happen, a teacher's colleagues and superiors must, in turn, treat her with the same kind of care she needs to give to her students. This is how caring goes from being more than a motto or a program to being an institutional culture. Being part of a caring school allowed that little boy to express his own caring and turn it into action.

It's always been hard for me to understand how schools can articulate a calling and then not live up to it. I once met with the principal of a school in the Bronx to discuss his students' declining scores. During the meeting he got up and pointed out a window at the nearby housing project. Before *that* went up, he said, this had been a good school. Now there were too many parents from the Dominican Republic who barely spoke English. They were illiterate. They came to school in bedroom slippers. How was he supposed to raise reading and math scores with people like that coming in the door?

I fired him on the spot. I did it because he lacked true care for the children and families in his school. He was unable to see the power that his words had in shaping their lives. They weren't "normal" to him; he had not met them as human beings, equal to him in value. If that principal didn't care about his students, his families, his faculty, and, essentially, himself, then *they* wouldn't care. I was paying him to care, and if he couldn't or didn't want to, then he was wasting taxpayer money.

Caring isn't always a soft skill. One way a teacher and classroom provide caring is through structure. How schools organize themselves says a lot to kids about whether they're cared about. If you roll out balls, say, "Do what you want," and then walk away, the message the kids get is that no one cares enough about them to even organize an activity. On the other hand, a structure so tight that it makes children feel as if they're on a conveyor belt will result in the same feelings. Structure does not necessarily equal caring, but by tuning out the static and letting the work of the adult-student relationship get done, it goes a long way toward making it happen.

So how do we insert caring into classrooms? Well, not with "projects," all tricked out with school assemblies and banners and mission statements. For many years I was involved with Eunice Kennedy Shriver and her organization Community of Caring, which helps schools build caring environments through a structural program. In short, school leadership instills caring as the norm by saying quite simply *this* is the way business is done around here by *everyone* involved in the system, whether you're the superintendent, the principal, or the janitor.

Everyone must care. Though much of the literature about the philosophy of caring makes it seem as if women have some sort of exclusive monopoly of it while men must develop the ability to care for others, I'm here to tell you that's flat wrong. The care my father gave me and my sisters was as complete and rich as could be imagined. And I've seen football coaches display more care for students than gooey-sweet first-grade teachers. So I expect care out of the school janitor and administrators in suits just as much as I expect it out of cuddly kindergarten teachers. Care is a human quality that each person manifests differently given who he is and who he's caring for. Playing gender politics about this basic human impulse solves nothing in the daily lives of our children.

At the core, we must drill into people's heads (in a caring way) that caring leads to development. Indeed, care is an end in itself in our lives. We should be caring people, and I'd like every child to leave school as a caring person. But if we've come to any crisis in caring, it's that we ask teachers to make a false choice between either being caring or getting their kids to score high enough on their tests. There's a kind of sad, utilitarian truth to that, but it reduces the possibilities of what education and a good teacher can do. Teachers shouldn't be choosing between those two things when in fact it's caring that makes real success possible. True care is where nurturance and cognitive instruction meet. "Caring relations," writes Noddings, "can prepare children for an initial receptivity to all sorts of experiences and subject matters." This initial opening, in turn, leads to a child who can then become engaged not just with other people but with ideas. A caring adult-student relationship, therefore, produces development in all four of the qualities of a mature and conscious contributor to society. Children learn and grow best when they believe their classroom is a place of healing and balance. Caring gets results.

HIGH EXPECTATIONS

I saw a little boy in New York one day wearing a shirt that said, "I'm an Underachiever and Proud of It."

Picturing that boy waking up one morning and picking *that* shirt out of his drawer literally hurts me. But children don't just come to that place on their own. More often, they have that attitude pressed upon them.

On the first day of third grade at St. Mary's in Poughkeepsie, Sister Mary Elizabeth had us draw a picture of what we'd done over summer vacation. That summer at Blueberry Cove I'd seen a place on the coast called the Spouting Horn, where the ocean comes crashing in between the rocks and creates an enormous spray that my mind could then only compare to a thousand cans of 7-Up all shaken and popped at the same time. The counselors had taken us there at night once to see the moon through the spray, and it had just blown my mind. It was "luminous," one of them told me. I remember wondering where in my neighborhood I'd use such a word, or if only white kids could use it. Well, I jumped on that assignment. I drew a picture of the Spouting Horn. I drew a picture of the rolling hills in Maine, the blueberry patches, a lobster boat, a mainsail and jib. I labeled each drawing. I worked hard and I was ready.

The next day Sister Mary Elizabeth walked up and down the rows, giving us kids a chance to explain what we had done and to show our work, and to each she'd say, "Great job," or "Oh, how interesting." And I'm sitting there, the only black kid in the room, just waiting for her to come by so I can describe the Spouting Horn and tell everyone what it's like to ride a horse bareback. When she finally got to me, the nun took one look at me, one look at my page full of drawings, and said, "Rudy, you have a wonderful imagination."

With that one sentence, she said to me in front of everyone the worst thing you can tell a poor child: "You can't." And at that moment she lost me. Sister Mary Elizabeth expected nothing of me. "You can't." Understand how long and lonely life is for a third grader when nothing is expected of him. How long the school day is, how enraged your heart can become. How mortified you are to have everyone around you convinced that you have nothing at all to contribute. How those words play over and over in your mind. "You can't." It was a very long time before I was found again by my father.

Expectations make or break a student's experience. They show love and faith and belief that a child can do great things; they are an expression of caring, and without them caring can become pity. High expectations are critical because they deal with one's self in the moment, and learning is all about being in a moment where the task is *yours*, the victory is *yours*, the feat is *yours*, the effort is *yours*. You have to *want* to be smarter. You have to *want* to get better, and as an aspect of the student-teacher relationship that belief is not just about the kid. It also has everything to do with the teacher, as an adult person in the child's life, believing that there's

something within that child that she wants him to go find and bring
back to the task at hand so together they can figure out how to
crack that nut. If you believe you can do something and the significant adults in your life believe you can do something, it strengthens your resolve to do it, and that's really what you want—a zone
where the kid and the teacher both have great resolve. I love it
when teachers say to me, "I wasn't able to get this kid this year, but
I'll get him next year." I love to watch teachers match wits with a
kid, allowing the kid to come close enough to winning to say, "I'll
get you next time." Because there *will* be a next time.

Creating expectations begins with creating excitement, and
great teachers convey a tremendous sense of passion for their work
without losing productivity. Younger teachers often have an easier
time with the excitement part than with the mechanics. Maybe the
best example I've ever seen of a teacher creating excitement and expectations was in Tacoma, while I was superintendent there. I
hadn't gone to the school to see this woman in particular, but as I
was walking past her room, I looked in the window and saw her
sitting in front of a couple of dozen first graders and putting on a
hand puppet. I like a good puppet show, so I went in and watched
as she addressed the kids on the rug.

"Boys and girls," she said, "today you are going to have the
most fun that you have ever had!"

This got their attention, to say the least.

She turned to the puppet, a tiger, who said, "What are we
gonna do?"

And she said, "Today we are going to learn to *read*."

Up went the puppet's hands. "Oh! I don't know how to read!
Is it going to be hard?"

The teacher shook her head. "Boys and girls, we are going to
have a day where even the *hard* things are gonna be easy."

For fifteen minutes she went on like this, and I couldn't leave
the room. In that little space with one hand puppet, she had created
a Zen moment for those kids, a football locker room where they all

sat amazed and excited and completely full of their ability to do this enormous, difficult, utterly life-changing thing.

When my father would wake me up in the morning, telling me that something good was going to happen, he was doing exactly the same thing as that teacher, but in his own way. Eugene Crew was not about hand puppets and smiles. When he told me to go for that A in algebra, he was setting expectations for me, this smallish, stoic man from Macon, Georgia, who never made it past grade school, who never took an algebra class himself, and he was not playing. He was telling me that my brain was untapped, my gas tank was nowheres near empty, and as long as he was gonna buff floors and clean bathrooms to help me out, I was gonna give him the Big One in return. Good enough was not enough.

At a certain point in life, hand puppets don't work for our kids. We have to say to them, all of them, whether they're working to eke out a diploma or coasting by on God-given talents, that good enough is *not* enough. You got a roof over your head, food on the table, love and forgiveness from your family. No, you don't have money. No, you don't have Nike swooshes on everything you wear. No, you don't have the latest car or anything, but you got *everything* it takes to get an A. You got everything it takes right here right now to get an A. If you *do* have all of those things, then what's your excuse? "You got a typewriter," my father would tell me, which was true. Somebody at IBM had given him one and the ribbon never worked, but I had one, and he created in me the wonderful sense that the power was inside me to do anything with it. If your light shines within, then it can shine outside just as well.

Making excuses for our children does them no good. Wrapped around the Civil Rights movement in the 1960s and '70s was a wider unhappiness with the "establishment," and our public schools got caught up in that. Though we broke down outmoded systems and opened up the windows, we unfortunately threw out more than we should have. In urban schools and large systems the sense emerged that we were asking too much of our students. We gave ourselves permission to give up on minority children and children with special needs by saying, in effect, "Oh, poor little black ghetto kid, *pobrecito*, we feel so guilty about what's happened that here's our form of reparations: We'll feel sorry for you. We'll dumb down the curriculum. We'll leave you alone. We won't demand you take your hat off when you walk into a room, or speak the King's English. We won't offer you SAT prep or honors classes. We won't ask you to compete." If you were a poor black or brown kid with too much intelligence for them to dismiss, they'd pat you on the head and call you a credit to your race. The result was confusion. I know, because I was there. Were we supposed to keep rising or sit back and wait for someone to lift us up?

Plain and simple, we must expect more from our children. Expecting less and settling for less are as treasonous as not giving kids the opportunity to succeed at all. Making excuses for your underperforming child doesn't make him stronger or happier or smarter. Making excuses for your spoiled, rude child, your lazy child, your child who watches TV or plays video games all day won't connect that child to the real world or to himself. I'm not asking you to pack more ballet or cello or tae kwon do into the day; just expect more from your child as a human being. What are your expectations for your children not just as scholars but as people with Personal Integrity, Civic Awareness, Workplace Literacy, and Academic Proficiency? Congratulations to you if they're hitting all your marks, but I'd say most of you could find ways in which your children could do better.

My father expected me to get that A in algebra. He wasn't looking to empower me, or affirm me, or make me feel good. There was nothing complicated about it: he'd put everything in place for me to succeed, and now he just wanted the damn A. Setting clear expectations in the classroom frees both students and their teachers from having to guess what their goals are and lets them get down to the hard work of reaching them. That's the point of measurable outcomes, especially when it comes to qualities such as

Civic Awareness and Personal Integrity. A teacher can't guarantee that a student will be a good person, but a teacher can train a child to say "please" and "thank you" and to behave appropriately in the public arena. Teachers can't, or at least shouldn't, teach young people whom or what to vote for, but they should be able to close the door on the last day of the school year knowing that every kid in their class knows how this democracy is supposed to function. Not only our classrooms but our *nation* should establish measurable standards for all the four qualities of a mature and conscious contributor to society.

But it isn't enough to set goals. For too long, we've taken high expectations to mean saying a motto loudly and often. "*Everyone succeeds!*" "*We're an ethical community!*" "*Failure is not an option!*" These are education's version of Nike and Eckō—brand names that people wave around to keep you from looking too hard at what's inside. The more you say them, the more it sounds as if you're trying to convince yourself of something you don't believe. High expectations may begin with a message, but they're meaningless if the steps a child needs to reach them aren't in place. That's the hard, tangible aspect of high expectations that we must require educators to deliver. Teachers who forget the tactics but remember the mantra don't have high expectations; they're just cheerleaders. I know I'm in a school that is setting high expectations when I see a tactical approach to developing children—when, for example, I see AP classes and a policy that children in this school will now work against international standards. What's really fabulous about what's happening right now in Miami is that kids don't just *believe* they can read or *think* they can read. They actually *can* read. They know how to decode words instantaneously and routinely, and they can do it with enough fluency to finally be able to tell themselves they are reading. Having high expectations helps turn belief into action.

That process is hard work, and a caring school expresses its high expectations as more than just demands. It teaches perseverance. Every word and deed of the educators in that school says: *We aren't going to give up on you, and, even more important, we aren't going to let you give up on yourself.* The trip up those steps may not be easy, but you have to keep trying. You have to persevere. Kids drop out or say to me that they're not good enough to learn algebra or take AP physics because they haven't learned perseverance. And I say right back to them that algebra is not going away. There is a way to scale AP calculus. There is a way to get through gerunds and participles and whatever is required of you before you are considered a mature and conscious person. I expect that you will establish a sense of discipline, learn to carry your own weight, and develop the ability to finish a task, lessons as important to Personal Integrity and Workplace Literacy as they are to any course work.

During my last year in New York there was all kinds of craziness going on around me, and I remember saying to myself one day, *You know what? Let me get out of my office. I just don't feel like ten hours of bad news.* So I went to a school in Bed-Stuy and walked into a fourth-grade classroom. The students were doing a math assignment, so I started going around and looking at the kids' work, trying to see if they were really engaged in it. I noticed this one boy erasing away at his paper.

"Son," I said to him, "what're you doing?"

And he said, "I'm doing this math problem. But I don't get it. I don't get it. I do not understand it."

I said, "Well, did you study?"

He said, "Yeah, I studied."

"Did you have homework in it?"

"Yeah," he said, "but I just don't get it."

So I looked down at him and said, "Don't worry about it. You just stay at this, son. You're gonna get this."

After checking out several other kids, I could tell it was a really good class with a very, very good teacher. As I started walking out, the boy grabbed my coat.

"Who are you, anyway?" he asked.

"I'm the chancellor of New York City schools."

He looked at me, this little black kid, with eyes big as plates. "You must be the Man!"

This was definitely one of those days when I was not feeling like I was the Man. I was getting my butt beat every day, but I thought, *You know what? Yeah. I still am the Man.*

He said, "Do you like your job?"

I took the question seriously. "Yeah, I like this job. It's a hard job, but I like it."

"Are you any good at it?"

"Well, that's another question, son. There are days when I don't think I'm very good at it at all. Other days I think I can just manage."

With the wit and charm and graciousness of a young mind, he looked at me and said, "Well, you stay at it. You'll get it."

That boy had the *stuff*. I wasn't there to see it, but I'm sure he cracked that problem, and he was lucky, because boys especially are struggling right now with perseverance. We're seeing more and more mental fatigue in young boys because this culture of Fast, Quick, and in a Hurry places no value on perseverance. Since they don't develop any mechanical ways to approach challenges, they quit very early in a task, and then, almost out of disgust, they resort to trying to manipulate the problem physically. Whether they bully their peers or play mind games with their teachers or some other adults, what they're really saying is, I don't have a handle on this, and I don't know how to persevere.

When I played football, our coach used to say, "If you quit on me on the field, you'll quit in the classroom." And he was absolutely right. Quitting is a pattern. It's saying, I don't have an answer to this challenge. I can't make it to practice. I can't work out in the hot sun. I don't want to lift weights. Well, that's no different from I don't want to do the homework. I don't care about an A. I don't care if I win or lose.

Kids learn perseverance by having to regularly put forth their best, by having to prepare and practice and study, to work in teams, exhibit passion, and commit themselves for the long haul, learning to manage anger and frustration along the way. The arts, sports, debate, even homework, are places where kids learn not just the skill set to assume risks and develop approaches to getting the answer but also the ability to go back to the drawing board with dignity if the answer is wrong.

Unfortunately, we've gutted too many of the items on the school menu that offer opportunities for kids to do all that. And yet kids still need to learn perseverance. So what do they do? They find another place to practice. Where? Out on the street at two or three in the morning. What are they practicing? They're practicing their resilience and perseverance. They're practicing their sportsmanship; they're practicing the art of success and the art of failure, but in perverse ways, oftentimes in a culture of drugs, crime, and abuse.

Setting high expectations for all our children must include restoring those traditional ways of teaching perseverance throughout their lives. Children need people to catch them so that they can learn through failure. Unfortunately, that support network rarely exists now in our public schools, and reestablishing it is at the core of transforming them. Today's process of schooling offers few opportunities for youngsters to experience a network of support that runs not just through the school but through the home, churches, synagogues, and other places in their communities. All of these locations in a child's life must be aligned and in constant communication so that when problems start bubbling to the surface, all parties can participate in a conversation with the child and help him learn the tactics needed to work through a given situation. The nation should never have to experience the horror of Columbine or Virginia Tech again, or lose another dropout.

The classroom should be the place that restores balance in a child's life, where young people can learn that they're not stupid, that they have value even without the latest Adidas or if they failed a test or didn't get asked to the prom. Schools are about guidance, not judgment, but budget cuts have rendered guidance for middle school kids little more than a babysitting service just at the moment in their lives when they need that extra voice as much as any academic instruction. Creating a culture of high expectations from home to school also means that we have to recognize that current student–guidance counselor ratios of 350 or 500 to 1 are ridiculous. We need more guidance services and counselors in our schools, and particularly in our middle schools.

TEACHERS SHOULD HAVE HIGH EXPECTATIONS THAT THEIR STUDENTS WILL

- *Give their best efforts.*

- *Complete their work.*

- *Pay attention.*

- *Ask good questions.*

- *Listen to feedback.*

- *Say when they don't understand something.*

- *Remain confident in the face of failure.*

- *Ultimately succeed.*

DIVERSE APPROACHES TO LEARNING

Every child can learn, but all children do not learn the same way.

For at least a century now, psychologists and philosophers and neurologists and educators have been studying—and debating—how intelligence is formed, and for me it all boils down to that one line: all children do not learn the same way. I base that not just on the work of Howard Gardner, whose influential and well-known model of seven kinds of intelligence has worked itself into the mainstream understanding of how our minds function, but also on the work of two others. The first, Jeff Howard, developed a formal system of creating intelligence based on the statement "Smart is not something you are; smart is something you can get." His organization, the Efficacy Institute, works with the Harvard Principals' Center and other educational institutions in helping schools develop a circuit within each child that connects confidence, effort, and development, clearly a cycle I hold with. The second person is Ron Edmonds, who back in the 1980s created the concept of Effective Schools. Like Howard, Edmonds believes in every child's ability and desire to learn and places the responsibility for fostering those two things on focused, demanding, and nurturing schools that work closely with parents. Between the bell curves and IQ tests and all the other garbage produced by philosophers and psychologists and educators more interested in advancing their own agendas than in really learning about the human condition, we've had to wade through a lot to get to this point of understanding, and I'm not fighting those wars over again. I say, "All kids can learn," and that's that.

But saying "all kids can learn" means nothing if we can't move on to *how* they do it. You have to make it real. A good classroom expects each child to succeed, but it doesn't expect them all to take the same path there. The issue of a diverse learning strategy is for me the heart of the matter in the relationship between a kid and a teacher, the unit of production we are trying to offer to all of our children. A caring teacher builds the confidence for risk taking and sets the expectations, but no two children will acquire any skill the same way, so the instructor has to figure out which path of understanding the concept of pi or the process of mitosis has to take to get into your child's brain. Providing each child with the specific tactics he'll need to meet expectations is the truly fine work, the art and science of teaching, and it's a more complicated task than it was eighty years ago. Our children function now on such a multi-sensory basis that they need a multitude of ways to make meaning out of content. Too many children are wrongly placed in special ed-ucation, wrongly placed in special-needs programs, simply because we haven't figured out how to access the way they think.

I was nearly one of them. Until I was twelve, I hated reading. When young readers sit down with a book, the act is twofold: pro-nunciation and comprehension. On the one hand, they take a word in a sentence and decode the word so they can pronounce it. When children just start reading, you see them focusing on this aspect, spitting out syllables and sounds, but if you ask them what they've just read, they have to take the time to replay the sentence in their heads before they can answer. All they've been doing is applying the rules of pronunciation to each word. Until you're fluent in de-coding *both* aspects—a word's sound *and* its meaning—essentially your brain struggles to decide which way you'll use your head. When I was a kid, meaning always won. My urge was to immedi-ately turn the meaning into a picture. If we were reading *Animal Farm,* for instance, my love of horses would draw all my attention to imagining the horses in the barn talking to other animals. How did they do that? Did they unlock the door first and come out? Did they visit like we do, just go to the neighbor's house? Were they able to just speak, or did they actually have to get in front of the chickens so that they could see their mouths? I remember thinking all these things. But I was so wrapped up in the imagery, the com-prehension, that I couldn't pronounce or decode the meanings of the particular words.

Enter my father. This time he cleaned floors at a local high school on Saturdays in order to pay a Vassar student to tutor me. She tried an approach totally different from what I'd had in school, and she found a way to dissolve the conflict between language processes and comprehension that made reading an invitation to create images with words. Soon I could read aloud and silently without the shame of being the slowest in the class or the one kid who couldn't answer the questions at the end of the chapter.

The prerequisite for all this fine-tool work is caring. As Noddings has explained, "Caring involves stepping out of one's own personal frame of reference into the other's." Caring, not ESP, is what lets a teacher get inside the child's mind and decide what will work. Teaching is a matter of what works more than what's right. One primary math program is not philosophically superior to another one; what matters is that your daughter can achieve certain standards in math. There's a host of proven strategies, programs, and technologies; teachers must have a diverse enough repertoire, the resources to employ it, and the caring to determine which approach is most effective in getting your daughter to those standards. This is especially true when it comes to teaching special-needs children. It's only in the last twenty years that we've realized that *all* kids can learn, including children with autism, neurological issues, learning impairments, and so on. These children have taught us that one size doesn't fit all.

As a teacher, I was constantly asking myself how I would know if and what my kids were learning. To try to figure out what had worked, I needed feedback. Classrooms must offer our multisensory children a myriad of ways to show their teachers that they understand the material being taught. Some students—for example, in a math class—will demonstrate their comprehension through their use of a calculator or a ruler; others will do it by solving problems on the blackboard or on a computer. In other classes the students' grasp of the material might become evident in a variety of settings: working in groups or making a model or acting something out onstage. However it's done, the child has to express his comprehension in the method that best suits his way of understanding, and the teacher must have the training, the skill, and the desire to take in that feedback and assess it.

The best bundle of tools we can offer our multisensory kids to express their knowledge has nothing to do with hardware or computer programs. Because they require putting knowledge to use in the classroom rather than simply repeating it, the arts are the most potent tools we have when it comes to diversity of approach. They're an engine for making meaning, a lens that lets you look at math differently, at social sciences differently, at language arts and virtually every other discipline differently. The arts create patterns of information that make concepts vivid and tangible in a child's mind. Children who go to a play learn how to sit in the audience and pay attention; they learn how to listen and follow a plot. They learn the need to enunciate. They see risk taking and discipline and trial and error and concentration all put into practice in a very public way. The introvert as well as the highly verbal kid who has nowhere to go with all his words can see how a human being can build herself into someone who can do something that looks difficult or intriguing. As an official at Carnegie Hall once told me, children involved in the arts have a mirror in which they can watch themselves grow.

And yet the arts are the first thing to go when the budget needs to be cut. Instead of giving every classroom this standard set of tools, we assign the arts to second-rate duty as an extracurricular for kids who are already interested in them. It's a mistaken approach with a damaging impact that goes far beyond the walls of the band room or the art room. Studies done over the last two decades have shown that arts integrated into curricula produce strong gains for disadvantaged children, and have proven more popular and more beneficial academically and developmentally to low-income students than athletics. A 2006 study by the Guggenheim in New York showed that students involved in an arts program that the museum sponsored had made clear gains in literacy and critical thinking. Cutting the arts means undercutting academics.

But we don't need the arts to simply boost test scores. The flat world is about global relationships, and the arts are where we learn to see ourselves as a part of mankind. They let us visit one another in the human sphere, and as global business turns away from the battlefield paradigm, the value of the arts multiplies. Business-people play golf to connect with others, not to beat them. They make deals as much by knowing what will create a relationship as by knowing their product, and so we need to teach the human curriculum.

The arts don't just offer an infinite number of opportunities for intersection; they show us how to find them. The things that often frighten people about the arts—how they express differences and similarities, how they don't pass judgment—are exactly what we need our children to learn to survive in the global economy. As a jazz musician in the 1940s and '50s, my father saw a lot of things and met a lot of people, and the only time I remember him letting himself relax was next to a glass of sweet tea with his eyes closed, humming "Satin Doll." He may have waxed floors, but he was an artist to the bone, and he taught me to see with an artist's eyes. When I was young, a woman named Gloria Castro lived in our building, and one day I had to go up to collect her rent money, but before I did, my father pulled me aside.

"Now, son," he said, "the world is made up of lotta different kind of people. Miss Castro is a woman." I nodded; so what else was new? "But she really likes to dress like a man. She's a good human being, pays the rent every week, keeps a clean room. And you'll see, she'll be nice to you."

He told me that she'd had a tough time getting a place to stay because people were afraid of her, thought they might become "that way" if they even touched her. But my dad approached her the same way he approached every person he met, like a fellow artist with her own song to play. He didn't ignore who such people were or how they were different; no, he went dead into that place, greeted it head-on, and tried to find the melodies and rhythms they could play together.

"You see, Rudy, she's a human being just like you and me. She's just different. Just like I'm different, and you're different." Hell, I don't even remember what Miss Castro was wearing when I went up to see her. But I do remember she was perfectly nice.

So as valuable as technology can be in providing new ways into seeing what and how our kids think, it's paintbrushes, recorders, and a stage that we can't afford to lose. The arts can't just be a subject area that we try to work into the schedule once in a while, not a budget line that gets cut out when things are tight. One of the first things I did when I took over the New York City schools was to get the arts back into the classrooms, and when I visit there, people still thank me for that. We owe our kids the opportunity to be human artists, to know how to make sense out of the tapestry of human patterns available to them, for our souls and our bank accounts. All schools need the arts. Period. *Punto*.

Your son deserves to have caring, high expectations, and diverse approaches to learning in his classroom; anything less is educational malpractice. Classrooms clicking with all three of these things produce students who set personal, academic, civic, and even workplace goals and do their best to reach them. Classrooms without them become tiny cracks in the bottom of the boat. More and more students seep through without what they need, and a sense of failure spreads throughout the school as more and more classrooms come apart. Another school sinks into hopelessness, and it doesn't take long for that hopelessness to spread throughout an entire system.

Many Americans have reacted to that by homeschooling their children, but as I said earlier, a good classroom provides balance in a child's life by combining public and private. The student learns personal skills through interaction with a teacher on one intimate level while also learning to function and be part of something larger with a group of her peers. She learns to negotiate between her needs and the needs of the group; she shares in group expectations—not just her own—and she can test her growing adequacies and her ability to care. Most of all, though, the classroom provides balance by giving the child a healing place to belong to.

Kids are desperate to belong. To what? It almost doesn't matter. They just want to belong, and when we don't have opportunities for them to do that, we see that natural desire to lead and influence and belong degrade into the perversity of gangs. A young man can't become senior class president, because he doesn't have enough credits to be a senior. He can't become a member of the football team, because he doesn't play well enough. There isn't a chess club, because it got cut in the budget. The art program is nil because it got whacked, too, and now you have a kid who wants to belong somewhere, but there's nothing. Gangs are an innovation of boredom and loneliness and a sense of alienation. As perverse as they are, they answer the bell. They give a child the chance to say: I belong to *this*.

Belonging is a basic need of every child. When I went to Babson College, only the children of the most affluent people in the country went there, and I was one of the first African-Americans. I'd been the only black kid in my class at St. Mary's Catholic school and over the years had come to expect that I'd often be the only African-American in a room, but to the credit of my school and fellow students, I didn't encounter much overt racism during my four years at Babson. Given that the son of the president of Johnson Publishing Company, owners of *Ebony* magazine and Afro Sheen, attended the college, the fact was, the color people cared about there wasn't white; it was green. Of course I didn't have much of that, either, but in my first semester I tried with varying success to weave my way into the social fabric of the place, assuming that I would always be in some ways an outsider amid all this power and privilege.

Well, fast-forward to Thanksgiving. Like most of the other kids, I was in my room packing, getting my stuff together for a trip down to Poughkeepsie to see my father, when a kid in my class knocked on the door. He was the grandson of an incredibly famous man, and the word "wealth" doesn't really describe what he had: exquisite clothes, gold cuff links, the total WASP package. Though we weren't what I'd call friends, he was a nice enough guy and we got along. Anyhow, he came into my room wearing one of his beautiful suits and said, "Can I come home with you for Thanksgiving? I don't have a place to go."

My jaw all but hit my chest. At that moment, seeing this rich kid so lonely among all the mahogany paneling and old leather— *his* world, I was sure—I felt comfortable at Babson for the first time. It wasn't that I was happy to see this guy in distress—I liked him well enough—but I thought to myself, *You're as hungry as I am, man. You feel as lost as I feel, and no amount of money can buy you a family to belong to at Thanksgiving.*

The "connect" in *Only Connect* has to do with more than phone lines or the sense of personal balance E. M. Forster meant when he coined the phrase in *Howards End*. To me, it's about how a child belongs to something—how she's connected not just to the classroom but to the world. The demonstrative, consistent, and caring adult relationship at the center of the classroom is key to making this connection for a child. The teacher checks on the student, wants to know about her. She pushes her, refuses to accept her answers all the time, and does so lovingly, setting high expectations and trying different strategies to reach her. Back in the 1960s and '70s, the Model Cities program created rec centers and community centers that gave kids the chance to play under the supervision of adults who literally watched them to see when they came and when they left, what they played, how well they got along. Those kids *belonged* to something in their world, and they knew it.

To sum up: Here is how the classroom must work. Each child enjoys a personal, intellectually intimate relationship with an adult who, as the psychologist Urie Bronfenbrenner says, is crazy about the kid. The teacher builds a safe place for the child by acknowledging him as a person, builds the confidence in him to take risks, and then sets expectations that he must reach through a considered, tactical approach that's right for the child. The material, the expectations, and the approach all have aspects that require interaction with others so that the child is learning not just philosophies or facts but how to live in the world. All of this takes place within a caring culture; caring is something that everyone in the class lives and does. And so while the classroom is a place of great risk for your child, it's also a place of balance for him, a place where he learns to be comfortable within himself, to belong to himself (Personal Integrity), and to be comfortable as someone who belongs to society (Civic Awareness). The classroom is where children learn that the world cares about them and that they care about the world, and that their words and actions must express this.

But how do we offer true service opportunities in the classroom beyond clapping erasers and collecting papers? How do we introduce children to the world of work and generative growth with more than class projects and bake sales? There's much that can and should be done in the classroom, but textbooks and lectures are only two of the tools now. How do we open the doors and truly bring the world into the classroom?

Connected Schools.

CONNECTED
SCHOOLS

Alot of people have imagined what our schools should look like in the future. Usually there are computers. In fact, there are *always* computers. Lots of them. And they're new and they're all hooked up with Wi-Fi and tricked out with iThis and iThat and the kids can do PowerPoint presentations with the three facts they pulled off the Internet and wow! They're all ready for the future! And there are ten kids in every classroom, and the principal and the teachers have created a perfect curriculum for them because the evil bureaucracy of the school system has been defeated by the swift-thinking charter school people, who truly know what children need. And there are no more unions because all the teachers love teaching so much that they don't even want money to do it, that's how much they love the children, *your* children, who now go off to Brown or Harvard because of their unmatched preparation as young nuclear physicists or international relief aid workers and those years of free-range chicken and healthy salads in the cafeteria.

All you need to do is find a place to land your spaceship, and you're set.

In a world where a working toilet or a sharp pencil is an educational fantasy for many, many children, excuse my lack of enthusiasm for pedagogical daydreaming right now. I'm all for theory. It's important to create goals and ideals that can then be worked into mainstream thinking, but when delivering quality education on a day-to-day basis to tens of millions of Americans is so difficult a task, I think our heads need to come out of the clouds. You can spend all day telling me how to hit the bull's-eye, but when half the time I'm not even hitting the target, I think you need to change your focus. This culture isn't going to fight off the darkness of ignorance when the majority of us don't know how to use our weapons. I want results.

So far we've established in Chapter Two what we want out of education, and in Chapter Three the unit of production we need to get it. The truth is, there's nothing futuristic about any of what we've discussed to this point. Some Greek philosopher in a robe could have taught his students all four qualities of a mature and conscious contributor to society under a tree in Athens, using caring, high expectations, and diverse approaches to learning, and I believe that's exactly what they all did. Those four qualities have always in some form or another been the goal of education, and the three basic elements of a good classroom are nothing but the timeless qualities of effective teaching that exist beneath any serious theory of pedagogy. Caring, high expectations, and diverse approaches do exist now in many, many classrooms within our struggling public school systems, but their effectiveness in creating twenty-first-century people is limited by the nature of schools today. Nor are they distributed equitably, and therefore efficiently.

In order to create a smarter, swifter, stronger future for public education in America and distribute quality education to all children, we'll have to view the challenges of education not as a matter of philosophy but as a matter of engineering. And that means we'll have to fundamentally change our relationship with our schools.

For generations, public education has been a passive part of the community, happy to get its budget line every year and graduate a new crop of workers and taxpayers every June. Any talk of school reform has always boiled down to a desire for more money so spare parts—be it personnel, curriculum, or governance—can be swapped out. No matter how parts of the system may change, what never changes is the school system's role as supplicant. Every budget season, as the big boys in their shiny suits debate the "important" things, here comes the superintendent in his tweed jacket or her sensible skirt, hat in hand, asking for money to take care of the city's or state's children as if begging for charity. For a few seconds, the lawmakers stop writing massive checks for boondoggle projects and corporate subsidies and grudgingly peel off a few bills for education that come with warnings about performing well—or else. At which point Superintendent Tweed Jacket is shooed away and that's that. *There have to be schools, right?* is the attitude. And so schools are treated as one of the difficult and sometimes even unpleasant realities a community has to deal with, only a notch or two above garbage removal. Don't get me wrong—very often the schools walk away with a good piece of money, but it's usually poorly leveraged, wastefully applied in how it pays for the same thing over and over, and with no bearing on what is actually produced.

Very few people see the basic fact that we established in Chapter One: nothing is as important to the life of the nation, state, or locality as the functional populace produced by its schools. It's a simple equation: if your citizens don't have the skills to find or hold a job in your community, they're going to leave, and soon you won't have much of a community. And whatever investment was made to educate those children will have been, in terms of the locality, squandered. School systems that don't integrate day-to-day learning with the needs of the economy, so that kids learn to function within the context of low-, middle-, and high-end job requirements for going into the surrounding community's economic base, whatever that is, lose their leverage and ultimately lose their way, leaving their communities high and dry. I've seen many businesses in New York and Miami leave for a different state or even country where they could get workers on a consistent basis who could outfit their technological offices, their front-end phones, their customer service phone calls, and the like. And the problems just cascade down from there as the social safety net begins to strain under all the weight of the people we didn't train to succeed. The reason we want to make schools better is not just for their own sake; we want to make schools better so our cities and states and nation as a whole function better. Gold stars are nice, but the real point is prosperity and efficiency for all.

To move public education forward, we must pull it out of the nursery and put it right in the middle of every town and city and rural stretch of this country. Instead of considering public schools as a budget line or a handout, we have to see the distribution of educational services as an integral part of the machinery and value of local government. Schools and societies share common goals, and we need to focus on creating the relationships that will bring the right resources of our communities to bear in the right places in our schools. This is the connection, the central focus, that I discussed in Chapter One—the need for everyone, from statehouse to schoolhouse, from boardroom to home, to share a common interest and vision for the central role of the schools. It is the need for everyone to understand that resources must come from all quarters and be used wisely and mutually, and in return schools will produce mature and conscious contributors to society. There is, I believe, no greater work to be done in this nation.

Okay, that sounds great, but when I step off the soapbox, what does all that *mean*? What does it mean on a day-to-day level for your kid? What does it mean for teachers and taxpayers? How does such a relationship happen not just in theory but on the ground?

For our schools to be connected to their communities, they must be connected in the intimate, functional way the heart works within our bodies, constantly receiving and producing and ultimately proving that we're alive. So our school systems must consciously enter into a network of formal relationships with the elements of their communities, both local and federal, governmental and business, arts, educational, you name it, as well as with their families and students. Not a promise or a letter of intent; photo ops and good intentions aren't enough anymore. I've learned that when you want to make a deal, you get it in writing. I mean we must sign a series of binding compacts or partnerships that gives each of us a full understanding of what we can expect from the others and what will be expected from us in this great undertaking of educating our children. Every aspect of society must accept its responsibility for creating mature and conscious contributors. In return for a broad spectrum of investments, financial and otherwise, that all these various facets of the community make in the school, the school will, first, produce the measurable outcome of children equipped with the four qualities. Not theoretically. Not because the schools tell us that they've done their best. We'll know it because the schools will prove it with quantifiable results in all four qualities. The children will have shown their abilities not just academically but in the other three areas through the testing, the course work, and other educational opportunities, be they occupational or service and community oriented, that we create through the partnerships. Later we'll look at some specific methods that can be used to open our classrooms to the world, but the exact details and process a locality uses in its schools to do this should be of its own choosing. It's the network of direct and meaningful relationships that must be created around every school in America that's the point here. In addition, our schools can offer services to the surrounding community that extend beyond good grades and quality kids.

This is how we're putting this into practice in Miami. After I had that first meeting with the Chamber of Commerce about the vast number of unemployable kids our schools were producing, I sat down and identified all the players in any educational system in this country:

1. Federal government

2. State government

3. Local government

4. Local business community

5. Arts community

6. Postsecondary-education venues

7. Faith community

8. Service community

9. School system, including superintendents and school boards

10. Individual schools and school administration, that is, principals

11. Teachers

12. Families/parents

13. Students

14. The community at large

The first question was, how could we create a oneness of effort on the part of all of these elements that would put schools at the center? Before I came to Miami, there had been issues with the school board in the district involving the relationship between the board and the superintendent and land deals gone sour. Now the city and its citizens were primed to clean up and start doing things right. I needed to do more than steer a big old ship in a new direction or turn everything over to the private sector the way they're doing these days in New York. Looking around Miami, I saw terrific assets and a great will to change, but all in various kinds of loose ends, plugs that needed sockets and sockets that needed plugs; businesses that needed workers and kids who needed jobs; concerts that needed audiences and children who needed beauty. It seemed to me that the work involved in making Miami's schools function was not about test scores, not when our jobs, the jobs we needed to create a healthy community, were flowing out to other countries just as thousands of new immigrants were arriving. Our schools were more important than that; the business community had in effect said so. My job, then, was not to put up banners and drive children to ulcers over the FCATs. My job was to make connections, to identify needs in our system and the resources in the community that could fill them, then put them together so that all our kids would graduate up to speed in all four qualities and enter their city and nation prepared to contribute.

There is a model for a similar type of arrangement called, aptly enough, community schools. Very much a product of the 1960s, these schools still exist, and in many cases thrive, around the country, using schools as clearinghouses for a whole range of social services by providing them on-site. While I like the idea of schools offering a range of services that goes beyond traditional ideas of teaching, I wanted schools to be more than clearinghouses; I wanted to redefine the role schools play in the community. I wanted the whole city plugged into the culture of its schools, and the schools plugged into the city.

So instead of throwing the philosophical blanket of the community schools over all our schools, we decided to atomize before we synthesized. Miami is made up of thirty-five different local municipalities, each run by a city government and mayor and so forth, and each of the thirty-five has its own relationship with the Miami-Dade County Public Schools district (M-DCPS). I went to all of the thirty-five mayors as the representative of an independent entity, not a fellow civil servant, and offered them a different way of looking at the M-DCPS. Our value to the community isn't just that we educate children, I told them; it's that we offer educational services, and those services have a bandwidth that includes services to parents, the community, museumgoers, and on and on. We are a service provider, and so I asked them not just what they really wanted from their schools in terms of quality for their residents, but to think of other services we could provide. At the same time, I asked them what resources they had to offer to help us realize their goals. Were there ways we could help each other? Places we could pool resources or needs in order to save money (another serious concern for the system beyond student performance)? I didn't walk in hat in hand, nor were these meetings about crossing our fingers and hoping for results; I walked in with a vision and a set of outcomes I thought I could consistently offer within a certain time frame in return for cooperation from this other entity. Our goal was to get our school system built up strong enough with a useful and appropriate menu of real options for parents and for children so that it could become a serious economic draw for the community.

Then I took this message to the business community, the faith community, the health-care community, the arts community, even the sports community. Wherever I went, Miami understood immediately where I was going with this. Within a year our network was up and running. Instead of plodding along and punching the clock, M-DCPS became an active player in the life of its communities. Here are some of the connections and initiatives and lines of communication that we've created in Miami between our schools and our community:

- Right now 3,887 business and community-based organizations have formal partnerships with M-DCPS through our business partnership program, Dade Partners. These partnerships help provide the internships, mentors, and real-world experience that M-DCPS students need to learn Workplace Literacy and Civic Awareness.

- We have formal Education Compacts with four local governments. Instead of M-DCPS being simply a passive recipient of tax dollars, we entered into these "mutual support" agreements as a partner, as an independently functioning entity, collaborating in areas such as economies of scale, training and development, and education and facilities. Economies of scale allow us to save taxpayer money; joint training sessions let us cut even more costs. Our agreement with the City of Miami includes the development of a series of specialized high schools which focus on law studies, or medical research and technologies, or international finance—each drawing on the local business community not just for money but for expertise and real-world guidance into the job market.

- In partnership with the Children's Trust and the Miami-Dade Health Department, we've created Health Connect in Our Schools, which, through a school-based health team, will ensure that a coordinated level of health care is consistently available at every school. We'll be at 100 percent of our schools by 2010.

- Working with the Early Childhood Initiative Foundation, we've created Ready Schools Miami, which brings together families, schools, early-learning centers, and community organizations to provide support to children from birth to third grade.

- We've created the Parent Academy, which helps teach thousands of parents how to become more engaged in their children's lives, not just in their homework. It's supported entirely through private-sector funding. Chapter Six will go into more detail.

- Our new Community Workforce Pilot Program will create long-term employment opportunities in the community base around new school construction and renovation.

- The Beacon Council, a group of over one hundred business leaders, provides educational outreach for businesses working in and considering Miami.

- The Miami Dolphins, the Florida Marlins, the Miami Heat, the Florida Panthers, and the University of Miami Hurricanes all have partnerships with the M-DCPS to provide not just ways to honor teachers, students, and schools but tutoring, speakers, and incentives.

- Fifteen local college and university deans work with the M-DCPS through either the Parent Academy, Curriculum and Instruction, or the Zone, a special support organization within the school system for schools working their way out of low-performing categories.

- We have partnerships with the Harvard Graduate School of Education, the University of Florida's Lastinger Center for Learning, the University of Miami, Miami Dade College, Barry University, the Council for Educational Change, the Miami Museum of Science, and Mathematica Policy Research, Inc., for various training programs that will involve our principals, teachers, administrators, and paraprofessionals.

- I hosted a faith-based orientation and keep in regular contact with over seventy-five of the region's faith-based leaders, as well as more than fifty community-based organizations such as Big Brothers Big Sisters.

- Over 150 of the region's top CEOs have signed on for my CEO Roundtable Briefings, which put me in one-on-one contact with all these business leaders.

- I've established a Blue Ribbon Council for Internships and a Legislative Business Outreach Council.

And I'm just skimming the top. The result is a web, a network of community, business, government, and individuals that meets in our schools, with effects that range from improved teacher and principal training to job opportunities and training for those who live around our schools. We've even gotten involved in hurricane preparedness. Our schools—Connected Schools, I call them—are becoming community hubs, creating relationships that help everyone around them, redefining, really, what a public school can be, while our kids are learning that the whole world is their classroom. Inside the schools, the offerings are widening, our scores are rising, and, much more important, our children are benefiting from the sharper focus on them as entire people, not just FCAT scores. Miami is proud of its schools and education. The city is putting its best into its school system, and I think we're doing a good job of giving back. In 2006, for the first time, Miami's reading and math scores on all levels were above the national average. In 2005 the percentage gains in Miami-Dade were twice those of the entire state of Florida, and we registered the highest number of Hispanic and African-American students scoring 3s or higher on AP tests of any school district in the nation. What we're doing here versus other systems is the difference between a symphony orchestra and a one-man band. The latter has lots of noise and moving parts and things going on, and you can appreciate that any one of them can make noise, but all of it together isn't making music. Our goal is harmony, all the different parts working together at what they do best to create one sound.

Given the different kinds of possible relationships, there's an almost infinite variety of ways these partnerships can work. The private sector gives money and manpower and expertise. A township may buy or donate the land for a school or fund an initiative that works within our strategy for achieving a mutual goal. For example, a particular school in Miami had been for many years ranked as an F under Florida's school grading system. I wasn't happy about it, and neither was Manny Diaz, the mayor of the city of Miami. But instead of just hoping things would get better or pointing fingers, he committed himself and the City of Miami to helping us turn around that school. Mayor Diaz put a lot of the city's money and time into mentorship programs and after-school programs, and by God, that school got off the F list. Since then, the M-DCPS and the City of Miami have made a commitment to have absolutely no schools graded lower than a B. That's a three-year project of great value to Miami because of what it can say to the rest of the state and the nation and the kinds of residents and businesses the city will be able to attract. Our role at the M-DCPS in this agreement is to replicate effective practices that we already know work, while the City of Miami provides the kinds of specific support elements that helped get that school off the F list. The Greater Miami Chamber of Commerce and Merrill Lynch co-sponsored a Principal for a Day program that brought 345 business and civic leaders into the schools. As well as programs to strengthen Workplace Literacy, we created a link with United Way that has turned into the nation's largest student United Way Campaign and the county's largest employee campaign. Those are our students learning about Civic Awareness and Personal Integrity and service, alongside the adults in their community.

So what's happening in Miami? The success in our schools is not just a matter of kids trying harder or cities handing us more money. Our students aren't being taught the four qualities of a mature and conscious contributor to society; they're *learning* them by living them in their communities. Growth and change are coming out of conscious, voluntary, and committed action, not through the inevitable grindings of a government bureaucracy. For example, Paul Cejas and Adrienne Arsht, president and vice president of the Miami Business Forum, have created accountability standards for legislators and enlisted the support of major business representatives in directing attention to the issues and outcomes of public education in Miami. Instead of the old system of action-reaction (pour in some money here and wait to see what happens; hire a new person there and wait to see what happens), we're getting a lot of things done at once, attacking on all fronts by strategically enlisting the right help for the right tasks. What we're seeing is a school system that reacts to *specific* needs and desires in its community, and we're seeing a community embrace its school system while at the same time expecting more from it and getting excited about the possibilities. And that's creating results. The community is now coming to us with ideas and ways in which we can benefit each other. The M-DCPS gives out awards every year to our top ten partners; our school system has the strength and confidence to recognize others, not just ask for more for itself. Caring and high expectations are coming together as people use diverse approaches to solve problems and move ahead.

There's a harder edge to this as well. By making people look at our academic results as a product with a direct impact on the quality of their lives and pocketbooks, we've taken education out of the welfare line and put it into the marketplace. We make deals with businesses on our terms, to receive goods or services from them in return for the delivery of informed workers and consumers. Individual communities have specific needs related to education, and we work with them to deliver what they need on a cooperative basis. It's smart; it's nimble; it's delivering specific services where they're needed, the kind of thinking that the business community engaged in ten or fifteen years ago but that never reached the towers of academe. No more passing the buck on the part of a community telling a school that it has to perform or close but without offering any kind of extra assistance. And no more passing the buck on the school side, where we throw up our hands and say, "Oh, well, sorry, we tried." Now the school system operates within the market, but without privatization. We work according to the rules of supply and demand, but without selling ourselves out for someone else's profit.

As unique as Miami is in its governance, compacts and partnerships can work anywhere and *should* work anywhere. When I was in New York, whenever the mayor was upset with the school board or the school board was angry with the mayor, they'd operate as if there were no mutuality in the delivery of services to the people of the city. Their petty grievances and slights ended up roiling the lives of little children in the Bronx, and while they bickered, they missed how desperate members of the business community were for quality schools and a reliable workforce, how willing they were to do more than just write checks and be principal for a day.

That said, there need to be real incentives and consequences for cities and businesses to work together to help schools, and for the schools to help their communities. Mayors talk all the time about remaking their cities, but schools are the natural and most effective places to do that. Government must say to businesses: We want our young people to be in your place of business so much that we'll provide you with a tax write-off for offering internships, for having your workforce groom the next level of workers that are going to be coming in. I have no strict program in mind for how that should work—the individual school system, companies, and government can work out the details—but the point is that businesses must tend our children, too. They need to help us while our children are still on the vine.

It's time for someone in a place of power to point us forward, to say that we must arm the schools and the parents and the business community with what they need to get the nation's educational engine pumping again. After three decades of our schools decaying both physically and attitudinally, three decades of dumbing down, we've been left with an empty vessel, underfunded and undercapitalized and generally led by people with no business smarts and no connective tissue with the business community or the infrastructure of cities. We're lucky to be mediocre.

The formal compacts and partnerships of Connected Schools are ways to focus everyone on the work of recharging public education with at least the same attention as the community would give to a new shopping mall. They are real agreements to join work to a specific outcome that will occur in a specific time frame, and they embody the need for the mutual financial arrangement necessary to accomplish those outcomes.

Of course, all communities have those strands creating the web through and around their schools, but they differ in their particulars. The nature of the business community, the structure of local government, how many kids are in the system, how wealthy the tax base is—all of these factors will determine how individual localities structure their own compacts. And the success of such compacts requires leadership at all levels of the school system. Just to start, the superintendent must have the vision, the power, and the ability to solve problems and create opportunities by forging agreements with the whole range of relationships the world offers beyond school walls. Unfortunately, too many superintendents come into a school system without knowing enough about the community and its resources and the grass roots that already exist and instead set their own agenda, which sours opportunities for mutual thinking. But a compact, a web of partnerships, initiates a dialogue. It brings together all the multiple divergent interests of a community in one brick-and-mortar location and asks the question: How do we each improve our quality of life through this convergence? This is simply good government. A government that has no relation with its public school system loses out on a conversation with thousands, even millions of its people whom it might otherwise touch.

A warning bell might go off in some heads at the idea of this level of collaboration between government and business. I agree— to a point. Centuries of history tell us that when those two estates get too chummy, it's the little man who pays. That's something my father was always on about, watching out for the little man, so when I talk about learning from business or using business models, I don't mean selling out our kids as captive audiences, where they're watching commercials in the classroom or only able to get beverages in school that come from the one soda dealer the city does business with. I don't mean sweetheart deals and kickbacks. I mean schools and school systems working with businesses, and in an effectively businesslike fashion. It is important that we understand how schools interact with the other power centers in society, and understand their relationship with their clients—the students and their families. Putting school systems into a market mode, making them think of themselves as entities that are not custodial or faucets of public money but results oriented and pennywise, has the great benefit of making them offer their services to their students rather than handing them their education like so many blocks of government cheese.

To this point, we've been discussing the institutional relationships schools need to create, but that's only half of the strategy. The other side is the relationship between the school and the students and their families. And the question is, How exactly do we get caring, high expectations, and diverse approaches to learning into our classrooms and functional young people walking out the doors? Over the years many schools have lowered their expectations for themselves and their students to the point where they offer a limited menu of classes and activities. These schools are the educational version of the worst institutional cafeteria you can imagine, dumping big lumps of cold and unconsidered facts onto our kids' trays and then wondering (if they even bother to care) why the kids aren't touching them, why they're finding their intellectual and emotional nourishment off campus. This problem can't be solved from one direction, because parents are at fault in this situation as well. Parents have let this happen to their schools, and together the schools and their clients are spiraling further and further down.

Two things have to happen, and they have to happen simultaneously because that's how complex relationships improve: schools have to rethink what their role is in relation to parents and students, and parents have to become actively engaged in their children's education. I'll go into more detail later on both of these, but for now let me simply say that rather than handing us their children and expecting an adult to pop out at the other end, parents must participate at home and within the school and community to support the school effort to bring not just their children to maturity but all their community's children to maturity. They must demand things from themselves and from their children, and from their schools and their school systems as well. You've heard it before—the squeaky wheel gets the grease. Well, that is very true in education, and the parents in Scarsdale and Winnetka know it very, very well. They demand performance from their educational professionals. Whether they expect too much is another question, but one so small in the greater scheme of our educational crisis that it's not even worth discussing. Instead of parents who passively hand us their children, we need Demand Parents, parents who expect market behavior from their schools, in the range of services offered and how well they're offered. In Miami one of the partnerships we have created with local businesses is the Parent Academy, which we'll examine in depth in Chapter Six. One of its goals is to give parents a greater understanding of the issues and skills needed for successfully engaging in their child's education, from what they need to know about homework and the FCATs all the way up to college admissions. By increasing their knowledge about schools and schooling, they will be in a better position to make decisions about their children's education and drive thoughtful demand of school services. Demand Parents make better partners in the process of education, and they are as crucial to the concept of Connected Schools as any organizational partnership.

As schools widen their portfolios of offerings and their parent clients are better able to express and act on their needs, the schools can then, like any entity that works in the marketplace, adjust their offerings accordingly regarding specialization, curriculum, and even structure. Once we have school systems with a variety of schools— magnet, charter, local catchment, specialized, you name it—that offer a variety of classes and activities and services, all with a track record of achievement, and, on the other side, parents able to choose from among these the educational experience they consider best for their children, then we'll have true school choice. Then we'll have a living, breathing school system that is smart and reactive to the institutional and personal needs of its community in a three-dimensional way.

Think of schools as a business offering a variety of services, almost like a franchise that tailors its business slightly to each particular locality. If I look at M-DCPS that way, I think of all the possible services schools can provide, and I'm talking tangible and specific educational services. How many AP classes are offered in our high schools? How many programs for gifted children do we have, and what varieties are there? What's our menu of summer school offerings for our kids? In urban systems you've often got kids coming and going all through the year, so what are the venues for entry into the school? The list can go on forever, and it should be examined and retooled and adapted constantly. This is a school's product line, and schools that plan on leaving no child behind have to have one. This is where equity becomes efficiency. If I don't see a wide array of choices offered in a school, I don't see equity. This is where market behavior in schools and the equity we've talked about come together. Making our schools work means offering choices to everyone. It means creating demand in all communities for high-quality education and educational tools. It's not a matter of token programs, of offering something here and there; it's a product line, a menu of services that the schools constantly check, measure, and then reform or redesign as necessary before they're put back out onto the market.

Take, for instance, AP classes in Miami high schools. One of the things I'm most proud of is that in 2005 we had seven high schools recognized by the College Board for having the largest number of Latino and/or African-American students who scored a 3 or higher on their AP exams. In 2006 enrollment in AP classes was up by 13 percent. That didn't happen by magic. We put AP classes into schools that didn't have them, we offered that product, we addressed the equity problem posed by these classes not being made available to low-income kids, and what happened? They were a success. The demand was there, the classes succeeded, the kids succeeded, and now AP will continue to spread in acceptance where many assumed it was a waste. But this requires constant monitoring from the schools, so that we're looking not just at the scores but at the efficiency of the AP offerings. Where are we growing AP? Which schools are having success with this, and in which fields of study? Right now we may have only five kids in a class, whereas in other AP classes we may have thirty, but we have to track the efficiency of the offering and in time decide whether to continue that class in that place or not. The market force will determine whether we keep that particular class going, but only after we've given it a try. If we do this well—if we offer the right classes in the right places and post high expectations for parents and students—it won't be very long before the lowest-performing schools have as strong a demand for AP classes as the highest ones.

Let's stop here for a moment and look at the nature of choice and the marketplace, because if we're going to introduce those two aspects into the educational system, we must do so with our eyes open. What I've laid out above is the goal, and we're getting there in Miami, but let me give you an example about the realities of choice in America. Fifty years ago grocery stores in the United States carried a fairly limited selection of produce, the same old apples and heads of iceberg lettuce that we'd been eating forever. And then, in the 1970s and '80s, new kinds of fresh foods began to appear in grocery stores: arugula, endive, radicchio, kiwi fruits, and all sorts of other wonderful, tasty new things that people all around America started to regularly eat.

But not everybody in America, because these great new foods didn't appear in every grocery store. They appeared where the corporations selling the foods assumed that, one, they could create a demand for the products and, two, the people could afford the prices they were charging. So if you shopped in Harlem, chances are not too many dried porcini mushrooms or star fruits appeared on your shelves, and they still haven't. Could you afford them? Would you buy them every day if you could? Who knows, because you've been written out of the equation. No one will ever know, nor will they even ask. You might love dried porcini mushrooms, but if you want to participate in the free market and buy them, you'll have to pay extra to go to a neighborhood—and let's just be honest and say white—in the form of a cab ride or subway ride to get what someone there can get just by walking. Moreover, the products that are actually in your stores often cost more than they do in other neighborhoods. So, to review: your food shopping choices in the "free" market are limited to higher-priced, lower-quality goods, and within a fairly limited selection as well. When this inequity is pointed out, the usual answer is, But those are the goods those people want—they don't want the porcini mushrooms. Yet there's no proof to the statement, and unless you market the materials in the same way as you market them elsewhere, how can you tell? Why was the assumption made in the first place that kiwi fruits wouldn't be popular in Bed-Stuy?

I'll let you answer that yourself. But this illustrates an important caveat about the free market and how we apply it to the common good. At the end of the day, this supposedly color-blind, faceless, totally impartial force called the market is regularly channeled in ways that profit specific groups of people. Those "business decisions" based on groundless assumptions and self-fulfilling prophecies are the bloodless boardroom version of old-time racism. These kinds of decisions are made in education all the time in the form of uneven divisions of common goods based on an assumed lack of demand or ability. I can understand the economics behind the fact that there are no fancy private schools in inner cities, but that doesn't mean that there shouldn't be great public schools simply because the people living there can't afford the fancy brand name. The inability to afford private school education doesn't mean people don't want that level of education. People in New Orleans don't just deserve the same quality of public school as people in Beverly Hills; they want it. Why is it that whenever a charter school is built, there's a rush to the lottery? Because there is a demand there, but it's consciously undersupplied. Just because people can't speak English, or they're poor, or they live in a rural community doesn't mean they don't want quality public schools. When we create a system of approaching education that requires certain market concepts of supply and demand, speed and resources, we need to guarantee equity with real choices that offer quality to all comers.

Now, while I might be unhappy about the relative availability of produce, it's not illegal, and if you truly let the market work and find, all things being equal as to price and availability, that a product sells better on Beacon Hill than it does in Roxbury and you adjust your distribution and pricing accordingly, I have no problem. But when it comes to government services, when it comes to the common good for which we all share the burden of support, then equity must be guaranteed. Then we must guide the power of the market the way we guide a river that floods every spring. I will not stand to see us give lip service to equity, to holding up a handful of shining cities on the hill, beautiful schools that people are stabbing their neighbors in the back to get their kids into, and calling that "choice." That's false. That's a choice between life and death, not a choice between an emphasis on science and an emphasis on communications. Creating the kind of transforming equity we need in our public schools rests on five very simple ideas:

1. **All Kids Can Learn.** *All* of them.

2. **Don't Underestimate the Power of a Caring Relationship.**
You can make a difference. The days of looking at urban communities and saying, There's nothing I can do—those days are

over. The effect one teacher can have on a child can have enor-mous repercussions that literally last generations. The days when America could coast on its money and power are quickly sliding away. We can't afford half-baked, half-assed, or half-interested.

3. Measure Outcomes Rather Than Inputs. Testing and assess-ment will always be necessary. We can't throw away the con-cepts of success and failure, but we will make testing a tool, not the point of the system.

4. Investments Must Be Strategic. I won't kid you—to estab-lish the conditions on a national level that we need to make this concept of schooling viable, we will have to make a serious fi-nancial commitment. But considering what we as a nation have spent our money on the last five years, I can't think of anything more valuable. If you want quality results, you pay for quality work. Everyone knows that. When was the last time you heard the military offer a low-bid contract? We have to pay for qual-ity across the board. But equal is not equitable. We have chil-dren living everywhere from American Indian reservations to tenements to soybean farms, and so the point is not writing the same amount on every check. It's to make strategic investments that will produce the same outcomes across the board.

5. Schools Are Intrinsic to the Local Economy. Schools are part of the infrastructure of a town or city, and they have a di-rect impact on real estate values, unemployment, wages, and countless other economic factors in the life of a community. Healthy schools are as much an indicator of economic progress as people at work.

Slogans. They're all slogans. I know that. They've been posted on blackboards and T-shirts for years, and most schools and school systems just change the artifacts, just change the marquee and put up the banners and hold the pep rallies, and make effort a proxy for outcome. People will feel good for trying, not because they're getting the job done. Well, I need to see behaviors. Tell me all day that your son has Personal Integrity, but if he doesn't shake my hand or open a door for an elderly woman and structure his time wisely, I won't believe you. It's the same with schools. The federal government can tell me all day till next week that our nation's resources are being brought to bear equally on the problems of education, Miami or Washington, D.C., can tell me that it's changing its inner-city schools, but the proof is in the behaviors they display. If I go into a struggling school where I once saw the worst teachers fumbling through the day's lessons, now I expect to see the best teachers the system has to offer. The behaviors, not the words, of a school system display its true intentions about equity—and therefore the kind of efficiency we're looking for to deliver quality education to all our children. For this strategy to work, those five true statements need to become behaviors all across America. They are the rock-solid foundation of equity on which we'll create the wonderful architecture of partnerships and community involvement in our Connected Schools and high-functioning classrooms.

The next chapter will discuss how that foundation is laid and how we will know it's in place.

WHAT THE FEDERAL GOVERNMENT WILL HAVE TO DO

I remember when I was young how long the school year seemed. I'd walk in the door in September, and June was off on the other side of the horizon, past Thanksgiving and Christmas, beyond even the first days of spring and Easter. The leaves would fall, there'd be trick-or-treating, snow, mud—everything I could imagine before I'd finally get out and head back up to Maine. And that was just *that* year. Some quick calculations in fourth grade showed that I had twelve more school years ahead of me before I'd be out into the *real* world, where *real* things happened. I mean, twelve years was longer than I'd been *alive* to that point. It seemed unbearable.

But in high school, once I was working at M. Schwartz & Co., I started to notice something a little upsetting and a little comforting at the same time. The real world I was so eager to dive into really wasn't all that different from school. Socially, there were cliques and clubs, people who thought they were cool, and the lone wolves, just like at Arlington High. And figuring out what my teachers wanted wasn't all that different from figuring out what Mr. Morris wanted, or my father. At the time we owned a rooming house in Poughkeepsie. The bottom floor was ours, and my dad rented the top two out to boarders—small-time hustlers, cabdrivers, folks down on their luck—so my other job from when I was maybe six years old until I went to college was to collect the rent, deliver linen, sweep the floors, and do whatever else my dad said needed doing. Work was work, I finally understood, whether it was writing a history paper or sweeping a hallway or boxing a suit. The same expectations were there, the same connection between effort and reward, and all work required commitment whether you got a grade at the end of the week or a paycheck.

This was upsetting because it completely demolished my idea that life once I was out of school would be radically different, as if somehow the adult world really did function by another, better set of rules. But it also demystified the whole idea of education for me. School stopped being some kind of trial by fire, a sprint where the hurdles just kept getting higher and higher until you reached the end and passed out. The walls around my classrooms were only made of brick. I was there to take advantage of what was being offered to me in the way of knowledge and a safe place to test my abilities as a scholar and as a person. My teachers weren't the enemy; they weren't evil authorities. It was simply incumbent upon me as a student to figure out how to get the information I needed out of them while still working within their parameters. Life would not begin the day I graduated; it had started the day I entered my first classroom. School was for me to use.

The classroom is not a world apart from the "real" world. Like a garden, it's a guarded space of designed and nurtured growth, but it's still subject to the same rain and sun that fall on the wilder world around it. The purpose of our Connected Schools is not just to make sense of that fact but to take advantage of it. And this means that the strategy we use in reenvisioning public education is as applicable on a large scale as it is on a small one, and, in fact, the elements of caring, high expectations, and diverse approaches must exist structurally and culturally everywhere in the system before they can exist in every classroom. One caring teacher working inside a school with no culture of caring around her will remain a single candle at midnight. A teacher can't set high expectations when the state legislature thinks so little of education that it doesn't allocate enough money for the arts or technology or even textbooks. In order to see the behaviors and outcomes we want from our students and teachers in the classroom, we have to see those same behaviors modeled throughout the network we create around our schools. We have to see that they matter, that they're accounted for in looking at student progress and used to determine who can lead and who can teach. Caring is a country that never lets a child be in a classroom without a caring adult relationship. Our Connected Schools become places where our partners can offer their best selves.

This begins in the broadest terms. We as a nation must do for the entire public education system what we want to do for each classroom—guarantee that caring, high expectations, and diverse approaches to learning exist, though they'll go by different names. Caring, on a national level, is equity, the belief that all children matter and deserve to succeed. High expectations are the five ideas, outlined at the end of the previous chapter, that serve as the foundation of all this work: all kids can learn, the power of a caring relationship, measurement, investment, and the structural value of schools. Diverse approaches to learning are exactly the fine work of creating Connected Schools and functioning classrooms that we've just been discussing that then allow, on the next level down, the fine work of teaching. As it is with students, there are many ways to make this happen. States will have to work closely with their local governments; local governments with their school systems; schools and governments with their local arts, business, and service communities—all in order to find the right combination of support for their schools. Caring, high expectations, and diverse approaches to learning must telescope up and down our educational system, from the mind of the student up to the national will. Changes we make at the top will have a direct effect on the educational experiences of our children.

Now, somewhere there's a teacher reading this with bags under her eyes, test papers from her seventh-grade class piled on one side of her kitchen table, her own bills on the other, and she's ticking off in her head all the problems we have in education. High-stakes testing and NCLB compliance. Teacher pay and the lack of good teachers. Inadequate funding. Outdated, often dangerous facilities. On and on it goes. She can barely think straight about her students' school performance for all the noise and struggle that surrounds her job. It's begun to seem to her as if those theoretical debates and policy arguments are really the point, and they're all impossible to solve. So then, what *is* the point? Caring and high expectations are nice and all, but she has to literally beg for art paper. How can we build when we're so busy putting out fires?

It's not just educators thinking this, the whole nation is. We've hit a point where all our endless conversations about educational problems and theories overshadow the true work that needs to be done. The best we've managed is a weak, cobbled-up law that's been trampled on by state politicians. The problems can't be solved, we're telling ourselves, so what's the point? And so everyone's losing hope and making a mad dash for the lifeboats that are vouchers and charter schools and private schools.

Here's my answer to all these unsolvable problems: Let's solve them.

If we're going to tend the common garden with the fine work of Connected Schools and classrooms, it's time to stop arguing, pick up our tools, and clear the ground of seven deep-rooted issues that right now we're all just scratching our heads about. We all feed from a national economy. We all service the national debt. We enter into trade and military agreements as a nation. The movement of the dollar up and down affects all of us on the most grassroots level. Education is at the core of our national existence—in fact, in 2005 the National Academy of Sciences issued a report that said our "strategic and economic security" was at risk if we didn't start producing more effective graduates. We can't let ourselves drift any longer. With the stroke of a pen, JFK sent us on our way to the moon, and that's what we need now, a vision that will create educational expectations for this nation and the stair steps to reach them.

If we deal with the seven issues in this chapter on a national level, we will anchor equity and efficiency into our educational system and allow local schools to do the fine work of educating our children in a new and more connected way that will prepare them for a global economy. These seven points must be in place before America's public schools can enter the community as the active and independent players we need them to be. They're the measurable behaviors that will prove if we've taken the five ideas at the end of Chapter Four seriously and are truly building on the solid foundation of equity that will be necessary for twenty-first-century schools and not leaving any child behind:

1. National standards

2. National assessments

3. Teacher pay

4. Teacher certification and support

5. Universal preschool

6. Facilities—repair, renovation, and new construction

7. Middle school

Too simplistic? Well, I know God is in the details, but we need to turn the details back into the means, not the end. Right now we need clear expectations for ourselves as a nation so that we can all focus on how to get the job done. Years have been wasted on discussions about assessment and teacher pay and tenure, and nothing has come of them. Even worse than the chatter is our profound structural confusion. Because so many vital aspects of education are in the hands of the states, we have fifty different solutions to the same problems, fifty different solutions whose alleged value as being more responsive to the needs of local constituents is marginal at the very best, and at worst, as we see, confusing and disruptive to the greater work. With fifty different state standards and state requirements and state inaction and state inefficiency, the possible outcomes on any given educational issue keep multiplying until it's impossible for us to have any sort of quality control on the most important product of all that we create in this country—mature and conscious contributors to society.

Take pre-K, for example. While the research overwhelmingly shows that early learning is vital to a student's future success, only thirty-eight states spend money on preschool programs, and that in a fashion I would generously call patchwork: local schools, faith-based care, private preschools of wildly differing quality, day care, you name it, all distributed with no plan, all teaching—if we can call it teaching—whatever they want. Some offer pre-literacy and pre-numeracy skill development and prepare their kids for kindergarten. Others have no bearing on that world at all. They have no standards and simply roll the ball out and let the kids play. Have a nap, milk and cookies, and then the parents pick them up. We go about academic assessment the same way: different tests for each state that end up costing hundreds of millions of dollars, instead of one national test that would cost less and give us better data about our international performance. Facilities that range from shameful to the sublime. Salaries that have some teachers in the stock market and others in the poorhouse. *It Depends*, we're told, on how much money the state has. *It Depends* on our technological structure. *It Depends* on the leadership. *It Depends* on the budget. *It Depends* on the next election. *It Depends* on the polls. For the sake of our democracy, our economy, and our security, we can't allow education to be a passive, "It Depends" kind of business.

I am in favor of choice and exploring a wide variety of options. Under the right circumstances, choice and variability give us creativity and smart solutions. But we must decide *where* in the entire structure of American education we want them. The kind of creative variability demanded by Connected Schools must be there by design, not through lack of effort or lack of thought or lack of concern or lack of money or the discrimination that hides behind those. If you want children to express themselves artistically, you don't just put them in the art room and say, "Go do it." You focus the effort. You care enough to put out crayons and paints and paper and define an object or experience or idea for them to draw. As counterintuitive as it may seem in a free-market culture, good structure eliminates meaningless choices and sets conditions that let people get down to the real work of innovation and addressing specific needs. In the early years of this nation, people used coins from all around the world and the states as currency until the obvious benefits of a single currency became apparent. Creating one track standard let railroads stretch into every corner of America; creating one Internet standard let us explore the possibilities of connectedness instead of battling endlessly about which software platform we'd use to do it. In the seven critical areas listed earlier, we need that common coin and common goal in order to function not just most efficiently but also most creatively. We can't let our children fall further and further behind while one state works on teacher shortages and another spends all its time on its science curriculum and deciding whether to incorporate a Christian-right philosophy or to follow the standard, research-based philosophy of science.

I know from experience that reducing variability works. Instead of cutting loose troubled schools in New York and Miami, I brought them together into what I called the Chancellor's District. We applied a uniform approach to instruction and set uniform expectations that allowed everyone from administrators to students to tune out the noise and get down to producing results. And it worked. Mayor Rudy Giuliani and I had a great relationship for several years during my tenure as chancellor in New York. He was a strong mayor and a very bright man, though with a limited understanding of how school systems work. One day he called me into his office and simply said, "What do we need to do to get this right on behalf of the children of New York City?"

I explained that there were three things we needed to do and do them quickly:

1. Concentrate on literacy and focus specifically on preschool through grade three

2. Get our arms around the lowest-performing schools and either shut them down or improve them

3. Return the arts to the curriculum as an integrated approach to literacy

All *he* wanted, the mayor said, was to improve the situation and be known as the mayor who ended social promotion and cracked the code of low performance in urban schools. Essentially, the deal we cut that day was that I got to focus on that work without any interference, and whatever we achieved would go to Giuliani's list of political accomplishments. In that meeting Rudy and I created a clear, unalterable (I thought) vision that went across the system and reflected a common theme of implementation from the mayor's office to the chancellor's office directly into every community and every school in every borough of New York City.

This kind of across-the-board approach allowed us to do some great things in New York, and it's what America needs right now. Reducing variability in the seven areas I outlined will create equity, and therefore efficiency. By operating on a shared foundation and resources, we'll be able to tailor each of our schools to the specific needs of our communities. Our national conversation should be about one thing: using caring, high expectations, and diverse approaches to learning in every level of our public school systems, from the home and school to the superintendent's office and the statehouse, to produce mature and conscious contributors to society. With federal oversight of the seven basic elements, all of us will be able to consolidate our work into the few essential things that every school ought to be doing, that every parent ought to be doing, that every community ought to be driving toward with Connected Schools so that kids are equipped for the complexities and challenges ahead. A common belief in the necessity of this work must meet the individual effort of millions.

NATIONAL STANDARDS

No matter how much money is spent and how many tests are administered and reports issued, it simply does not matter whether fourth graders in Iowa test better in math than, say, fourth graders in Arizona or Missouri. Not a bit. And it is inexplicable to me why a child in Arkansas or Utah should leave school with a different base of knowledge from a child in New York or Michigan and how that serves the national good when the whole point is whether or not we can compete against China or India or the EU. Imagine if Notre Dame spent its entire athletic budget on intramural flag football and then stuck helmets on the champions and sent them to a bowl game. It's an ugly picture, but that's what we're doing by playing state versus state instead of focusing on the big picture. And trust me, the other guys are crushing us early.

Somewhere along the way, we dropped the ball. In our postindustrial culture, where we push buttons to buy things from all corners of the globe, we have forgotten to ask how things happen, how they're made, how they work. Instead, it's all about style and surface: all we care about is how pretty the dunk is, not whether we win or lose the game; which college sticker is in our rear window, not what our children learn. The flat world means, quite literally, a level playing field across the globe; people have learned who we are and what we do, and they're doing it better because they care more, they're learning the basics, and they're trying harder. We don't play that way anymore, not on the court, not in our schools, not in our businesses.

Instead of helping us wrap our arms around this issue as one people with one set of standards, NCLB sent fifty states home, and they came up with fifty *different* sets of academic standards for their children, many of which, as we've seen, were either bogus or manipulated after the fact. It was absurd for the United States to let individual states decide *what* those standards would be. This is too important. I have yet to see anything that remotely resembles the consistent national measure of third, fifth, and tenth graders in America that we need to direct their improvement up to levels where they'll be internationally competitive. Meanwhile, the student body president of a high school in North Miami presides over students who come from thirty different countries and speak fifty different languages. America's future will be spent in a small world that will demand portable knowledge and skills. So in one voice, we as a nation have to state our expectations to our students that they *will* compete in the global economy. To get us back to playing Xs and Os basketball again, the kind of hardworking, fundamental ball that wins championships, we must establish national standards that are benchmarked internationally to the set of tools—reading, math, and science—our young people will need to navigate the globe. National standards simply state what our children must know to survive in a world where good enough isn't good enough anymore.

Now, what you probably don't know is that we already have national standards, challenging, tough national standards that can be compared internationally so we can gauge where we are next to other nations. A provision in NCLB made the annual National Assessment of Educational Progress (NAEP) tests the control. State results are placed next to the NAEP numbers, and that's where those enormous gaps came from that we saw in Chapter One between state "proficiency" and the true international performance of students throughout America, such as Tennessee's claim of 87 percent "proficient" versus 27 percent on the NAEP test. When I took over in New York, I put the NAEP standards in place voluntarily for our school system, and they're what we use in Miami. Many localities don't want to use them, though, because revealing their actual proficiency levels would be too damaging politically and economically. I say, "Too bad." We have what we need at hand without getting bogged down in micromanaging every detail of what constitutes Academic Proficiency. We don't need committee meetings and congressional hearings. All we have to do is put those NAEP standards in place across the board as the standards every child in America is reaching toward.

Not long ago national standards were a political hand grenade. The left distrusted standardized testing, and the right hated the idea of federal control, but while we've spent the last few decades arguing, the rest of the world has overtaken us on the things that we actually do agree on, things like 1 + 1 = 2. As we harvest the poor crop that NCLB has given us, voices from all over the political spectrum—from Bill Bennett and Rod Paige, two secretaries of education in Republican administrations, to the progressive Robert Gordon, an education adviser to John Kerry, to Diane Ravitch of NYU and the Brookings Institution—are calling for national standards and national assessment. Standards are how we start stitching back together our common vision of America.

They'll be pointless, though, just another mountain of numbers, unless they're used as part of a leveraged and funded set of strategies based on the belief that all kids can learn, as the goal of a cohesive, coherent national policy driven by rewarding success instead of punishing failure. Right now we're all over the place. None of us—educators, parents, students—know what we're aiming at, and so we've let education become a race to the riches that you either win or lose. There's no national leadership, no shared sense of what education means. Wherever I go, I see the popcorn effect—local politicians who pop up on the stage as the "education mayor" or the "education governor" and then quickly disappear when the bad news comes. Politics drive too many of our decisions about education. Progress and momentum that took years to build can be wiped away in a day to serve other ends that have nothing to do with teaching our children. One state claims great results, while its neighbor is mired in a hopeless battle over issues that should have been settled long ago. Our upper crust of kids and schools may be as good as any in the world—but we just don't have enough. If we don't start moving more kids up from the middle and lower rungs, those kids—and all of us—will lose in a bigger way than we ever have before.

National standards will eliminate all that intellectual and political clutter and force us to focus on the technical issues surrounding the equitable distribution of quality education. The color of our cars won't matter anymore; what will matter is what makes the engines go faster. At every point along the way of creating Connected Schools, we'll have to ask: What are the optimal strategies for students and schools to reach those national standards? What do we know right now that optimizes the student-teacher relationship? What are the things that optimize school performance? What optimizes a state's relationship with a local school system?

They'll also clarify our often questionable sense of accountability surrounding education. On the face of it, I'm not against bad consequences for poor performance. Anyone or anything that persistently fails and shows little or no improvement over a reasonable time period should be held accountable. Connected Schools are built on an intricate web of relationships predicated on all parties being accountable for their roles in creating education. But simply holding people accountable for failing isn't a strategy for improvement in and of itself. Unfortunately, it's the only strategy most states have in place right now, and to make it worse, it usually carries an implication of ill will, as if failure by a school or a student were somehow willful.

America needs to say flat out that we believe *all* our children *do* want to learn, that we believe *all* our teachers *do* want to teach, but intentions aren't enough in the global economy. Because there's no substitute for high-performing children in our country, state departments of education will now, instead of obsessing on compliance and punishment, concentrate on providing technical support. A technical support team is an entirely different thing from a state education department barging into a school, snapping pictures, and taking names as if it were at a crime scene. If a student doesn't get his algebra assignment right, you don't drag him out of the classroom and punish him. In fact, that's the exact *opposite* of what you ought to do. Instead, you should intervene in a way that assumes there's a mechanical problem with how the student views this topic or how his mind sees this particular formula. Algebra is a series of formulas and equations that you have to get a rhythm for. The student doesn't have that rhythm, so we now have to intervene in a very methodological, technical way. Since caring assumes that all kids can learn and that there is a will to learn, from now on we're going to approach failure the same way as a teacher sees failure, as a learning moment, a chance to see whether a different approach is needed. Failure is an engineering problem, not a behavior problem, and no matter what happens, we will approach academic failure within a school system with our eyes open for a technical solution, not a moral or philosophical or political one. There's still accountability and, if necessary, punishment in the system, but punishment is not the goal; everything is done to serve the true goal, which is reaching those national standards and creating mature and conscious contributors to society.

Ultimately, this is a matter of national will. We've known something has to happen, but we haven't really wanted to bother attacking the problem, so we set out guidelines that have all the teeth of the nutritional pyramid. If we need a model, we should look instead at how we as a nation reduced smoking. Once smoking was identified as not just a voluntary health risk but one with

stacked odds that was taking an immense toll on the nation's economy, the national will changed, and we—not as one, but as a majority—expressed that through the limitations now placed on
tobacco use. In education, we have even more reasons to demand
change. Public money, both local and some federal, goes into the
system. As I see it, we will need a massive ("massive" only in relative terms to what's been done so far for public education; pennies
compared with what we spend on tank prototypes and corporate
welfare) commitment from the federal government to accomplish
our goal. Therefore, serious national standards that everyone will
have to reach are the quid pro quo for national support.

We've been afraid to set national standards for another reason
beyond the personal politics of local leaders afraid of their own accountability and the larger divisiveness of party politics. The fact
is, we're afraid our students can't reach them, and we're afraid our
teachers can't teach them. We don't have the system in place to deal
with it. Who will read the papers? Who will deal with the fallout?
The questions and doubts go on and on, but believe me, they'll go
away when we say, "We will have national standards." When I
took over as superintendent in Miami, we were desperately short
of places, what we call student stations. During my first couple of
weeks on the job, I asked the head of the building department how
many new stations they had planned for the coming year, and he
said five thousand. "How many do you think we'll need?" I asked.
He shrugged and said probably at least ten thousand. So I asked
him, "What would it take to get those ten thousand? What would
your department look like? How many hours would you have to
work? Who would you have to fire and hire?"

I may as well have asked him to build the Brooklyn Bridge with
his bare hands. He'd have to reorganize this and reprioritize that
and expand here and on and on and on until I cut him off and said,
"Your goal this year is fifteen thousand stations. And just so you
know that it's a *real* goal, if you don't get them, you're fired."

He staggered out the door, and pretty soon he left the district.

I brought in someone else, and at the end of the year we had eighteen thousand new stations.

Necessity often creates magical powers in people and organizations. When you *have to* do something, the questions are all about how, not why.

NATIONAL ASSESSMENTS

Success in life is not about penciling in dots. But every year, in every state of the Union, the lives of families and schools are thrown into utter disarray by high-stakes tests mandated by NCLB. Parents are frustrated; their kids literally worry themselves sick over whether or not they're going to pass the tests and what will happen to them if they fail. Teachers teach almost exclusively to the test, gutting arts and elective programs from the curriculum for all but the most talented children and replacing them with—you guessed it—test prep. Some schools place children in low-level prep courses designed to build their skills toward a passing grade but whose real effect is to break their confidence. Most fourth graders in public schools spend the entire year being taught what will be on the mandated tests that spring rather than anything new; in effect, it's a lost year in their education because anything outside the range of the test is considered a waste of time. The results, after all of that, are reams of numbers based on watered-down state standards.

Is this really what we want out of our assessment process? All-or-nothing academic tests that warp the purpose of education and create more anxiety than learning? Our insistence on testing not only encourages maniuplation and waste, it also doesn't help us compare to our real competitors overseas. NCLB may define what adequate yearly progress is, but since each state has a different test, we spend, according to *Education Week*, something like $500 million a year on versions on the same test, which still vary widely in their ability to differentiate actual skills from simple memorization.

That's good for the testing companies, who drive range wars between states as to how many data items they're collecting and the like, but it's bad for the rest of us.

Worst of all, though, is that the way we test now doesn't assess where we are in producing kids who can walk out the door at the end of the school year really knowing what they need to know to build on next year, and enter the global economy once they graduate. The current testing structure has no way to assess where our kids stand on Personal Integrity, Workplace Literacy, or Civic Awareness, those "soft skills" that are the true measure of their ability to survive.

As we go forward into Connected Schools, we will need to assess our children in new ways.

First, we need one commonsense national assessment. It would come naturally out of national standards, and it would give us real numbers to compare with the rest of the world. And every high school student should have to pass a test on the U.S. Constitution in order to graduate. Period.

Second, we need to test for things beyond raw Academic Proficiency. We need to assess, on a nationwide basis, where our children stand when it comes to Personal Integrity, Workplace Literacy, and Civic Awareness. Without assessment in these areas, we're only looking at one tiny slice of the whole child and pretending to know his or her prospects for future success. But these qualities aren't "extras" anymore. They're now as determining as any math or reading skills, and they demand measurement and the accountability that goes with it.

Again, here's a place where a federal approach will open up opportunities for local creativity. With a standard national assessment, communities with Connected Schools will then concentrate on devising new metrics for measuring the four qualities of a mature and conscious contributor to society—detailed, specific measures that can look beyond the walls of the classroom to ask how well the child is applying the qualities in the "real" world alongside the school's connected partners. For example, in Miami we have eleven schools involved in a pilot internship program. These schools will now have students serving internships as part of their curriculum, which includes a capstone project that's the equivalent of a thesis. Teachers who have these senior interns will mentor them through their capstone project. In effect, they're pushing past the traditional limits of period-by-period teaching and providing something akin to doctoral guidance. The program has created major challenges in how we deploy resources, and it's making us ask a whole different set of questions around assessment. Instead of just asking if the students are academically prepared, we're asking whether they're Workplace Literate. Do they have a sense of Civic Awareness? Of cultural literacy? Do they know how to work in groups? Take initiative? We need to be able to draw a rounded portrait of each child—his or her strengths and weaknesses as a scholar and as a person who will be operating in a flat world.

Finally, we must view assessment as exactly that: a method to determine where, at this moment in time, a child is on the journey to becoming a mature and conscious contributor to society. Assessment cannot continue as the Darwinian, survival-of-the-fittest exercise it is today. As most states do it now under NCLB, testing works like counting mortality rates in hospitals. It doesn't tell you how to be successful; it just tells you if you've failed. Imagine if we dealt with obesity the same way. Somebody'd be outside your house with a bullhorn, making sure that everyone heard loud and clear that you were overweight and that you'd better eat right and exercise. And then he'd leave you standing there on your doorstep, wondering what to do.

As much as I dislike high-stakes testing, I'm not against assessing children. If you'll recall, it's one of the five ideas underlying the creation of Connected Schools, so in fact, I want *lots* of assessments. I asked for *more* assessments within the Chancellor's District in New York, monthly and weekly tests. I put in quarterly assessments when I came to Miami. But the point of assessment, whether it's of the hard skills of Academic Proficiency or of the soft skills of the other three qualities, is not to identify failing children and schools so they can be punished. It's to find the boy who can't divide whole numbers when he's still in third grade, instead of finding him in eighth grade, so we have a chance to fix the problem before his entire experience of math becomes a tragedy. Constant interim assessments ask kids to stop and demonstrate where they are in their learning process, instead of dancing for their lives. They allow us to diagnose *our* work as educators, to see what's working and what's not. The child's brain is only one part of the understanding equation; assessment lets us work on the variables we can control.

TEACHER PAY

Whether you're in Iowa, Minnesota, or New York City, no teacher in America should make less than $40,000.

In the summertime when I was a boy, I'd go and sit out on the porch with one of the upstairs boarders, name of Mr. Gatewood. Mr. Gatewood used to be a cabbie in New York City before his legs got bad on him and he had to quit, so now he was looking for just about any kind of work. Problem was, he couldn't read. The man had a really good math mind, could do all sorts of figures in his head, but he couldn't read, and he wanted to learn in the worst way. So this one day we were sitting out, and Mr. Gatewood stopped in the middle of a story.

"You know what I need?" he said. "What I need is I need some Lucky Strike cigarettes. Would you run to the store and get me some cigarettes?"

I said sure. This was my *other* other job, running errands for everybody in the building, and they'd give me a quarter here and there. So I ran to the store, got him his package of Lucky Strikes, came back, and gave him the change. He opened his pack of cigarettes, lit one up, and then held out both fists.

"This is for you," he said. "Tap the one where you think the money is."

So I tapped one, and there's a nickel. "Thank you, Mr. Gatewood," I said. "I appreciate it."

"Well," he said, "you finished?"

"Yeah, I got my money."

"Naw, you got to keep going." So I tapped his other hand, he opened it up, and this one had a dollar in it. "This is for another reason," he said. "This one is if you help me learn how to read. You teach me to learn to read, and I'm gonna pay you a dollar a week."

I sat down. I didn't know how to teach anybody how to read. I was about ten, and I remember having a deep pain in me about the idea of a grown man not being able to read. I had enough problems with my own self, and here was this grown man coming to me for help. The pain of being illiterate became so real to me. *How you gonna get your job?* I wondered. *How you gonna pay us rent? How you gonna be a* man? I tried really hard to work with Mr. Gatewood. Though I never took his money, because I could barely read myself at the time, for the next few months I would bring my books and sit with him and show him how to sound out letters and words, until one day Mr. Gatewood moved out and I never heard from him again.

But none of that had anything to do with my becoming a teacher. Heck, I went to Babson planning to come back to Harlem and open a barbecue restaurant with my dad. I finally became a teacher when I decided that I wanted to *make a living* as a teacher.

Teaching is a profession. It is not charity work. It is not something you do until something better comes along, nor is it something you do when there's nothing else *to* do. Teaching should not be a matter of expiating guilt, doing good, or making a difference. It is a highly skilled, vital vocation, and I want serious, dedicated, brilliant professionals who have a stake in the success of their efforts. Please, no more touching tales of white men bringing order to the chaos of ghetto schools, or stockbrokers leaving it all behind to pat heads and zip parkas. If you want to teach, don't do it out of pity. Do it as you would any other profession, with the same focus and drive and determination you brought to the trading floor.

There are tens of thousands of teachers working in America today who *are* brilliant, motivated, and inspiring. But we need a lot more. And we need ones who are even more talented than many of the ones we do have. Our nation is full of good, smart people who really would make terrific teachers. Every day I have the frustrating experience of meeting men and women who would be amazing in front of an English literature class or an intro biology class or a roomful of third graders all ready to learn fractions, but they're in marketing or pharmaceuticals or some other part of the private sector.

The problem is we pay charity wages for professional work. In Miami entry-level teachers with a bachelor's degree make $34,200, and those with a doctorate make $41,200 per year. That's not a living wage in a city where the average house costs more than $400,000 and the average apartment is about $1,100 a month. Teachers need to make enough money to buy a home and live and work in their community, but they're just about the only group of professional employees who can't. Look at what we're asking of them: We're asking teachers to do incredibly hard, fine work, often in dismal, underfunded conditions, and drive two hours to do it. Then, after five years, they'll still be making less than what they'd have made five years earlier if they'd gone straight into the private sector. And we wonder why we can't attract the best people to teaching. In business terms, we are undercapitalizing the industry. Talented, skilled people in the sciences or mathematics have career and salary options that far outstrip what's possible for them on a teaching track. After my second son was born early in my teaching days, I realized that it was time to get out of our apartment and into a house. Once my wife and I finally found a place we loved, I pulled out the salary schedule. Some quick and depressing math made it clear that not only could I not afford that house now but it would *always* be just out of my reach. And so I was faced with the choice that faces thousands of teachers and potential teachers every year: keep doing the work I love or provide for my family. Luckily, I had graduated with a degree in business management that allowed me to stay in education by moving into administration, but I'm the exception. Who knows how many great teachers we've lost for exactly this reason.

For us to revitalize the profession, we need to do more than drop apples on teachers' desks. We need to capture a bigger share of the best and the brightest, who can in turn push our children forward. *A national pay structure for teachers, including performance-based pay, will help us do that.* I think that the requirements of the democracy, the requirements of the transformation of the human mind are such that the society has to put a base value on this work. The high end should be a function of collective bargaining, but as in any other profession, the scale should increase with tenure, credentials, and performance. While test scores would have to be one element, pay should also reflect how much a teacher uses his or her skills in the classroom. A doctor is paid for the ability to perform specialized kinds of surgery; it's the same with an architect or a lawyer who handles certain kinds of cases. Like any other professionals, teachers have tools of their trade, and there must be some provision made for teachers with high levels of technical proficiency. Programs such as housing and tax credits for educators, entry-level mortgage loans, and assistance with insurance can all do a great deal to defray bottom-line costs, but in the end most of all the federal government must subsidize a national wage scale for teachers.

The elephant in the corner is the issue of unions, and it's the reason why we can keep raising education budgets and yet still have the constant turnover that most undermines the quality of our current teaching stock. Unfortunately, far too many local unions are driven by the needs of senior teachers, who have traditionally been underpaid. This has forced unions to distribute meager resources in ways that don't serve the continued need to bring new teachers into the profession. As the system is structured now, teachers cannot vote in their unions until they've been teaching for five years. The young people coming in the door usually earn something in the $30,000s, and their salary structure isn't generous with them in terms of incremental raises on these bottom rungs. But since the members of the voting bloc that elects union leadership are all teachers who have been around at least six years, when more money is made available by governments for salaries, if I'm a union president, I have to make sure my voters are satisfied. So if the superintendent puts 17 percent over three years on the table— 5 percent first year, 7 percent second year, 5 percent third year—the money will be distributed very heavily among the senior teachers, and the crumbs are tossed to the five and unders, who immediately head for the exits. Hence the constant turnover and the lack of experienced teachers that grows more acute every year. It isn't the top end of teachers who are leaving. Those folks are invested. They're not walking away from their retirement. The people leaving are in that first through fifth year. Their jobs are incredibly hard, the learning curves are incredibly steep, and dollar for dollar, incremental year to year, their salaries are so minimal they don't see the purpose of hanging in.

Every union I've ever worked with and every union system I've ever been in has taken its dollars and distributed them along this kind of continuum. That's why the answer isn't just handing teachers more money. It's a matter of making the best use of our educational dollars, of leveraging our investment. As long as the unions allocate salaries in this fashion, even if we open up Fort Knox, the issue of teacher pay won't get solved.

In every other industry around the country, attracting talent out of the limited pool of qualified workers is harder and harder. This whole book is predicated on the fact that this nation is suffering a shortage of talented workers. And so how do we expect to attract talent to education in a more competitive environment when we force teachers to put up with what is essentially five years of donated work before they're able to make a living wage?

Unions have every right to a higher wage, every right to appropriate working conditions, I don't argue with that. I was a teacher, so I do understand the need for those things. I've also talked a lot in this book about paying dues and working your way up, and I can see how senior teachers would view those first five years as a probationary period to see who's really talented and serious. Perseverance, expertise, experience—these should all be rewarded. But not at the expense of losing the new blood coming into the system. This is ostrich thinking at its sandiest.

Unions have to change. They have hurt themselves in the last several years because they've established a primacy of purpose around building up the union as opposed to the building of the human mind, and so we're constantly poised for war against each other instead of against the tyranny of ignorance and the challenges of the flat world.

Unfortunately, the forces of reality are not strong enough to make unions change. They have a lot of money in their coffers. They can buy off politicians, buy off school board elections, but when they exempt themselves, they really are exempting teachers from professional development; they're exempting people from real training they need to do their craft. Unions destroying their own industries is nothing new. Industries such as the airlines are dying on the vine because both the cost of doing business and the way you have to do business drive the actual cost through the roof. Remember, I was raised by a New Dealer who loved Paul Robeson, so I can talk about the Struggle all day, but we can't let education go down that road. The world has changed. The constellation of forces that make up the ability of a school system to attract and hold on to teachers are different, but unions fail to admit this. The need for performance in return for pay has heightened, but unions fail to admit this. The need for stability and a consistent student-teacher relationship—and therefore the end of free transfers by teachers with tenure—is paramount in a child's education, but unions fail to admit this.

You can't ask the beast to be something it isn't gonna be. You can't ask it to be an egalitarian organization at the same time it's a union. Therein lies the problem, and I've had too many years when we've put all the union demands on the table, and what you never got was a better system. And it was never enough. It was an empty hole. To some degree the union movement has become as perverse and greedy as the management quest for profit, and neither of those worlds will endure in, or add sufficiently to, a flat world. We need to pay all our teachers more, but we also need a national pay structure so that someone else does the allocation.

TEACHER CERTIFICATION

In return for a living wage, the government needs to establish national certification standards for teachers and school leaders.

We've spent too many years throwing money at this problem, and I don't propose increasing teacher pay in that spirit. I have high expectations for my teachers. Again, teaching is not something you do instead of waiting tables until that "real" job comes through. It's not a hobby or an indulgence. It demands competence, professionalism, and commitment, and those willing to offer those qualities to the general good should be paid accordingly. But there's no place in a classroom for a teacher who doesn't know how to teach the material or—and believe me, I've seen it—a teacher who doesn't even understand the material itself. I've witnessed teachers sleeping at their desks, reading newspapers while the kids ran wild, or just standing up at the front of the room and winging it, chatting away with no plan or focus whatsoever. I've seen a teacher literally throw a child across a room. We must either help those who aren't qualified get qualified or show them the door.

Certification is not a gotcha game. Struggling students and struggling schools need help, not punishment, and the same is true for teachers. While we need to elevate the standards of our teachers, it must be in the context of developing career educators, not creating further burdens on people who are already carrying heavy loads. We need to make teaching a profession, just like medicine or the law. Chapter Eight will explore this in greater detail because establishing teaching as a viable profession demands lots of angles and input. We need to create leverage at national levels to support our teachers financially and professionally. Left to our own devices, we are too slow, too entrenched, too bureaucratic, and too unwilling to effect the change ourselves.

UNIVERSAL PRESCHOOL

We can no longer afford—in all senses of the word—to think of preschool as babysitting.

Back when my kids were in diapers, you hung a mobile over the crib and figured it would keep them busy until they were old enough for blocks, and then, before you knew it, they were in school. Recent research, though, shows that young brains can do a lot more than we thought, and what does or doesn't happen in the preschool years can have a profound effect on a child's school experience and, therefore, life. One fascinating study with deep implications often comes up in reference to this topic, notably in a 2006 *New York Times Magazine* piece by David L. Kirp. Professor Eric Turkheimer of the University of Virginia did a series of twin studies regarding the IQs of twins in wealthy homes compared with those in low-income homes. While the variations between the twins in wealthy homes were all within a certain range, the scores of the twins in low-income homes varied widely, with the identical twins varying as much as the fraternal ones. The conclusion, then, as Kirp writes, is that "the impact of growing up impoverished overwhelms these children's genetic capacities. In other words, home life is the critical factor for youngsters at the bottom of the economic barrel."

Clearly there are many things missing in the lives of those children, but Kirp identifies one shocking difference discovered in another well-known study made by two University of Kansas psychologists, Betty Hart and Todd Risley. They found that "by the time they are 4 years old, children growing up in poor families have typically heard a total of 32 million fewer spoken words than those whose parents are professionals." Add to this what we've learned from brain research and early-literacy work, and it's clear that the achievement gap that's cleaving us apart doesn't begin in the job line or in high school or even in elementary school. It's starting when children are toddlers and just opens up wider the further kids go. A 2003 National Academy of Sciences study showed that good preschool does prepare children for what lies ahead of them in elementary school and beyond, and it's especially true with at-risk children.

This, of course, has sent the upwardly mobile off to buy Baby Einstein tapes so Ashley and Jason will be assured their place at Yale, but there are wonderful, exciting implications in this work that are much more profound than any fads. We're being offered a remarkable opportunity to teach and prepare our children in a way that can someday minimize so much of the catch-up work education must now do with older children. Not only are the bell curve and genetic determinism junk science and not true—all kids can indeed learn—but if we start offering our children educational experiences at a younger age than we had ever thought sensible, we can have a major positive impact on their lives, and therefore *all* of our lives. A 2006 cost-benefit analysis by the Committee for Economic Development (CED) of three high-functioning preschool programs showed a public benefit per $1 invested of between $2.69 and $7.16. When you include the child herself in the calculation, it rose to a high of $10.15 per dollar invested.

Very simply, preschool is where we start if we want to address inequities in education and reduce poverty's crushing impact on learning.

I don't believe that we should mandate preschool, but we must do two things on a national level that will hopefully get more of our young children in. First, create a universal preschool program. Right now only Oklahoma and Georgia offer preschool to all their residents. Out of twenty million preschoolers in America, just under one million are in Early Head Start or Head Start programs. These are only offered to low-income families, which is important, but this issue goes wider and deeper than helping the poor kids catch up. We have to offer *all* our kids more. Dealing with a flat world doesn't just mean getting more kids into engineering schools; it means creating literacy and numeracy earlier in the lives of all our children so they'll be better equipped to handle the kind of rigorous education they'll need to compete later. As the CED study says, "It's better to get it right the first time than to try to fix it after the fact." We're always trying to catch problems in our children, but we'll never truly "fix" a boy who can't read in eighth grade; we're in triage mode at that point, trying to stop the bleeding. Remediation is a major drain on our educational system, all the way up through postsecondary schools—teaching fourth-grade math in eighth grade cannot be the norm. But if we can put the basics in that boy's head when he's three or four, his chances of being able to read when he's six or seven go way up. We'll also be able to identify and diagnose learning disabilities and issues such as autism and other disorders earlier. Other nations understand this issue better than we do. Great Britain, China, India, Indonesia, and even Bangladesh have all recently put preschool at the top of their educational agendas.

The value of universal preschool promises to be immense. Instilling confidence in our youngest, sending them forward with a base of knowledge, can change everything. The difference between a child learning how to read in first grade versus fourth is enormous, because once that genie of illiteracy gets out, it quickly turns into "I can't," and the loss of confidence multiplies like a virus. It latches onto high drug use, teenage pregnancy, and the other ways kids who feel inadequate make themselves feel adequate, functional, as if they belong. This isn't brand-new information. It's time this nation says we're losing too many children and losing them too early. This is an appropriate intervention at the root of a national crisis.

Second, eliminate the variability. As I mentioned earlier, we have no national standards or requirements for any aspect of pre-K, so our children now bring a huge variation of preparation when they come into school, widening the bandwidth teachers have to work within and spinning off problems in all directions. The preschool we offer must be governed by a set of standards for the instructional programming and the people trained to deliver it. Preschools aren't to be understood as simply babysitting operations. These are now pre-literacy providers. The elitist backlash to early learning is holding kids, especially boys, back so that they are more controllable or will be able to do the work more easily. I've read interviews with affluent parents who hold their children back an extra year in preschool under the guise of letting their kids enjoy childhood longer. I think they have a different agenda, though, and it's about making sure their child stands out throughout school to get into the "right" college. But while a child who goes through his educational experience without being challenged, without having to work for learning, might stand out in his peer group in school, he'll have quite a shock waiting for him outside, where he won't get props just for doing work that's below his ability. Show me the parent in Appalachia or East St. Louis who doesn't want her child to do better than he's doing right now.

Universal preschool is not about rushing children. It's about trying to add to the basic skill set all children bring into school so we can better prepare them for the world in which they're going to live. It can't be at the expense of play and creativity and developing self-awareness. Instead of concentrating on how much education our children should have, we should focus on identifying and delivering the things that are absolutely critical for a quality education. Universal preschool is one of them.

FACILITIES

If you want proof that equity doesn't exist in our public schools, look at our facilities.

The Department of Education did just that in 1999 and reported that 70 percent of schools in poverty-stricken areas and more than 50 percent of schools with mostly minority populations had facilities that needed at the least serious repair and more likely replacement. No question, we have some beautiful public school facilities in America, but the Department of Education is quick to point out that since most school building budgets are locally provided, the disparity between haves and have-nots is dramatic, to say the least. Wealthy communities by and large have clean, well-maintained, well-equipped schools, while the middle and low ends of the spectrum get what they can scrape together or what's handed them. And what they're handed is often shocking. When I was in New York, I saw schools with coal-burning furnaces, bathrooms closed because the plumbing didn't work, blackboards that came away from the wall. In one school a water leak flooded classrooms. But that wasn't enough. Cracks in the walls allowed in winter air, so that the next morning the teachers found their rooms turned into ice rinks. Across America, schools report infestations of rats and roaches and mold. Ceilings have collapsed within an hour after class was dismissed. Air-conditioning is a luxury; ventilation is bad. Overcrowding is putting stress on facilities that causes them to degrade sooner than expected. I could go on.

From 1950 to 1980, America built a huge number of schools. What we built was architecturally appropriate to the needs of the time and the school population, so we had science labs with Bunsen burners and glass beakers and auto and wood shops, and we were sure that we'd be set, if not forever, then at least until it was somebody else's problem. Unfortunately, that *somebody else* turned out to be all of us who went to school in those buildings. Between 1980 and 2000 we had a period of not-so-benign neglect. No one put money into maintaining or updating facilities, either in terms of simple physical plant or in terms of technology. In cities, those schools that dated from before the baby boom were located mostly in low-income areas and therefore suffered the most from the lack of financial support and upkeep. Any schools that were built in this time were largely additions just to deal with overcrowding, and more often than building, we used mobile facilities that turned our playgrounds into trailer parks.

By the late 1990s, when the Department of Education did its report, we were finally waking up to the reality that our schools were falling apart. As much as I'd like to believe we suddenly developed a conscience, it was in fact forced upon us by rising enrollment and new technologies that schools lacked the physical resources to handle. Bunsen burners and beakers are nice, but schools now need computers. Schools can't be anachronisms; that defeats their entire purpose. If technology and science change in the world, then that's what and how schools must teach. Now America is in a phase of hurry up and build, hurry up and modernize, as we try to compensate for twenty years of letting our infrastructure decay.

But the problem isn't just that we didn't do anything to our schools for twenty years. The problem is also that we *were* doing something else, and that was having babies. In late 2006 America passed 300 million citizens, and an estimated 55 million of them are in K–12 school. Unlike Europe, where an aging population will bring serious financial and cultural problems in the coming decades, we're lucky to have youth on our side, but they'll only be on our side if they are well served and trained. Right now they're not, because too many of our schools are overcrowded, which, on a purely physical level, is taxing our facilities. The rise in immigration from Mexico and Central America means that much of that youth will be going to schools in the West, which is also, sad to say, the region of the country with the facilities most in need of repair and replacement. In the big cities, and especially those in the Northeast, overcrowding comes from a different demographic shift and is more linked to the realities of urban real estate. As white flight in the 1960s and '70s pulled people out to the suburbs, suddenly many urban schools were left underpopulated. The school systems then consolidated the schools and sold off buildings and land that they decided were no longer needed, figuring they could get back into the market if they had to. And then came two things, hand in hand: the new rise in population, which consists mostly of immigrants who increased the density in the same urban areas where schools had been consolidated, and the real estate boom. Despite what they'd originally believed, school systems can't afford to buy new land in dense and highly valued urban markets, and the land that *is* within their reach often requires expensive environmental mitigation. Maybe the lot needs ground cleanup because of toxic chemicals, or the empty factory that's available is contaminated with lead paint or asbestos and needs a complete abatement and removal program before it can be used. By the time you've done that work, the cost per square foot is astronomical.

This isn't just an urban problem. As we push out into the suburbs and exurbs, growing school-age populations there force communities not so much into hasty repairs as into programs of quick building to assure newcomers that the home they just bought has a school attached to it. While land costs are lower than in the cities, the sheer speed and quantity of the work that needs to be done and the tremendous demand for architectural companies and land developers, as well as the parcel taxes that will have to be levied, all start to raise square-foot prices there as well.

The reasonable drive for smaller class size is also putting a new sort of stress on the system. I agree that it's all but impossible to get caring, high expectations, and diverse approaches to learning into a classroom being held in a hallway or in a room with forty kids. Reducing class size, and even school size, will have a definite positive impact on equipping our kids with the four qualities of a mature and conscious contributor to society, but we need to be mindful of the realities that silver bullet throws off. Smaller classes mean more classes, which mean more teachers in a labor market already begging for qualified teachers and more classrooms in a national building inventory that's overcrowded and outdated. On the face of it, you might be happy to hear that your daughter's class is going down from thirty-three students to twenty-five, but will you still be happy if her classroom gets divided in half to make that happen? What if her class now meets in a bathroom? That happens now in schools, such is the problem, so if we're going to talk about class size, it has to be included in the blueprints of change, not treated as an afterthought.

And so, on all levels—equity, efficiency, meeting the challenges of a global economy—how do we leave no child behind when it comes to facilities? We know the ticket to success in the twenty-first century is a technology ticket, a math and science ticket, a literacy ticket. All American children deserve that, for themselves and for our own general good. Right now we're asking schools and school systems and cities to figure out how to compensate for several decades of neglect, and the way we're approaching this, in states like Florida, is to simply pull funds from the richer counties, where there's greater property-tax revenue, and send that revenue to the rural counties, thus taking dollars once again out of urban areas. Now, the fact is, according to the Department of Education, 78 percent of rural schools need repair or modernization, and out of the 250 poorest counties in the United States, 244 are rural. Make no mistake, rural schools need money. But deepening the problem in other parts of the country isn't the answer.

If we are to have national standards of academic achievement for our children and national certification standards for our teachers, we must require national standards for the physical structures of our schools as well. Schools, like hospitals, need to have standards for functionality, safety, and cleanliness.

AN ELEMENTARY SCHOOL MUST HAVE

- *Properly functioning heating and air-conditioning.*

- *Clean, working bathrooms* with hot and cold water.

- *A classroom for each teacher.*

- *A library.* There should also be enough up-to-date, grade-appropriate textbooks for every child.

- *Multipurpose rooms.*

- *Appropriate technological underpinnings.*

- *Working telephones for parent communication.*

- *Space for the arts.*

- *A nursing/health-care facility.*

A MIDDLE SCHOOL MUST HAVE ALL OF THE ABOVE, PLUS

- *Small group space.*

- *A gym.*

- *Up-to-date technological infrastructure.*

A HIGH SCHOOL MUST HAVE ALL OF THE ABOVE, PLUS

- *Science labs.*

In 1999 the Department of Education estimated it would take $127 billion to bring all our schools up to where they should be.

It's a lot, but the federal government needs to make this onetime investment. The number we need is closer to $100 billion, spread over five years, which we invest purely in the infrastructure of our public schools.

In return for this huge injection of funds, we'll have to be creative and nimble in how we spend it. Unfortunately, for all the business sense we supposedly have in our government now, I see too much of the brand of leadership that knows how to squeeze out profits and drive share value but is clueless as to how one creates a thriving, ongoing concern that profits not just the owners but the workers and the community it exists in. Smart businesses are flexible, not disposable. They learn how to serve demand and create it at the same time, just as we're doing in Miami with our Connected Schools. And when it comes to infrastructure, smart businesses don't let it rot. They invest in it, keep it maintained and current, and Miami's doing that, too. Since I arrived in 2004, we've built ten new schools and added thirty-eight thousand student stations, with sixty thousand currently under construction. Now we've begun a new program that uses prototypes to add to our building stock while keeping costs down. Our design teams looked at innovative school plans all around the globe and developed a new group of school buildings that can be put together in different combinations and customized to suit different needs and sites without having to start from scratch with every building. In our first dozen prototype schools, we estimate that we saved $9 million in planning costs alone, and using standard materials for all the buildings lets us save money by buying in bulk. Saving money, though, wasn't the only goal. The classrooms have more windows and aren't the old-fashioned boxes you might be accustomed to; instead, they're shaped in Ls and Zs to create more intimate spaces for student-student learning and student-teacher learning, as well as integrated learning opportunities for children with special needs.

These are the kinds of lessons Connected Schools need to learn from business, and these are the kinds of partnerships we should be entering into on a local level regarding our facilities, not sponsorship deals that simply pour money into general funds. Connected Schools will have to create multiuse centers, community-friendly places that take into account the range of uses of our surrounding school network. New schools will need to be able to expand and contract; populations do ebb and flow, and a little forethought will pay off later. This onetime federal investment can create equity throughout America, equity of a sort that goes beyond matters of black and white to embrace all of us, rich and poor, urban and rural, and everyone in between. Don't ask our kids to care, to bring their most serious and responsible selves to school, when they see the adults around them more concerned about flowerpots at the strip mall than the hole in the roof of their classroom.

MIDDLE SCHOOL: THE FORK IN THE ROAD

The middle school years are a volatile blend of childhood and adulthood that can be as frightening as they are wonderful. That's why middle schoolers need a lot more people running alongside them than they have right now.

The primary grades get a lot of attention. All those rows of little babies just starting to come up, laughing and losing their teeth; it kills us to see problems there. And high school, well, it's easy to picture those kids walking the streets without a job—we're already aware that we have to prepare them for what's next. But those kids in middle school, those tweens—they are *bad* news. They're loud; they smell funny. No one, including them, has any clue as to where they're headed, and they are, to a child, desperate to know. But the fight for success in high school, in and out of the classroom, is won or lost for most kids in middle school, and the marketers and media have noticed their vulnerability much more than the rest of us have.

We need, as a nation, to pay attention to all our middle schoolers. Unlike the six other areas we've covered in this chapter, there's not one action that can be put into place to improve the situation. If we want to put our arms around it, we must offer middle school students the same level of developmentally appropriate guidance and instruction that we offer in elementary and high school. This will take many forms.

These years are the fork in the road for many of our children. They were for me. When my older sister was in high school, my father took her to a fancy hotel in New York to meet with some college admissions people, and I was dragged along to watch a movie about campus life. To be honest, I hadn't been all that excited about going, as I was fixated during those years, to the exclusion of almost everything else, on how much we didn't have. But that was until the movie started. Seeing this place called college, with people riding their bikes under the elm trees, walking into beautiful old buildings with books tucked under their arms, changed that bitter hunger of not having into a desire for something more than just a new leather jacket. There was a world out there beyond the broken glass I had to sweep off our sidewalk every morning. I spent the rest of the time there wondering when we were going to be thrown out, told that we couldn't afford it, but to my amazement we weren't. A greater life for me began that day; things were made possible because I was guided to them.

The elementary years are about finding your knowledge: I'm smart. I can learn. Here's how I learn. I know that fact. I know how to learn that fact, and so on. Hopefully, you've been exposed to the concepts underlying the four qualities of a mature and conscious contributor to society—you've been to a play or a museum, you know that you're part of a nation and a state and a locality, you've been introduced to the idea of service and fundamental ethics. You've moved from literacy in the first grades to gaining content by third or fourth; you're not so much learning skills as using skills to gain knowledge. But now, in middle school, it's time to apply what you've been learning to your life. Arts become not a matter of exposure but a means of expression. You can actually perform some type of meaningful service in your community and should be expected to display your Personal Integrity in daily life—you have chores, use manners, and so on. Like it or not, issues around health at this point move past basic concepts of health to young people using their bodies for sports and intimacy. I'm not advocating the latter, but you're blind if you don't know that it's happening, and schools must play a role in teaching our children responsible ways of applying sexual and physical knowledge as well. Girls who are already maturing physically have best friends who wouldn't stand out in elementary school; overnight, boys get muscles and low voices. All their relationships are unstable—with peers, family members, teachers, you name it. He likes me, she doesn't like me, I'm in, she's out, who's cool, where do I belong?

Teaching or parenting these kids is not a passive act. Too often, though, because people at this age are beginning to roll on their own, we act as though they're already adults, able to make reasonable, mature decisions, while in fact these years are about learning *how* to be independent, not about being that way. As much as they push away for independence, these kids are also terribly needy and in fact very eager for more adult contact time, just at the point when many adults are mistaking their desire for independence as a desire to be left alone.

These kids are in an environment where they're always putting their wares out on the table, always having to show what they know and apply it publicly. They need people who are attentive to the gravity of this, who are talking to kids, looking behind their eyes—not just checking them off a list, but really *knowing*. When parents put their kids in private school, what I really hear them saying is, I want somebody to look behind my kid's eyes. I want that kind of attention paid to my child. That's not necessarily a selfish, narcissistic desire; it's a human one.

But that requires professionals smart enough to do fine, nuanced work while dealing at the same time with a wide range of development, mood, ability, you name it, so some of your best teachers have to be in middle school. But even more, these kids need guidance. Someone must meet with them on a regular, individual basis and look behind their eyes. In most school structures, though, that one adult who puts it all together for students has melted away. I'd like federal funds to pay for enough quality guidance counselors so that each middle school student has an adult who's in touch with him or her every week, or at least every month. Such a counselor would ask how students are feeling, ask what's up with them, notice when they're not in school and want to know why. In other words, he would convey the caring and high expectations that are essential to a successful school experience. We need someone who can track a child's development in all four qualities and begin preparing him or her for the outside world.

Keen, proactive guidance through the middle school years will also begin the process of building greater value into the high school diploma by allowing early detection of academic, psychological, or development issues and their immediate remediation before high school. The inadequacies of many children go undetected until they hit high school and experience a devastating dip in ninth grade when they're unable to function, let alone compete. High school then becomes a matter of learning what should have been learned in middle school. In Miami we're trying to provide more guidance for exactly this moment, catching problems in this transition period early and then providing guidance sessions on the University of Miami campus in the summer between eighth and ninth grades and guidance intervention as the school year begins. If every kid enters high school doing high school work, we'll have taken an enormous step toward success right there.

Guidance is only one part of the middle school focus. As middle schoolers well know, many things wait for them outside the walls of school, and they can feel them, are maybe even trying some of them. What they need is something I addressed in the discussion of Workplace Literacy—they need to know that they will have a life in the future. And the way to impart this knowledge is to expose them to the world of work. To hit this head-on, I propose a national occupational prep curriculum for the middle school years. In sixth and seventh grades, students would be exposed to the myriad of careers out there in the world. Throughout, there'd be research about careers, visitations, lectures, all with the goal of giving kids a sense of how their academic work fits into the world around them and into their own future. Basic aspects of Workplace Literacy would be covered. In eighth grade the emphasis would shift from career awareness to selection. What do you think you'd want to do? What do you want to do with your life? Students would do specific research tailored to their interests; they'd examine their choices in terms of dress, colleges, universities, and what they'd need to do. What does it take for me to do this job? I have to wear a smock? Every job is going to require me to speak, or work with some sort of group, small or large. I'm going to have to do more writing than I thought, and so on. The guidance system would be aligned with this project and would now include a mentor from the local business community, a Mr. Morris, if you will, who's been given a tax break by the federal government for hooking into our Connected Schools in this way. He'll be a part of the process so that each kid will have an adult who tests his or her ideas—this doesn't sound like you, why don't you look at this field or that occupation, here's what you'll have to do to do that. This is about the journey, not the destination. (We don't want kids selecting their lifetime occupation when they're twelve. We'd wind up with a world full of quarterbacks and fashion models.) We'll tell the students we expect a report at the end of the year, but the real result we're looking for is the start of the process of elimination.

I want kids to enter high school with three years of experiences that make them knowledge-driven about their futures and what's possible in life instead of just leaving it up to chance. In high-demand cultures, where families do this work almost without thinking about it, parents make sure kids are exposed to a wide array of possibilities. They meet doctors and lawyers; they're aware—in a realistic sense—that people become airplane pilots and college professors and franchise owners. But in those parts of the nation where parents can't offer those exposures—or even know that they exist, believe it or not—many children don't even know they could become a doctor. The concept is so beyond their world that they may as well aspire to be queen of England or emperor of a distant planet. That hurts us as a nation. Let's eliminate this variability in career knowledge and reintroduce the old idea of economic mobility. It will create new dreams and new opportunities for all of us.

Addressing middle school is how we cut down on teenage pregnancies and dropouts; it's how we recharge the high school experience and add value to a high school diploma. A little prevention will save us time and money, and lives. Leaving no child behind means just that, that no child gets lost, no child walks through the halls of a middle school without a clear vision of what she might want to do with the rest of her life.

A MIDDLE SCHOOL CURRICULUM SHOULD INCLUDE

- An introduction to careers.

- The ability to begin to define the steps to be taken toward the attainment of a career goal.

- More attention to social deportment.

- A longer day than elementary school.

- Segments of time devoted to instruction related to social behavior.

- Instruction on how to write a résumé and balance a checkbook.

- Researching and declaring a major interest of study.

- Intense guidance and mentoring from the local business community.

Let me be clear:

Culture wars may swirl around us, but the truth is we really don't have that many differences among us as to what constitutes standards in reading, math, and science. I may not like what you let your child read, but I certainly want your child *to be able to* read.

I do not advocate the federal government controlling public education.

I do not advocate the federal government telling states and localities how to reach standards.

I do not advocate the federal government becoming a national school board.

I do not advocate the repeal of NCLB.

But I *do* believe that for us to succeed in truly not leaving any child behind, we can't work piecemeal. If we're serious about moving our educational system into the future, we can't wait for states to catch up. The federal government must lead us forward.

How will we pay for all this?

Let's be honest. The day America decides to *really* change its public school system, America will pay for it. As my father would say, "Anything worth having is worth paying for." There's a definite correlation between per-student spending and achievement; I think *that's* worth paying for. But what *have* we been paying for with our tax dollars the last few years?

According to Citizens Against Government Waste, we've spent $105.9 million since 1995 on a plan to harness the energy in the aurora borealis; $13.5 million in 2006 for the International Fund for Ireland, which helped pay for the Donegal town waterbus and the World Toilet Summit; $5 million to improve transportation at the St. Louis Zoo; $500,000 for a teapot museum in North Carolina. Even though I grimace when I think of what could have been done even with that money, I know that earmarks aren't really the point. A recent study by the Kennedy School of Government estimated that the war in Iraq will cost between $500 and $700 billion. Once the subsidiary costs on the economy are added in, the bill could easily pass $1 trillion. American corporations receive billions upon billions of dollars in tax rebates, much of which is then passed along in compensation to CEOs. And at the same time we have students, young Americans, with no books, no pencils, no desks. Make no mistake—we're subsidizing billionaires at the expense of our future. How hard would it be to offer a tax incentive to corporations and businesspeople, to the arts community, and to universities, big and small, for accepting their responsibility to enter the network of support for the schools in their communities? Eliminating variability in our patchwork educational system, building a nation of Connected Schools, will do more than save us money; replacing millions of nonfunctioning adults with ones who not only don't take money out of the public coffers but generate it by working, spending, saving, and starting their own businesses will repay any investment hundreds of times over. If you want to cut taxes, you cut the *need* for taxes. You don't turn your head away and thereby allow a segment of your population to devolve into a crushing burden. You invest in the growth of your nation and let the people create opportunities for themselves and for their fellow Americans. Investing in Connected Schools makes good business sense for our nation.

DEMAND
PARENTS

Toward the end of my eighth-grade year, my father came to my school to meet with my guidance counselor. I can't say I liked the woman, but I can't say I *didn't* like her, either. She just didn't exist for me. For someone whose job was supposedly to help guide me through some of the most treacherous years of my life, I barely knew who she was, and obviously it was mutual. Whatever little light I had, any individual qualities or abilities, was to her buried under my less-than-impressive grades and the one visibly unique thing about me at St. Mary's, which was that I was the only black kid. The message was simple: I would be put on the vocational track in high school instead of the college track.

"Your boy's just not college material," she said, and then she riffled through the pages of some manuals and showed my father guidelines and score cutoffs—and in my part of town, you knew that when They did that, you were dead.

Well, if this woman knew only the minimum about me, then she knew nothing at all about Eugene Crew. He gave a quick glance to everything she'd laid out in front of him, like he was trying the tuna casserole just to be polite; then he sat up straight in his chair. "You know, ma'am," he said in a firm voice. "My boy is smart. His mother was smart, and I'm not too shabby myself."

The woman riffled through some more pages and showed him

all the same things she'd shown him the first time around, but this time he didn't even look at it.

"He's headed to college, ma'am. And you're standing in the way. Just give him a chance . . . Please." He'd added that "Please" because in the sixties black men didn't go into offices and tell folks what to do, but he was not a begging man. He wasn't asking me whether or not I wanted to go to college. I was going. And the school was going to help me get there.

To her credit, the guidance counselor must have seen the fire in my father's eyes, registered that his back was straight and his chin was lifted and he would not be moved, because when I started Arlington High that September, I was on the college track. If my father hadn't gone to that meeting with a vision of who I was and what he wanted for me, if my father in his one good suit hadn't been strong and courageous in the intimidating face of powerful people trying to make his decisions for him, then I would not be where I am today. He demanded a future for me and he got it.

When spiders build their webs, they spin out a few key strands that hold the whole thing up, and our Connected Schools are like that. The school is the hub, the place where all the strands come in and crisscross with all the other strands coming in from all directions. The government and the business community are crucial, fundamental strands, but they're worthless without one more, and that's the parents.

Life has changed, many people say, and our parents have lost their way as surely as our kids. They allow too much television and video games; they absolve themselves of their parenting responsibilities by giving in to the peer pressure around their children almost faster than the children do. Most people work too hard making ends meet to parent the old-school way, while on the other side of the gap wealthy parents let extravagance and entitlement direct their children instead of values. Some of this is said as an accusation—*those* people don't care about education; *those* people don't have a work ethic; *those* people have everything, so they don't have to try. Other times it's an excuse: How can we expect parents to parent their children when poverty and unemployment are so devastating?

And there's truth to all of it. But I don't think it's the whole picture. Yes, the cosmetics of life have changed. The rich are richer and the poor are poorer. We do very different things with our spare time from what we did twenty years ago, but the essential fact remains that parents want their children to have a good education. A 2003 survey of parent involvement by the National Center for Education Statistics reported that 88 percent of all parents said they had gone to a general school meeting; 77 percent said they regularly attended parent-teacher conferences. The vast majority report spending time with their kids and participating in some way in their child's education at home and at school, and so even if they're lying to the interviewer, at least they know that they're *supposed* to have a role in creating that good education. I've met poor parents in Liberty City who didn't have anything more than their broken English and their human presence, but they were willing to use it all to get a high-quality education for their child. I've met parents in affluent communities willing to go to court, or take their child to school every day, or be on the PTA to get the same thing. Rich and poor, the overwhelming number of parents are very willing to act on behalf of their children, but the problem is that too many don't know how to do it *effectively,* either at home or at school. Connected Schools rely on parents bringing that vital third strand into the web of support for their children and their school.

Some parents figure out how to do this almost instinctively. They demand things from us, and the system favors them because schools know how to respond to parents. Whether we give them what they want is another question, but at least we know how to tell them that there are policies and timelines and procedures to be abided by. We know how to interact with them on issues like safety and security and suspensions.

The parents we don't know how to deal with are the ones who demand nothing. I call them Supply Parents. Sometimes immigrants, very often poor and powerless and easily abused, Supply Parents often feel like outsiders in the very schools that are supposed to be serving them, and they're right. No one's letting them into the knowledge core of the system, the things you need to know to make the school work for you, nor are they asking. The technical realities of getting your children educated—from making sure they're medically eligible to getting them to the SAT test on time—form a whole second body of knowledge that Supply Parents don't even know exists. Supply Parents may not be able to speak English, don't know how to use the services or read the forms, usually have no history of education in their families. If they even knew such a thing as a gifted program or an honors program existed, they wouldn't know how to get their child into it. Mostly they just want their kid safe in school, and they want to know how much lunch is.

Those parents in our system are virtually nonentities. We don't see their cultural value, their point of leverage, whatever currency or cachet they may bring. And because of that, we essentially give their children schooling of a different quality. Not because we get up in the morning trying to ruin their lives, but because we simply say: We're gonna give you special ed because we don't know what else we can do. Or: Your kid doesn't seem to be doing well, and we don't know how to communicate with you. How do Haitian parents bring themselves to the table when nobody in the school speaks Creole? How do they play the game? How can they even get a chance to talk about the gifted program? They're suppliers, and their role ends at drop-off because we can't even talk with them. But language is only one cause. There are millions of parents who don't know how to make their public school system work for them, and many of them don't even know that it should. Some may be out-and-out apathetic or lazy, but for the most part school is just another opportunity for them to be told, "You can't."

I call the first kinds of parents, those who interact with the school, Demand Parents. Demand Parents demand things from their schools because they understand that they are indeed owed something and it is their responsibility to get it for their children. They demand things from their children and themselves. Like my father, the original Demand Parent, they don't just bring "You can" into the conversation; they bring "You're gonna do it." They're the squeaky wheels, the ones asking questions at the PTA meetings and signing petitions. They're the ones who don't assume that just because the speeches are given or the laws are passed or the money is allocated or the math homework assigned that the work will get done.

Good principals and teachers find it easier to work with strong, organized parents who know what they want and who operate with a sense of their power both as individuals and as a group. Parents who feel they're consulted and have real choices about their child's education can get past their initial anxieties and truly participate. Most high-functioning schools have a high-functioning parent leadership integrated into the workings of the school in ways that go well beyond bake sales and helping out on field trips. And underneath it all will be a structured yet open communication between parents and administration—in short, a partnership, challenging but not adversarial, to raise up children with the four qualities of mature and conscious contributors to society. If we're going to prepare our children for a more complex world by offering more choices, by creating a web of opportunities through and around our Connected Schools, then we need millions of Supply Parents to participate as educational consumers the way my father did. If you want to call it playing the system, go ahead, but that's how the system works, and we need everyone to know that. Parents sign on to Connected Schools by becoming Demand Parents.

In *The Shame of the Nation*, Jonathan Kozol, who's done great and passionate work waking America up to the tragic state of our schools, describes some inner-city children coming into kindergarten without the benefit of preschool as not having "even such very modest early-learning skills as knowing how to hold a pencil, identify perhaps a couple of shapes or colors, or recognize that printed pages go from left to right." Now, I think I've made my support of universal preschool pretty clear, so I don't disagree with his desire for every child to come into school prepared. The thirty-two million fewer words I mentioned in the last chapter are not forgotten. And I also agree that children's being unable to do these things reflects terribly on our society. But for goodness' sake, *where were the parents?* In five years no one ever sat down with those children and looked at a book? They never went to a library? Walked into a bookstore? Watched *Sesame Street?* Universal preschool can help address what's missing from the lives of children like these, but it doesn't deal with the fact that with such parental neglect, their problems will not disappear once they're in school and any benefits of preschool will likely dry up and blow away. To absolve parents of responsibility for their children is patronizing. If I believe that all kids can learn, I also believe that all parents can teach. Demand Parents understand and accept that they have an immediate and immeasurable impact on how their child learns how to be academically, personally, occupationally, and civically adequate. You don't need a college degree. What you need is an awareness of the responsibility you have assumed and the constant, mother-bear determination to make your child fit to survive in a world that we all know can be a hard and hungry place. Every word out of your mouth, every one of your actions, is a lesson to your child. Now, I can't teach anyone how to be a parent with this book, but I want every parent reading this to fully realize that you are your child's first and most important teacher. The caring and high expectations that a great teacher brings to the student-teacher relationship are really just extensions or variations of the parent-child relationship.

Being a Demand Parent does not mean commanding the mic at

the PTA meeting and harassing everyone around you to guarantee the success and comfort of your child. It means connecting the work you do parenting your child to the work your child's teachers are doing within the student-teacher relationships at school. It means actively engaging in both your child and her school, providing support for the developmental work only the school can provide while making sure the school supports the kind of work that only *you*, the parent and family at home, can provide. In many ways schools and homes have to operate as one unit. They don't have to agree that the same things are important, but they have to respect and support each other's values and clearly communicate that to the kids. The parents know that the school thinks homework is important or that science is really important or that being on time to school is really important. The school universe talks to the home universe, and the home universe talks to the school universe, and together they decide what they both have to watch, but no matter what, caring and high expectations carry over wherever the child goes. Failure grows out of schools not giving feedback on the things that the parent thinks are important, or the parent not paying attention to the things the school thinks are important. Private school parents pay for that symmetry between how their school looks at home and how their home looks at school, and I don't blame them. That's why I want *every* child in America to have that symmetry between home and school.

Ultimately, it's the parents' job to work with the school to create that single tissue of guidance and support and encouragement and discipline. They need to cross the bridge to us the way my father did every time he went down to the school and asked about course work he knew nothing about, about college entrance requirements he barely understood. His presence was my ticket across the bridge. Schools provide the service of education, and so, like anyone who uses a service, Demand Parents have to oversee the work, measure its success, cooperate when necessary, and stand as the ultimate accountability to the service provider. As consumers, they're how the system understands that its product is being received well in the market where it most counts, which is the home. If we don't get feedback from parents, then as far as we know, everything's fine. And I don't mean just your kid; I'm talking about the relationship between parent and school. Schools and school systems need to view this as a market relationship, and though we don't think about it in those terms, it's already true that Demand Parents shape the schools' response, response rate, depth of response, commitment, texture, and tone. Schools with high PTA activity, where there's a variety of school-based clubs and other activities that bring parents and children into the same fold, are, by and large, high performing. I don't care where it's located, how poor its families are; if you can get a critical mass of engaged, thoughtful, and knowledgeable parents to participate on a consistent basis, that school will be successful.

Schools, in turn, need to be able to demand things from parents in how they deal with their children. If you do nothing else, here are four things a Demand Parent *must* do:

1. Know where your children are in their growing process. I want you to be able to tell me that your son is shy or excited about the first day of school. I need you to know if your daughter is nervous about long division and bring that information to us at school so the teachers can do the fine work of caring and setting expectations with as much finesse as possible. Going to a doctor and being able to describe the intensity and location of a pain will get you healthier faster than if you just shrug your shoulders and say you don't feel well. Educators need parents to be able to know and articulate information about their children in the same way.

And please tell us more than just the bad news. One of the best things a teacher can hear from parents is that their child is excited about something that he's learning, that there's constant chatter at the dinner table about some major piece of information that's been planted in his brain and he's now feeding on it. That means that your son is seeing himself as a self-directed learner. The wheels of development are spinning because he knows how to have an impact on his own life, he's learning what he needs to become an even better learner, and he's communicating that to you and then you communicate it to the school. When that happens, the sky's the limit for him.

2. Do the things that are proven to add value to a child's education. In the broadest strokes: Have a place set aside with a good light where your daughter can always do her work. Make sure she gets enough sleep. Take her to a museum sometimes or the library. And if you do nothing else, make reading and literacy a part of daily life: Read to her. Read for your own pleasure and let her see you doing it. Have the newspaper around. Talk about what you read. Chapter Eight will go into more detail on action points.

3. Tell someone when it looks like your child's behaviors are coming off the track. Things that are very small to you and me—they didn't make the team, they're gonna miss a practice, they didn't get time to do the homework—are very large to our children. Since building confidence is basic to education, pay attention and tell someone when you see something that may have a negative impact on your child's confidence. His teacher, counselor, and school have to know that, because he'll be a different kid that day.

4. Care enough about your children to let them walk in and out the door of reality and not let it smack them in the face. They're going to be wrong a lot of times, and they'll have to pay the consequences for being wrong. They should pay the consequences, but it shouldn't be at such a high price that it knocks them out of the game altogether. A woman once came up to me and said, "I want my son to wear a motocross helmet, but he won't wear it, so I've said, 'If you don't want to wear it, then you'll just end up in the hospital and that'll be it.' " Suffice it to say, I didn't approve. That was too high a price to pay for this kid to learn this lesson. Of course she should have made him wear the helmet, but the way to do it was by insisting on it and taking the bike away if he didn't. You're the parent. *Punto*.

The other aspect of Demand Parenting is directed outward, toward connecting with the classroom, the school, and the community. When I began in New York, I hosted chancellor forums, the equivalent of town hall meetings, so parents could explain to me in person what they wanted done and how and why. One night in the Bronx, at one of the first meetings, a woman came up to the microphone. The place was packed, a couple thousand people; it was hot, the cameras were rolling, and this woman looked tired. Not that good tired from a day's work, but that squeezed sort of tired of someone who's been in pain for too long. Everyone seemed to see that, and the whole room went quiet.

"Chancellor," she said, "I want you to know that my daughter came home the other day with splinters in her legs and runs in her stockings from sitting on chairs that are so old and splintered that now they're coming apart in the children's legs. Now, I can't afford many more stockings. My daughter likes to dress up to come to school, which is why I buy her stockings. She's a young girl, but that's just something me and my daughter do, go out on a weekend and get our stockings. She's trying to be a young lady, but she can't get there when she goes to a school that won't replace the chairs."

Now she looked me in the eye, the way my father used to look at guidance counselors and nuns and anyone else who threw up a roadblock on my path.

"If you are here to help us," she went on, "then God bless you. If you are here to help us find the kinds of classes that my daughter can go to to get her into local college here in New York, then God bless you. If you're here to help my daughter and other children in New York City figure out how to stay safe from AIDS, drugs, from teen pregnancy, and all that, then I will harness my cart to your star. But if you are not any of those things, then I would ask you respectfully, do not deceive me. Do not make me have one more day's worth of hope, because it only then breaks my heart. I am willing to have my back broke with the work necessary to do this. But don't break my heart."

By the time she finished, there were tears in my eyes. Her pain was so clear and her words were so eloquent and she stood for so many people I had known. It was probably the most poignant thing I experienced as chancellor in New York, a sharp and undeniably powerful moment when a parent took charge of the night and set the moral standard for what it meant to be chancellor of New York City schools.

We can build a new sort of educational structure in America, but we need Demand Parents to breathe life into it. They do the work of applying caring, high expectations, and diverse approaches to learning throughout our system of Connected Schools. Their power as individuals is made possible by the federal government dealing with the seven issues discussed in the last chapter, but they also provide a check on its power by being able to consciously exercise their choice within their systems. By caring about public education and not considering it a lost cause or a monolith, they express confidence that it can work. By demanding quality education, they set the bar of high expectations for everyone from student and teacher up through the principal to, ultimately, the public officials who create budgets and policy. By cooperating and not just whining, they allow diverse approaches to be taken on all levels.

As you may have noticed by now in your life, things don't happen in this world just because they *should* happen. Connected Schools demand accountability at all levels, and in a personal way, not some generalized, pay-your-taxes, governmental way. The work is done by everyone personally, not through the proxy of a system.

Tangible, effective responsibility is shared by all partners. Kids are personally accountable; schools, teachers, parents, businesses, government, they're all personally accountable. And by their uniquely dynamic structure, Connected Schools express that truth in deeds, not just words, through the agreements they enter into. We've spent decades now talking about accountability as a public virtue, but if we're really serious about injecting it back into American life, this is where we start. A child who doesn't do his homework is accountable. A CEO who ignores his responsibility to his community is accountable. A parent who blows off curriculum night is accountable, as is a mayor or a governor who puts politics or money before the needs of his constituents. But this accountability in Connected Schools comes from more than just binding agreements; it must be guaranteed by the persistence and vigilance of Demand Parents.

One of the most powerful examples of Demand Parenting I've seen is the organization Mothers on the Move, or MOM. Started in the South Bronx in 1992 by parents concerned about the disparity between their school district and the wealthier and whiter district to the north, MOM mobilized around the question of how to become a strong voice for their children. They got clear on what they expected from the school system. They became uniformly articulate and understood the parameters of their demands for better conditions in and performance from their schools. Instead of just talking, they provided solutions and drew commitments from the higher-ups they dealt with—including me—and the result was real change for their schools, from increased security all the way up to the ouster of their district superintendent.

Demand Parents can direct their energies in all kinds of ways. When I was principal at Monroe Junior High in Inglewood, California, we went through a truly devastating period of budget reduction that started with Proposition 13 in 1978, the referendum that limited property-tax revenue in California and all but gutted public school budgets. Other states enacted similar legislation, and this is one of the major reasons why our schools slid into decline over the last twenty years. Anyway, Monroe faced the loss of a lot of money, and one of the strongest programs we'd had until then was our drill team. It was a real blockbuster for our kids. They did fantastic performances, and even though it may have looked like just a fun extracurricular, in fact it served a very real pedagogical value. The kids loved it, and they loved coming to school because of it. Without question those involved developed self-discipline, a better command of language, and increased capacities as learners. When the reductions came down, though, I had to decide which teachers to let go, which in turn meant eliminating programs that didn't include the entire school. Like the drill team.

So one day this very small, very quiet woman came up to me after school and said, "You know what, Dr. Crew? I feel we need to not lose the drill team."

"Yeah, I'm worried about it, too," I said, in the same way that you worry about a thunderstorm when the clouds are right over your head. I mean, this was happening, and I didn't see any way to stop it.

"No," she said. "We need to make sure we don't lose this program."

She said goodbye and that day began assembling a coalition of people that soon reached all the way into the arts industry, including Jane Fonda and the administration of the Dorothy Chandler Pavilion. And I still don't know how she did it. She was a working mom, but somehow her group raised enough money and frankly enough hell to save that program, and it was the hell that did the job. They wrote to everyone they could and raised the issue in the community in a way that I couldn't because I didn't have their street cred. That it came with money was gravy, but it was that mother's stand that won the day.

Demand Parents take a stand. They stand for things, and they do it in a way that doesn't sacrifice the needs of other parents. They make an affirmative statement. They say: This enterprise should include this program, or this value, or this event, and we feel so strongly that we demand it doesn't go away. Demand parents know how to leverage their credentials in ways that mobilize action, and once you have a body of parents who have mobilized around an issue, you have an engine that you can drive to other places, just like Mothers on the Move. Demand Parents are a force to be reckoned with. They are the power of public.

Before we go any further, we must address one more important point. If our goal is for every child to have the advocacy of a Demand Parent, then what do we do about those children who have no parents, or have parents who are unable to perform that role? Whether they are orphans, wards of the state, foster children, homeless, or displaced by a catastrophe like Katrina, these children deserve the same support, protection, and nurturing challenge that a Demand Parent offers. As much as I may pray that there would be an intimate, personal answer to every one of these cases, that someone would step forward and act as their surrogate in making the connection between home and school, the sad fact is that we as a community, as represented by our public social services, have to assume that work. Before that happens, though, we as a nation must act as Demand Parents for all of them by insisting that these children be treated as individuals of value. Enlightened people within our bureaucracies must make sure that every child has an adult demanding of the system, making a connection to the system, be it a social worker, a relative, or a guardian, and the system in turn must display extraordinary thoughtfulness in how it engages those children. This is the kind of place where we find out whether the phrase "No Child Left Behind" truly has meaning for America.

HOPE NEEDS HELP: THE PARENT ACADEMY

All parents want their children to do better than they did. They all want to find out how they can best work with their children's

school. But how do we get parents whose families have been ignored for generations to cross the bridge and join us? How do we
turn the Haitian mother who only speaks Creole, the unemployed
father, the migrant worker, the parent who can't read into Demand
Parents? This isn't just a matter of poor and non-English-speaking
parents; white middle-class parents are looking for help, too. I've
tried parent advocates and parent offices and parent coordinators,
but all that did was create another power position, stack another
layer onto the bureaucracy, and add one more line to the budget.
So the question is: How can parents learn to interact with, on the
one hand, their children and, on the other, their schools and school
systems in ways that leverage themselves and their resources into a
good-quality education that will result in their children having the
four qualities of a mature and conscious contributor to society? We
can give them what they want for their children through our Connected Schools, but the price they have to pay is crossing over that
bridge. If they don't, it's likely their kids will fail. The choice may
seem obvious, but it's a long walk for a lot of people, and if you're
afraid of falling off or of what's on the other side, your fears may
outweigh your good intentions.

In Miami-Dade we're walking out halfway and extending an
institutional hand to those people on the other side to help them
across. We're making a big, wide bridge to connect them to us,
with handrails so they feel safe, and we've put it close to home, in
their neighborhoods, their churches, and their community centers.
It's called the Parent Academy.

We got off to a very fast start during my early days in Miami,
making lots of changes to what was already a pretty complicated
system. Like every school system, M-DCPS has rules about summer school and transfers and attendance and address requirements
and graduation requirements and on and on. We've got about as
many rules as the IRS, but we're even less clear about how they
work, so I worried about how we'd get this information out to
the hundreds of thousands of parents, especially the ones who prob-

ably didn't know what was what in the first place. At the Meet the
Superintendent forums I'd hosted, I'd had two kinds of parents ask
me questions. On the one hand, I had parents basically saying, "I
like my school fine; it's a great place, but could we get some more
buses?" And then I had parents who asked harder, deeper questions like the one I'd been asked by that tired woman back in New
York. Their schools and their children were in wars of attrition
that they were losing, but at least they were fighting. Behind them,
I knew, were surely thousands more parents who weren't asking
questions, who weren't participating, who were going down without a sound.

They were the people I found myself coming back to. By now I
had begun to think of parents in terms of Demand and Supply, but
hand in hand with identifying the existence of Supply Parents came
the need to once and for all find the way to get them involved.
Every school has some Demand Parents who may as well work
there. But then there are those Supply Parents most schools see
twice: first, when they hand their child to us on that first day of
school; and second, if there's an emergency, if they need our immediate help because their son is failing or their daughter tried to
commit suicide.

Every once in a while, though, they'll come looking for something more. Maybe their son has some new friends and now he's
never leaving his bedroom; maybe their little girl, who's always
done well, has suddenly hit a wall; and you'll see them hazarding a
few tentative steps across the bridge. They need help of a very personal sort, and make no mistake, these are moments of enormous
intimacy, moments when the act of parenting is vulnerable and exposed and what they need more than anything else is a name and
a phone number, someone whose judgment they can work off of
for a second or two. The point is, *they* are the ones who need help.
The good news is that schools can usually provide that help. That's
what we're in the business of doing; helping in these moments is
one of our services, and it's a service to the parent, not just the

child. Once they're in, those Supply Parents learn about and often use the other things that we—and I'm talking particularly about Miami now—offer through our Connected Schools to satisfy their personal needs as parents and adults. And suddenly we have a Demand Parent.

In other words, it was possible for us to teach parents how to use the school system, how to interact with school and engage in their children's education, but to do that, we had to offer information that would be valuable to the parents personally, not just in service to their children. We had to turn school from a place of "You can't" into one of "You can," with "You" meaning the parents as much as the children. Turning more of Miami's parents into Demand Parents meant better showcasing of our marketplace of services. And we had to put our showcase right next to the bridge so we could lure more across. Hence, the Parent Academy, a department within the school system that would offer classes devoted to the needs of parents.

I laid this idea out in my cabinet meeting, and we decided to write it up, get it approved by the board as a concept, and then try to market it to parents and to the community. I gave it a name, pulled in TotalBank—which had enough heft to give it a real market niche—as a sponsor, and put it directly under a devoted manager. But instead of just creating a curriculum and tossing it out there, we met with parents and asked them what *they* wanted. What we heard was that they needed to know more not just about their kids but about their own lives. People didn't know how to buy a house or compute a mortgage, so we built classes around that. They needed to understand credit and basic things about how the economy functions, so we built around that, which in turn seeded ideas for what we need to teach earlier in life about Workplace Literacy. They wanted to learn English, so we hooked up with English for Speakers of Other Languages (ESOL) programs. We met with more parents and continued to add classes based on what they wanted, branching out into new locations in community centers and churches and wherever we could so that it would always be convenient and local to the people who truly needed the service. As much as we created content, we also tried to avoid overlapping efforts by finding existing groups that offered the kinds of classes our parents wanted and pulling them under our umbrella. Our role was to bring together parents looking for information and the experts who were offering it.

Now operating out of eighty sites around the county, the Parent Academy offers all parents in the county hundreds of courses, resources, and opportunities to foster their children's academic and life success, as well as their own. The classes are free, offered in English, Spanish, and Creole, and the course work falls into eight categories. Sample classes include

1. EARLY CHILDHOOD

- Parenting Your Baby with Special Needs

- Calming Your Fussy Infant

- Learning Games

2. HEALTH AND WELLNESS

- Preventing Substance Abuse

- Stress Management

- Diabetes Education

3. HELP YOUR CHILD LEARN

- Launching Young Readers

- Helping Children Prepare for Tests

- Monitoring Your Child's Education

4. FINANCIAL SKILLS

- Making the Most of the Money You Earn
- Understanding and Repairing Your Credit
- Financing Your Child's College Education

5. LANGUAGES

- English and Spanish classes
- Raising a Multilingual Child
- American Sign Language

6. PARENTING SKILLS

- Extreme Bullying and Violence Prevention
- Learning Disabilities and Self-Esteem
- The Importance of School Attendance

7. PERSONAL GROWTH

- Workforce Readiness
- Citizenship
- GED Prep

8. TECHNOLOGY

- Introduction to Computers
- Introduction to Microsoft Word

The Parent Academy also hosts a lecture series, a Lunch & Learn series, and a Summer Institute for parents of children in the

School Improvement Zone. Family Learning Events are held at various museums and attractions that allow families to enjoy a day together for free that they'd otherwise not be able to afford. Scholarships are available for supplies and certification classes, as are free transportation and child care, for qualifying parents.

In its first two years, more than twenty-eight thousand parents and caregivers attended courses at the academy. The results have been not just inspiring but visible. For example, Riverside Elementary in East Little Havana has gone in two years from being a C school to being an A school. Here's why: It approached the Parent Academy as an opportunity for the entire school community. With the help of CPC/All-Aboard, a local organization specializing in early education intervention, the parents of Riverside transformed the culture of their school from a place where once two or three parents would show up for PTA meetings to a truly active organization, headed largely by parents who attend Parent Academy classes. English classes have allowed many to take GED tests and even consider postsecondary education. Now that they can take advantage of what the school system and the community have to offer, they're learning how to look at their community through their own eyes and demand what they and their families need. Children are learning alongside their parents, and not just math and reading; they're learning how to play together at Family Learning Events held around the city at local museums and attractions such as the Parrot Zoo. Fathers are engaging more, learning problems are being diagnosed and addressed earlier, and a thriving, nurturing culture is in place that's helping not just the school but the community surrounding it. Parents with infants and preschoolers are taking classes as well, which will better prepare their children for school and support them along the way, pointing to a better future for the entire community.

The Parent Academy is a true expression of what Connected

Schools can achieve through partnerships between the private and the public sectors. Its budget right now is around $1 million a year, but not a dime is public money, and not all the contributions are monetary; space and expertise are also offered. TotalBank, other financial institutions, Knight Foundation, Blue Cross and Blue Shield, Alonzo Mourning, and a number of foundations have paid for all of it because they see this as an investment in specific outcomes that our schools can deliver. M-DCPS uses its money to bring together the resources of the community to train a workforce and to give parents a chance to be successful in their other job, which is raising children. We provide a sense of hope, and we're helping immigrants socialize more quickly into a pattern of parental engagement that may be very different from what was done in Haiti or Cuba or wherever. This will keep people connected to Miami; it builds stability, a market, investments, and all the value-driven intangibles of an established community such as East Little Havana.

Every community in the country should have a Parent Academy. It creates a way for parents to more freely engage in the activity of learning. Once they can play the game of learning themselves, they're more able to play it with their own children, and the wall between home and school comes down. At its core the Parent Academy helps parents develop healthy habits of learning that they can then model for their children, picking up in the process some new content that they can use for advocating for their children. Teaching and learning become integrated into the workings of the home, and simply by understanding the needs of their children, the parents better understand their own responsibilities and become Demand Parents.

The Parent Academy is also another example of how the culture of caring, high expectations, and diverse approaches to learning works throughout the entire system. Above all else, the Parent Academy is about building confidence in parents so they'll take the risks life demands, whether that means laying down rules and structures at home or getting a mortgage. By its very existence and its parent-driven content, the academy proves that it cares about parents, but in return we expect performance and engagement in this enterprise called school. It is not a social service outlet. It is a specialized, limited agenda that revolves around helping you help your own family move from here to there in reading, math, and science—and in preparing for high school, a possible college education, and a job.

The other day I gave the opening remarks to three or four thousand incoming American citizens. What was wonderful for me was listening to these parents tell me about their desire to participate in the public schools. Many were laborers who hadn't had the benefit of quality education but who believed that education was the key to not just their children's future but their own. So if they weren't telling me about their children's education, they were talking about going back to get their own at adult school or night school. These people hold a profound value for this nation; they bring a passion and a will that too many of us no longer have. We can't underestimate the school system's ability, and responsibility, to reach out to them, and Connected Schools offer an incredibly powerful tool for the socialization of millions of people who are currently on the fringes. Reaching out with cultural fluency to parents is part of the core mission of Connected Schools because participation strengthens the whole. Most of the new kids walking into our public schools have very different profiles—linguistically, culturally, and socioeconomically—from ever before. That's the "public" in public schools. We have to turn our talk about plurality and diversity into reality at the registration window, in guidance systems, and at so many other points in a child's life. The Parent Academy expresses to immigrant families, to families sinking generation by generation deeper into poverty, that we will expend the time and energy to share knowledge and trust with them. We don't much care if you're poor or rich. What we care about is your participation. The unit of value you bring to this enterprise is *you*. You are the most critical resource we want to exchange with. Please come across the bridge.

MONEY

CHAPTER SEVEN

How much did you spend on your children last Christmas?

Be honest. You swallowed hard, figured in your head just how much overtime you'd have to do to afford that PlayStation 3 or American Girl doll, and then you weighed that against the rush you'd get when your son or daughter tore off the paper. And you did it. Some other time during the year there might have been a cell phone, a birthday present, an Easter basket; every day there's some reason to buy something for your kids that will prove to them how much you love them. Weekly allowance. When my kids were young, I certainly did my share of indulging; just ask my daughter about those Janet Jackson sneakers.

Of course, when you sit down and look hard at what you spent your money on, there are always regrets; some things they played with constantly, and other things they didn't touch but once or twice or the stuff fell apart in a couple of days. The cell phone costs more than you ever imagined it would. The chores they were supposed to do for the allowance more often than not went undone. Adding it all up for a line in the family budget is way too scary to consider, and in the end, if you'd asked your kids, they'd probably trade a lot of what you bought simply for more time with you. But for parents busy trying to keep their heads above water—which means most of us—money stands for what we wish we could do with them, for all the things we wish we could give them from our heart; in short, money = love, and whatever we can pay to make ourselves feel better, we'll pay.

You'll have to look at yourself in the mirror on that one, we all do, but where it becomes my business is when we bring that same twisted-up, emotional attitude toward money and our children into the discussion of education. So far I've laid out an aggressive strategy for preparing our public schools for the twenty-first century. It involves rethinking how schools operate in our communities, and it requires a massive commitment from the federal government to guarantee the equitable and efficient foundation we'll need to create the individual networks ourselves. Now we have the difficult task of looking money straight in the face and putting a price tag on caring, high expectations, and diverse approaches to learning for all our children in all our classrooms. How much does it cost to give an American child the kind of quality public school education that will prepare him or her to compete and thrive in the twenty-first century?

Here's how we answer that question right now. Schools in America are largely funded by the state that they're in. Depending on the structure of its government, in broad strokes, come budget season, every state has its own formula for calculating its budget line for education. As you can probably guess, variability is the rule. Here's Florida's formula for the 2006–2007 budget:

FTE Students × Program Weights = Weighted FTE Students × Base Student Allocation × District Cost Differential = Base Funding + Declining Enrollment Allocation + Sparsity Supplement + Discretionary Equalization + 0.51 Mil Compression + Discretionary Contribution + Safe Schools + ESE Guaranteed Allocation + Supplemental Academic Instruction + Reading Allocation + Teacher Compensation + Minimum Guarantee = Gross State and Local FEFP − Required Local Effort = Net State FEFP + Discretionary Lottery Funds + School Recognition Program + Major Categorical Programs = Total State Funding.

Lurking inside that monster of a formula are more formulas. For example, the prevailing wisdom is that teacher compensation should be connected to the cost of living in that state and city, so states such as New York use the consumer price index; they look at the market basket, the total cost of around two hundred categories ranging from a bag of apples to car insurance, in each locality. That basket of goods will cost more in, say, Brooklyn than it will in Albany or Rochester, so the total compensation number is calculated by adjusting for the market basket in each locality. Florida has recently moved away from that model to what is called an amenities formula, which takes into account not just the cost of living in a locality but supposed quality-of-life intangibles. For example, since South Florida has beaches and sun and lots of tourists who pay good money to visit, teachers in that part of the state should be automatically willing to work for less than a teacher in Tallahassee; therefore, the amount allocated for teacher compensation goes down for Miami.

On the face of it, New York State's formula seems easier. It considers, according to New York State School Finance Reform, only four elements—foundation costs, pupil need index, regional cost index, and expected local contribution—but inside the actual calculation are "formula aids," such as this attempt to nail down a ratio for a more equitable distribution of state funds:

When the PWR (pupil wealth ratio) and the Alt-PWR (alternate pupil wealth ratio) are averaged together, the resulting average wealth ratio is called the combined wealth ratio (CWR) of the district.

$$\text{CWR} = 0.5 \times \frac{\text{DISTRICT AV/TWPU}}{\$346,400} + 0.5 \times \frac{\text{DISTRICT INCOME/TWPU}}{\$118,500}$$

Have a headache yet? Again, fifty different formulas to achieve the same goal, this time the state's total cost for education.

At some point during the year, the total number of students for the year is decided upon, either by attendance or by enrollment on a certain day, and then the funds are divided up, and the state then sends the money down to whoever controls it on the local level—in New York it goes to City Hall, whereas in Miami it comes straight to the M-DCPS. Once again, more formulas as to how the funds are distributed, at this point usually shifting more state funds to low-income areas.

On the city or system level, another set of rules and policies determines distribution based on another set of formulas that includes things such as the size of your school. Low-income schools are also eligible for federal Title I money—about $13 billion was budgeted nationally in 2006—as well as money for special education. If you, on the local level, want to put more into your schools than what the state has given you, if you want to raise teacher salaries, or if you need some additional after-school programs or want to keep the schools open twenty more days a year, then you have to either tax yourself or find a foundation or a sugar daddy someplace. In states with redistribution programs such as New Jersey, a locality may only receive 5 percent of its budget from the state, and the rest has to come from local taxes. Wealthy suburbs, free from the social service burdens of urban America, can afford to pour great sums of money into their schools, while some inner-city and increasingly rural schools may receive lots of state money, but their local contribution is lower or in some cases even nonexistent, and they're left treading water at best. Conversely, as real estate values boomed, so did property taxes in some areas, creating burdens on homeowners beyond a fair contribution to public education. Suffice it to say, all of these systems are imperfect, and eventually, by whatever formulas your town or district uses, what's left of the money trickles down to your principal, who applies earmarked funds and decides how to make use of what discretionary funds remain.

Good for you if you've kept up so far. Now, somewhere along the way, usually when the total state budget is calculated and the total school attendance is calculated, someone divides that total dollar amount by the number of students and comes up with how much each student will receive from the state, on average. That, at last, is our per-student expenditure. When you adjust that number for the local contribution and redistributions within the state, you get numbers that vary from around $5,000 in a place like Utah to almost $11,000 in New Jersey. Now, even with adjusting for the cost of living and other very real economic differences within our nation, and for the necessity of helping low-income students, it's hard to find any logic here, or any meaning in that per-student average cost.

So we're back to the question I started with: How much does it cost to give an American child the kind of quality education that will prepare her to compete and thrive in the twenty-first century? That strikes me as a reasonable question. If we're buying a few million of something, we need to know how much each of them will cost. But unfortunately that's not the number we've come up with when we calculated that per-student cost. What's been determined is *how much is being paid out*, which is not at all the same as how much it costs to educate a child for a year, nor is it anywhere close to how much it costs to give a child a year of quality education. We haven't asked any questions about how many children are in schools that haven't been painted in forty years. We haven't looked at how many of these children are performing way below grade level. The list of practical complications and contingencies in education is huge, but essentially all those things are by definition the fine work of good education.

Let's go back to that smoky room where the budget was being hashed out and Superintendent Tweed Jacket came knocking on the door. Let's get even closer to reality and imagine all sorts of well-meaning educators and social scientists and policy people sitting in that room, too. They dealt with all those practical complications of education, the fine work, by constructing intricate formulas that supposedly shifted resources around in a fair way, and then the politicians allocated and voted in whatever ways they thought would produce the best sound bites and get them reelected. The superintendents got their lump sums, and then had to figure out all the sticky details as best they could. And so the whole exercise of working out the year's educational budget has little to do with everyday life in the classroom. Rather, it involves a calculation on the part of the powers that be as to what they'll have to pay to make people happy or shut them up, so that the bigwigs can keep their jobs—and then maybe once in a while they'll worry about reaching a score level that looks good. For all the arcane calculations, the whole process is not about how much the state will have to pay to get a result; it's about how much the state will have to pour into the system. The rhetoric around this is always about doing the right thing by the children; it's about guilt and obligation and all kinds of indefinable things that supposedly show we care about our children. If they succeed, maybe we'll give them more, and if they fail, we'll take the money away as a punishment.

Remind you of anything?

Why are we using a parenting model—and a pretty ineffectual parenting model at that—in a place where we should be applying a business model? As it is now, our decisions as to how much we'll spend and how we'll spend it have no basis in the two things that any business would look at first when considering an investment: What are the actual costs and what are the outcomes? Ask yourself this: What exactly do our education dollars pay for? Keeping kids off the streets? Lip service? So our kids can reach some doctored-up "proficiency" goals? To make people feel good? The goal seems to have something to do with test scores, but that's as far as we go. We have no stated goal for our public education system. This country has not entered into a businesslike equation with the public school system. As a result, we hand our schools money—to the tune of hundreds of billions of dollars—more to show that we care than to realize any particular outcomes. Well, any businessperson can tell you that investing without a goal is not investing; it's simply an act of faith. Any serious investment has to be actively managed with a goal in mind. We take attendance at 10:30 on a certain day and base every school's funding for the year on that number. That's hardly what we mean when we talk about either caring or smart investing. Throwing money at education is purely symbolic; both caring and fiscal responsibility demand specificity and results.

If you wanted to start a business, the whole process would begin with a plan that laid down what product or service you wanted to produce along with a clear statement of your goals and a detailed budget of what it would cost in the way of investment to reach those goals. Here's what the machinery would cost and personnel and insurance and raw goods; everything would be in black and white. Then you'd meet with banks and investors and explain your plan, your methods, your expectations, the reasons why you think your business will create the outcomes you're offering. You're a smart person, so you'd convince a number of different parties to invest or partner with you, to tell you what you can have out of what you said you wanted. They would respond to your need, and as you built your company, they would check in periodically, look at the books, evaluate your progress based on assumptions and benchmarks that were mutually agreed upon up front. From all sides, you'd be looking at the same targets, and you'd have a budget that you could manage in terms of both the small things—how many ballpoint pens will you need to do the job?—and the big ones: Is our pricing competitive? Are we shipping enough units to Kalamazoo? If you hit your marks, investment would continue and maybe even increase, so you could expand the range of what you do and better serve your clients. If you didn't reach the agreed-upon levels, you'd face some unpleasant meetings.

There's no reason we can't approach the enterprise of public education in a similar responsible manner, but when you make that connection, hackles are raised and you face the mushy romanticism that cripples our schools as surely as those bloodless state budget formulas. How can you compare our babies to profits? Well, you can't and I'm not, but our squeamishness about applying money to education is part of the problem. By calling the work teachers do priceless, we reduce it to charity and absolve ourselves of the responsibility to pay for it. And by turning it into $(x + y)$ times the coefficient of wealthy districts divided by how good the politicians look, we distance ourselves from the possibility of real change in our educational system. We need to invest money in our schools in ways that will create the optimum situations for the real work of caring to be done, not to make people feel good or wish problems away.

The kinds of Connected Schools compacts I described in Chapter Four do more than answer curricular needs; they make good financial sense. Instead of allowing educational spending to collapse into a black hole in the government budget, Connected Schools systems predicated on business principles of efficiency and nimbleness let us leverage public money in more effective ways.

You can see how that works as we move from the bottom up toward our goal of all children graduating as mature and conscious contributors to society. By taking over the seven key issues I discussed in Chapter Five, the federal government lays down a new foundation for public schools in America. This creates a set of new possibilities:

- The nation will be equipped with schools that meet a baseline of safety and functionality and that are staffed with teachers who live in the community and who meet nationally established certification standards.

- Those teachers will be given a clear mission to create caring teaching environments that use diverse approaches to learning so each child can reach the high academic, occupational, personal, and civic expectations stated in national standards and measured through regular assessments, both national and local.

- Children will come into school with the preschool nurturance needed to hit the ground running.

- Special attention and guidance will be given in middle school so kids can enter high school without remediation.

- Some time in high school will be spent actively participating in the world of work so kids can demonstrate before they graduate that they have what they need to be mature and conscious contributors to society.

- To realize these possibilities, Connected Schools systems will sit down with their partners in the community to establish educational outcomes that satisfy the needs of their partners. The partners will provide specific investments that give the schools the resources they need to achieve those goals.

- The Connected Schools will enter into agreements with their state and local governments on multiyear sets of their own agreed-upon outcomes that will direct public funding.

These agreements, like those reached with other partners in the community, need to be mutually agreed upon, not just dictated to the schools. We need to drain the politics out of the funding process. Too often, state and local governments simply tell schools what they're getting, with little or no input from the schools as to their actual needs. For example, for no reason other than that it sounds wise politically, I'm instructed by the state of Florida to force teachers in failing schools to reapply for their jobs. So in the toughest places to teach, we're not looking for ways to help, we're looking for ways to punish. It will make a bad problem worse, but since I'm not holding the purse, my hands are tied. Together, and I stress *together*, schools and government must create their agreements, and funding every year will be driven by performance on whatever criteria are mutually set.

These criteria, these outcomes, have to be statistically measurable, but they should touch all elements of the educational process. Student assessment does matter, so, for instance, schools could agree to reading scores rising 8 percent in the third through fifth grades. A system could commit to increasing the number of AP classes offered and the number of students taking AP classes, with a 30 percent system-wide growth rate as a target. Here are the sorts of metrics we at the M-DCPS have committed to in our compacts with local governments and the state of Florida: the total number of student seats up by 25 percent; serious crime in schools down by 18 percent. These are real metrics, observable on an interim or quarterly basis, metrics that reveal the culture of the school, its climate, its productivity and growth. You can set standards for teacher stability and retention, as well as for parent participation, which would give school systems greater incentive to create something like the Parent Academy. Beyond test scores in purely academic areas, we can agree to measurable performance in the other three qualities of a mature and conscious contributor to society. As a nation, we've never created ways to measure Personal Integrity, Workplace Literacy, or Civic Awareness, even though they profoundly affect our gross domestic product and our ability to compete in the global economy. Turning what have been soft skills into tangible outcomes that have an impact on funding will focus people on them in a way we've never seen in America.

If the country really wants these to be the outcomes of our educational system and we really believe these things are important generators of a strong economy and a strong democracy, then we'll have to pay for them adequately, consciously, and responsibly. Where else in our system of government and laws, in our business sector, is that not the case? And if it's not the case in education, then why have generations of wealthy Americans paid top dollar for it? The trade-off would be a state scorecard not unlike what we have in Florida right now, an A through F grading system for schools that would match the scorecard for the district. The result would be a total shift in the culture of the classroom. Instead of looking to punish "failure," the focus would be on setting high expectations and identifying problems. It would be like looking through the other end of a telescope—what's viewed may be the same thing, but the perspective is totally changed. Change the perspective in the classroom and a conversation can open up between state, city, and district as to inputs and outcomes, investments and results. The grade on the scorecard might have an impact on funding for each local district, but this would be a variable amount on top of a set base per-student cost, to be paid by the state and the city in whatever proportion they agree on.

To decide what that base per-student cost will be, we must once and for all put a price tag on a quality public education. As I pointed out in Chapter One, economists have been calculating the financial impact of education on the economy since World War II, and it only rises higher, yet we've never looked at our investment in public education and analyzed the relationship between what goes in and what comes out. Education has a monetary value to both the individual and society. Private schools, preschools, and universities all calculate how much it costs to educate a child, and it is high time we approach the costs of public education with the same accountability and precision as private education.

Because we have no national educational system, we only have state numbers, which at best give us a range: at the bottom we have Utah and Arizona paying $5,067 and $6,331, respectively, per student, in 2003; and at the top we have New Jersey and New York paying $10,908 and $10,665, respectively, for each student. Again, none of those state numbers is created with outputs in mind. If you were designing a car, you wouldn't be so cavalier. You'd decide what you wanted your car to do; it would be safe and fuel efficient and be a certain size and perform at a specific standard and look a certain way and be made of certain materials. Then you'd price out the metal and the use of plastic, the weight distribution, the size of the tires, the labor costs, overhead, and distribution, and while you might not come to an exact per-unit cost, you would know before you pushed the Go button that each car would cost you between x and y to make.

We need to be that sharp on how we construct our educational budgets and compacts. While the actual base number is a moving target, I can tell you that it will be between $10,000 and $15,000. I also know that anything below $10,000 is too low and beyond $15,000 is at this moment probably unnecessary to do the work of fixing what's broken and sustaining a nation of public schools that can launch our children out into the flat world. At the same time, we must lock in standards around math, around reading, around science. In effect, we as a nation say to each state, city, and district: This amount is automatic. It is nonnegotiable—that's how important it is to our national security and the ongoing health of our economy. We know what it costs to give each child a quality education, and within the context of a binding agreement between the state, the city, and the district you're going to get that money in the form of a lump sum every three years, so you can manage it to the best advantage. In return, districts will provide quarterly reports to their states that say where they are on the established metrics. We gave you the money; you know what the goal is. Now we want to see our return on that investment.

This base funding will never be affected by the agreed-upon outcomes, no matter how high or low they are. We know how much it costs to do this work of educating a child. Taking money away from it only puts success that much further away, as does imposing state solutions that don't reflect specific needs and situations. School performance only affects a second tier of funding, a discretionary level that I call Value Add.

Value Add is how we create educational choice on the local level. True educational choice means a school system where Connected Schools compete with one another to provide various menus of services to students and their families. A superintendent adds value to a particular school by putting in an after-school or summer school program, or a technology program, or any kind of supplementary service that extends past the primary, core business into issues of family health and nutrition, parent education and the like, or specialization in a certain field. These programs stimulate the development of various individual school cultures that eventually make up a school system full of good choices. This is where we *want* differences. To pay for these extra programs, superintendents should have to apply for the funds, and then performance on all the agreed-upon criteria will determine whether the funding will continue.

Value Add is where Connected Schools bring in the local business community and local government to create local solutions and opportunities. Business and community partnerships will offer support as well, so the entire weight of the extra programs doesn't fall on the shoulders of the taxpayers. If we establish the basic cost of a quality education in America, then Connected Schools can construct their own menus of Value Adds that increase their ability to educate their children in the way the community desires. If the schools in Montclair, New Jersey, want to offer more and their final Base + Value Add per student number is ultimately higher than in Salt Lake City, then so be it. But it won't be at the expense of performance, or of students in other communities. The differences between large districts and small districts can be dealt with on a local level. High-performing schools and systems will be able to build their own Value Adds to address their own needs and desires and the inevitable demographic changes that all parts of America eventually undergo. Schools will have an incentive to do more than just produce scores. All this seems to me to be innately more innovative and more respectful of local needs than anything we have now.

Even though we're talking about billions of dollars and not your checking account, the problems that surround educational funding are really not all that different from the ones you have, and the solutions aren't all that different, either. Just as you and your husband or wife or you and your child need to be able to discuss openly and honestly your finances and your goals and expectations around them, so do our schools and the institutions that fund them. When the state and the city and the schools have a conversation about school performance, how to reach it and what the rewards will be if we get there, we're suddenly in a whole different—and a whole lot better—place from the one we were in when we were delivering edicts and handing down punishments and hiding bad scores. If my staff went to the state capital in Tallahassee every quarter and discussed outcomes with officials, there'd suddenly be a much more substantive discussion about money. And if that started happening in every other state in the country around a broad range of standards based on the four qualities of a mature and conscious contributor to society, soon millions more of our children would be getting a sense of Civic Awareness. More children would be taking courses that taught them the very specific behavioral traits of successful entrepreneurship. But to do it, this country will have to be willing to pay the freight in all ways, not just financially. We'll have to set educational goals for ourselves and live by them.

There are three issues related to money that have to be addressed in any discussion of public education right now: vouchers, charter schools, and philanthropy.

VOUCHERS

Now, understand, I *like* competition. When you boil it all down, this book is about competition: what we need to do to compete as a nation; what our public schools need to do to compete with private options; what parents need to do to prepare their children for competition in school and in life; how parents can demand services from their schools that will force schools to compete harder. For better or worse, competition is the nature of life, and it's true in education—all parents, not just the affluent ones, should be able to choose which school will best serve their children. All communities should have not just a variety of Connected Schools to pick from but an entire market mix of public, private, and charter schools, and then enjoy the benefits of competition between them as they work to improve labs and gyms and libraries and teachers and programs and otherwise draw students.

But competition does not have to mean survival of the fittest. True educational choice means selecting between equally viable alternatives. When you go to a restaurant, you pick the dish you think is going to take care of your hunger and taste the best. If you can't afford the filet mignon, you look for something else that works for you. Based on your preferences and pocketbook, you make a choice, and if the restaurant runs out of that one, there's a second choice that you may end up loving just as much. Now, what if the waiter told you that if you ordered one of the cheap entrées, you'd have a fifty-fifty chance of walking out alive? And the good stuff that doesn't cost too much? They only make a couple of those, so if you weren't in line when the place opened, you're sunk. That's a pretty tragic delivery of service. Real school choice will exist when it's a matter of deciding what *kind* of quality school you want, not picking between functional and failing.

Unfortunately, the idea of school choice has become attached to the idea of vouchers. Voucher programs rest on the assumption that redistributing public money to private schools will create that competition and ultimately result in better public schools. And I don't buy it.

Those in favor of vouchers argue that they serve to create competition. But how can they when their whole point is to drain money away from public schools? Vouchers take the dollars we need to do the work of rethinking our public schools and redistribute them to people who are "going to use them better." That doesn't create competition; it *destroys* competition. Every redistributed public school dollar isn't just a lost opportunity dollar for the revitalization of public schools; it's a two-dollar swing, in that every dollar we lose means a new one for the private school. And vouchers don't stop at taking money away from both the day-to-day functioning of public schools and our rebuilding efforts. Since their intent is to *penalize* failing schools, they further starve schools that are already desperate. No one can explain to me how that helps.

Let's be honest here: the point of vouchers is to rig the system for Us against Them. They're simply a way of busing money, of bolstering private schools while public schools decay from lack of funds and parents are left with fewer choices than they had before. Vouchers don't encourage choice; they encourage the abandonment of public education. Those who advocate such programs, especially minority members, are saying: I got mine. I won. And if you can't get yours, that's your problem. You just shoulda got in line early. I understand the fear that creates that kind of thinking, but better service for a few more people doesn't solve the real problem. We need enough good choices for *everyone* to have a quality education.

There's more. No voucher system proposal I've seen could handle the sheer size of what public school systems handle, and I've never heard a voucher proponent call for the closing of all public schools. So if we the people are not getting a replacement for our public school system, why should we subsidize programs that are destroying it? When I was chancellor in New York City, then-mayor Rudy Giuliani began to advocate vouchers. To explain how I felt about them, I made a simple comparison. "When you give me a rebate on my city taxes for moving to New Jersey," I said, "then you'll get me on board with vouchers."

If we want to talk about people making "better use" of public money and the free market, then let's get serious about supply and demand. If we want to really create educational choice in America, go head-to-head with private education. Use the same forces that shape the availability of goods and services in the economy and apply our tax dollars to making better public schools—Connected Schools—available *everywhere*. Make public schools so attractive and safe, so full of their own unique educational and experiential opportunities, that those lucky people with the luxury to choose will have to think long and hard about the cost benefit of a first-rate public school education versus big tuition bills and exclusivity. *Then* you have a high-performing system. *Then* you've spent public money responsibly, efficiently, and with equity. *Then* you've truly created competition and educational choice.

CHARTER SCHOOLS

Connected Schools are all about new ideas. They are based on the constant creation of new relationships with the world around them so that different schools can offer a variety of programming. Part of the charge of Connected Schools is to always ask if there's a better strategy they could use to service the needs of their students and families. Because under the current structure of most school systems charter schools are not directly answerable to the rules of the public school system they're in, they've done a lot of that work, trying new ideas without being crushed by the bureaucracy. For that reason, they've largely been a positive addition to the mix of community schools.

But as with vouchers, public money goes to fund these essentially private projects. And unfortunately, for a questionable return. A 2006 National Assessment of Educational Progress (NAEP) report showed that charter schools' scores were at best keeping up with public schools' in the primary grades, and by fourth grade had slipped behind in reading and math. It strikes me that for all the assurances from people who supposedly really understand how money works, both vouchers and charter schools lack financial sense for the greater good of the nation. Both require large amounts of money to produce substandard results for a small and hopeful segment of the population, while a few people walk away with the profits or the tax deductions.

I'm not going to bother with accusations, because much of the problem is structural. While administrative oversight can be sti-fling, it can also provide valuable accountability. Some charter schools have run into problems regarding finances, management, and administration that all point to two facts: running a business is not the same as running a school, and the supposed freedom from bureaucracy that charter schools offer doesn't guarantee results in the classroom. More often than not, stability is good for a school, and unpredictable administration, funding, location, and quality add up to a less than firm foundation. Charter schools that were not affiliated with any school district performed worst of all in the NAEP report, all but begging for a serious reexamination.

The bottom line is that charter schools can help but they're not the answer. One model high school in the Bronx that costs tens of millions of dollars, all paid for by a charity, may offer a lifeboat to 1,500 students. But there are more than 1.1 million students in the New York City school system. And what if that charity decides to fund some other initiative? The cost benefit of what the public and the private sectors will put in is debatable against what could have been achieved with that money if it had been applied in a broader fashion. That said, I do see a place for charter schools within a good school system; they're immensely useful as laboratories, and the good things that come out of them should be replicated. But don't overestimate their value.

PHILANTHROPY

It would be wrong for me to say that philanthropy hasn't worked when it comes to public education. Millions of Americans have benefited over the years from the generosity of others that has paid for buildings, books, instructors, research, and so on, and all of this in turn has obviously helped us as a nation to an extent that could never be calculated. The problem is that given the immense amount of resources that are brought to bear on education by philanthropy, literally billions of dollars by now, the overall effect has been so much less than it could have been. In New York City alone, millionaires trip over themselves to give money to educational charities—powerful, high-profile people with enough political and symbolic cachet to change the world, but all their speeches and checks and benefits have barely made a dent in how third-grade classrooms operate. It's not accountability I'm worried about; these are good works, and people are sincere in both how they give and how what's given is put to use. What disappoints me is the lost opportunity to create the deep structural changes that would really prepare our children.

Those millions of dollars have underperformed because most donors have a limited technical knowledge as to where to put their money for the highest leverage. Over the last ten years of cancer research, billions of dollars have been placed in the hands of very skilled people who knew exactly what they wanted to do with them, everything from buying laboratory animals to setting up labs to reaching out to various communities to creating new experiments and testing new drugs and so on. This is leveraging your money—applying it to specific goals that are worked toward by people with great expertise using tested strategies. You simply can't say that about much of the investment philanthropists have made in public schools. Not that they don't do it with the best intentions, but they simply don't have the benefit of knowing whom, exactly, they should give their money to. Researchers? School systems? Schools themselves? Should it support teachers, administrators, or students?

The quick answer to all these questions is all of the above. Schools need money; districts and states need money, as do teachers and principals. And educational philanthropy has responded to these needs by becoming, by and large, a general subsidy that helps schools continue to at least function, sprinkling water down to keep something coming up out of the ground, even if it's a meager subsistence crop. The Carnegie Foundation has spent an enormous amount of money for public education, but its gifts are so across the board that it's almost governmental.

What's clear is that we need this process of channeling philanthropy to be far more exact. What are the ideas that will really have an impact, really produce a yield on philanthropists' investments in education? Unfortunately, our educational environment and the research that's available have been anything but exact. And when philanthropists make decisions based on such research, the results can be painful. For example, the Gates Foundation, headed by the founder of Microsoft, Bill Gates, and his wife, Melinda, made reducing school size the keystone of their efforts to improve high schools. According to *The New York Times*, they have "invested $1 billion to persuade school districts to break up large high schools into small schools of 500 or fewer students." Small schools are a good idea, but they're only one piece of the puzzle. The fifteen hundred schools involved showed improvements in some areas but lost ground in others, and in one case, Manual High School in Denver, the breakup of the large school into three smaller ones resulted in not only no appreciable improvements in academic achievement but the eventual closing of all three. While it all made sense on paper, the economies of scale offered by the large school disappeared with the breakup; curricular and staff support issues hadn't been fully addressed, and within a few years students abandoned the schools. The reality is that change can never be made in a vacuum and any experiment that locks onto one aspect of education, as if changing one element would solve the whole problem, is simply not going to work.

I don't present this example as a criticism of the Gates Foundation. I agree with their commitment to rethinking our models of education, their goal of focusing education on today's workplace and strengthening the student-teacher relationship. I am grateful for their unmatched readiness to put their money where their mouths are. By pooling their enormous resources—some $60 billion at this point—Bill and Melinda Gates and Warren Buffett have positioned themselves to have an impact on the nation's education structure the likes of which have not been seen since Andrew Carnegie began building libraries across the country. Their commitment to direct-ing much of this money toward education is a special one that comes once in a generation (or more). Combined with the efforts of Eli Broad, their work is pointing the way to the investment neces-sary for a globally competitive public education system, and it has the chance to play a major role in effecting long-term structural change in public education.

But for private philanthropies to really leverage their money, they have to focus on outcomes, not simply on holes in the system where money is needed. This is where Connected Schools come in. Connected Schools are all about outcomes. And philanthropies' re-lationship with Connected Schools would be the same as any part-nership they would enter into in the business world: they would enter into a binding agreement with the school system to provide certain forms of support based on mutually agreed-upon outcomes. Philanthropists would have to stop viewing their donations as char-ity and instead see them as investments, applying the same kind of tough standards and processes they surely applied on the road toward amassing their fortunes. Instead of handing money out and crossing their fingers (hardly an accepted business practice), they could tell a Connected School system: Once you develop the infra-structure—once you redesign your processes and create the innova-tions that will bring you to this agreed-upon outcome—*this* is the kind of support that will be waiting for you. Yes, we'll put money into helping you figure out how to get there, we'll seed your idea, but the big piece will come when you show us that your innovation works. Our real investment will come both in supporting and in replicating the success of your approach.

Ask schools to earn their money. Some philanthropic organiza-tions, especially New York's Robin Hood Foundation, are taking this route. Over the years I've had ambivalent feelings about how the foundation has applied its resources to education, essentially focusing on only one or two schools. Recent system-wide initiatives, though, have the potential of influencing change throughout the entire city, which to me is a better use of its considerable power. By simultaneously making system-building investments and demanding results, the Robin Hood Foundation is a model for philanthropy. Recipients of its grants must draw up plans, set goals, and allow considerable oversight and auditing in order for the money to flow. What the Robin Hood Foundation, and others like it, acutely understand is that philanthropy can never be the backbone of the movement; it has real power only when it acts in conjunction with deeply rooted community and school transformation.

The true power of people such as the Gateses and Eli Broad and Warren Buffett and Oprah Winfrey, who has also taken a leadership role on education, is beyond the purely financial. Until now, there's been no one with the stature to lead this conversation about American education with any kind of legitimacy. Every mayor wants to be the education mayor, every president wants to be the education president, but no one has had the influence, independence, and willingness to stand up at the pulpit and say difficult things in a loud voice you can hear all the way in the last row of the balcony. If these people can bring the results-oriented, world-changing attitude they had in business to public education, if they can see the necessity of equipping our children with a sharper, smarter, more effective set of tools and work cooperatively with our schools to do that, then great things will be possible.

HOW TO CONNECT

I n late 2006 *BusinessWeek* predicted that by the end of 2007 "the cost of imported goods and services will exceed federal revenues."

What does that mean? It means that as large and important as our government will remain, the global economy is here to stay and only getting bigger. To survive, we'll have to adapt to that reality and concentrate the efforts of government, business, arts, service, home, and education on the place where our national character and national economy are created—in our schools. Connected Schools are the best way to do that.

The idea of Connected Schools wasn't cooked up in some policy think tank. It's a commonsense strategy to integrate education with life in a practical, effective, and yet entirely creative way. Good parents and good teachers have always known how to nurture the confidence and experience children draw from to naturally develop the four qualities of a mature and conscious contributor to society. Every moment of every day offers ways to learn things that you can use to realize your abilities, no matter if you lay optic cable, harvest artichokes, trade bonds, or paint pictures. And then you give those things back to the world, but now transformed by you. That fearlessness, that kind of flexible mind, is what wins in the flat world, and America was built on that marketplace of the human spirit. Thomas Jefferson and Benjamin Franklin—Founding

Fathers and certainly two global thinkers—would be right at home in our Connected Schools, merging thought and action, belief and deed, curiosity and character, so they could meet a changing world well prepared.

But Connected Schools need context. They teach context and exist within the context of a nation, a state, a local government, a business and an arts community, and all the other pieces of who we are as a society. One teacher up at the front of the room with a pointer can't make all the connections that a twenty-first-century education requires. But we all carry the light of our particular knowledge, and Connected Schools ask each of us to focus that light on the place called school so our children can see the world around them with the clarity and courage they'll need. Not because it's the "right" thing or a "good" thing, but because it's the only way we can ensure our vitality going forward. By marrying national standards and goals with local innovation and needs, Connected Schools will build on the best principles of America.

In Chapter Five we laid the foundation by detailing the seven things the federal government must do: set national standards and assessments; establish national minimum teacher salaries and teacher certification; create universal preschool; upgrade facilities; and support middle schools. In Chapter Six we established the need for parent involvement, and in Chapter Seven we laid out how we need to look at school funding. Now it's time for everyone from the statehouse down to your home to accept responsibility for preparing our children for the future through a system of Connected Schools. This chapter tells each of us in what ways we must put our shoulder to the wheel to advance the nation as a whole. It is by no means an exhaustive list. Because Connected Schools are grown out of their surroundings, each school and system will be different, and all the participants will need to create partnerships that satisfy their particular needs; there can never be an exhaustive list. You are charged with finding your own solutions. If aspects of this chapter are programmatic, it's because we have so much to relearn. Whether or not our federal government or even our national will rise to the challenge of this century, if we apply the lessons of this chapter to our own local schools—wherever we are, as much as we can—we will effect a change for the better. If we bring caring, high expectations, and diverse approaches to learning to all levels of public education, we will create a new generation of mature and conscious Americans, full of the stuff that once pointed us toward the stars.

THE STATE: SPREADING SUCCESS

The only people who can tell us how well we're preparing our students, whether we've given them the four qualities of a mature and conscious contributor to society, are the students themselves, but we need people to listen. That should be the state's job. State departments of education need to get out of the gotcha business and into the business of knowledge development and transfer by producing and sharing menus of exemplary practices.

Right now, all those FCAT and Regents test scores your child produces in school get collected up and go onto the state's desk. Now, imagine this was a classroom. A good teacher would score the tests, applaud those who did well, challenge those in the middle to do better, and analyze the work of those who failed so he could identify where the problems lie and create a new strategy to get the material across. He'd mine the tests to learn what strategies work well for most kids and which don't and where most kids slip up. The scores would matter, yes, but only as a part of a larger strategy of determining how the kids were doing and how he could spread success in the future.

Well, here's what the states do with all those scores right now. They identify the schools that failed, take away their money and their control, and tell them to do better or they'll get even more money and control taken away, or maybe even get shut down. And then all those reams of paper, I mean literally warehouses full of captured data, get taped up in boxes and that's that. Schools have been capturing data for years, but rarely have they converted those data into any kind of information that actually helps schools, teachers, parents, or students. Punish? Yes. Help? No. We have piles of statistics, but much of it with no relevance to the questions at the heart of this book, such as whether the students are leaving public schools feeling ready for college or the working world. Dropout rates, graduation rates, test scores, college acceptances—those we have, but we have little quantifiable data on *how* the children got there.

With a national assessment that identifies which schools are performing well and which need help, state departments of education will be freed from creating and administering tests and can refocus their operations. Yes, failing schools have to be identified, but high-performing schools offer the truly important information; they tell us how to succeed, and this is where the states should go. Connected Schools mean local communities using state tool kits to reach national standards. Instead of working out of a panicked need to act tough, states should reorient their efforts toward offering the successful ideas and practices of high-performing schools to other schools.

Information by itself is not enough, though. Just as our teachers and classrooms assume that all our kids can learn and approach their struggles with technical intervention, so we need the state to do that with our struggling schools. Punishment is antithetical to improvement. States must create technical teams that can replicate their exemplary practices. This means providing struggling schools with an intervention team that offers a menu of proven strategies from which the local system can choose. What I hear now is: "If the scores don't go up, the schools must be closed." Here's what I'd like to hear: "We've captured data on twenty-eight programs, but we've identified these seven as having the highest impact and highest value for children in this state, and we'll help you implement the one you select to best meet your local needs."

And let me be clear that this conversation is not just about Academic Proficiency. *All* our public schools are struggling with *all* four qualities in their own ways. We have children whose problems come largely from being overwhelmed by privilege. That's a real problem, as serious in its way as those faced by kids in inner cities, lost to poverty and crime and hopelessness. Hopelessness is hopelessness, whether it's in gutted inner cities or suburban communities torn up by crystal meth and soul-withering greed. All our schools need the same caring, high expectations, and diverse approaches to learning that individual students need, even if they apply to something other than reading scores. Different kinds of problems require different kinds of interventions, different kinds of teachers, different kinds of community-based collaborations and partnerships to create new and different outlets and opportunities for children to learn. All of those things are aspects of technical intervention, and they must be approached that way. Every child deserves a high-functioning classroom, and it's the states' job to lead the way by showing Connected Schools all the various, effective ways to achieve that.

Finally, states have to market this information about what works to parents, so they in turn can make the right choices for their children and demand accountability themselves. Where in your state can you find a listing of the exemplary practices in teaching math or science? Probably nowhere. If it's there, is your state actively sharing that information with the schools that need help? A state department of education should be able to tell a parent, just as an example, that there are five different kinds of programs that it's identified that best respond to the after-school needs of most parents in the state, and here's what they all have in common.

In short, the state facilitates the process of putting caring, high expectations, and diverse approaches to learning into every one of its classes. By believing that all its schools can succeed, aiming toward national standards, and providing information and intervention, states establish individual patterns of success for local systems.

THE SCHOOL SYSTEM:
KEEPING ALL EYES ON THE PRIZE

SCHOOL BOARDS

The only agenda of our public schools should be to produce children who can compete on a global level.

Now, go and poll the members of your local school board and see what *their* concerns are. During my years in Sacramento, Tacoma, Boston, New York City, and now Miami, I've watched school board members burn through hundreds of thousands of taxpayer dollars and thousands of man-hours over everything from costly, divisive hobbyhorses like "intelligent design" to political ambitions, from office locations to job offers for their pals.

And that's if you're lucky. Elected school boards are highly susceptible to corruption, too. When I came to New York City in 1995, New Yorkers had been investing hundreds of millions of dollars in their schools over the previous thirty years and were getting less and less from them. I wanted to know why. As the system was structured then, each of the city's thirty-two school districts had its own school board, so I sat down and reviewed the budget sheets for all thirty-two. One board in particular stood out. Huge sums of money had flowed through it, and the schools in this district were terrible, so I called the entire board into my office in Brooklyn to explain themselves.

Were they ashamed? Embarrassed? Even defensive?

No. What I got back was anger. "How dare you insult this board," said one of them. "This district has excellent music programs . . ."

I cut him off on that.

"If you've spent so much money on music programs," I asked, "where are the bands? Where are the student orchestras? Where are the concerts and ensembles and students going on to Juilliard?"

There might have been a spare tuba lying around in some corner, but all that money had produced not a single accomplished note. Instead, it was flying into other people's pockets. In other neighborhoods I saw boards where the parents had no real understanding of what a better school would look like, but they knew the person who could get them part-time work in the cafeteria. *That* was the sort of knowledge the system was run on. Principalships were bought and sold. There were too many examples in too many districts of communities that had been starved of ideas so a handful of people could get fat. I had no choice but to remove several entire school boards who were selling jobs, running their campaigns at district expense, and essentially using taxpayer dollars to advance their own political careers. Eventually I was able to bring the entire system under the chancellor and a single citywide board.

No other public interest, not the fire department or the police department, is placed under direct control the way our professional educators must report to local school boards. And while I could even live with that, the oversight often comes from people whose only qualification for a position directing educational policy is that they live in a certain zip code. Time and again I've seen individual members with no qualms about blowing past the limits of their own particular knowledge and the limits of what a board can or should reasonably do in order to advance their personal agenda. Most school boards spend more time haggling, whining, regulating, and politicizing classrooms than focusing on strategic planning that could lead to actual educational success. Imagine a group of people, each trying to steer the same car, usually in bizarre directions, and you'll be seeing the worst of a school board meeting.

What that means for your child is that the hands-on management of the school system, from superintendent on down, wastes more energy dealing with the board than making sure your child can read. The core business of whether our children graduate rich in the four qualities of a mature and conscious contributor to society is no longer the core business. Instead, it mutates into whatever the board says it is that month.

I've sat on corporate boards, and in my experience they operate with a clarity of purpose. The CEO and management are in charge of the corporate vision and how it's executed, while the board provides the accountability with, usually, a minimum of micromanagement. The members know the issues facing the company, they're familiar with the metrics, and their particular expertise is brought to bear where applicable. Robert Spillane, an extraordinary superintendent in Boston and Fairfax, Virginia, often says, "We've got to make the main thing the main thing." School boards must be modeled on corporate boards.

HERE'S HOW SCHOOL BOARDS IN CONNECTED SCHOOLS SYSTEMS SHOULD OPERATE:

- **They must have a strong and clearheaded sensibility about the work.** Dogged persistence, unfailing devotion to outcomes, a clarity of purpose, and respect for expertise—these should be the defining qualities of a school board. The core business of a school governing board, no matter its structure, must be about providing quality education for every child in the system. Anything that deviates from this mission is unacceptable.

- **They must act with one voice.**

- **They must be able to resolve differences professionally.**

- **They must not abuse staff or waste valuable time.**

- **Their members should be the people best positioned linguistically, culturally, personally, and professionally to further the dialogue between communities, not deepen rifts.** The board should help parents, community, and business get aligned, so the greatest value of board members should be their connections, in how they can provide both a power boost and a critical eye. At the end of the day, local governments have to own the desire to transform their schools for the new century. They have to decide that they want the management energy of their school boards focused on preparing their children for the global marketplace instead of whether or not they'll be in the newspaper tomorrow morning.

ON A TECHNICAL LEVEL, SCHOOL BOARDS SHOULD DO THE FOLLOWING:

- **Operate in a solely advisory role to the mayor.** This applies only to districts larger than thirty thousand or where performance has been consistently below standards.

- **Hire the superintendent.**

- **Provide information to the mayor and the superintendent** since they are composed of people whose presence on the board is supposedly based on their knowledge of and position within their community and some depth of knowledge in a relevant field.

- **Meet once a quarter to review very specific outcomes and measures** that have been agreed to by the mayor, the advisory board, and the superintendent, outcomes that will have a direct impact on funding.

That becomes the conversation. While they must keep their doors open to all the various segments of their community so people always know that they have a voice in this process, make no mistake, school boards shouldn't exist to simply provide a way to blow off steam. Their purpose is to discharge their fiduciary responsibilities regarding tax dollars, and they must hold the superintendent accountable for that within some sort of checks-and-balances environment.

The desire to help direct public education is an admirable thing. Connected Schools are assembled with that desire in mind, so I not only don't discount that desire, I encourage it. But Connected Schools offer a new governance model for school systems that allows people to add their knowledge as constituent members of the community while at the same time leaving the governance to those with expertise in education. By using the community to create a wider spectrum of choice and building a clientele of parents and students with the information and ability to exercise that choice, we're putting the schools on market terms and reducing the need for school board members to advocate for the particular needs of constituents; the constituents will vote with how and where they use their school choice. In addition, Connected Schools offer a range of major opportunities for involvement and direction, opportunities for high-impact, high-level work for those who might otherwise be inclined to sit on a board. Instead of giving gassy speeches about what he thinks should happen, a local businessman can create a direct partnership with the school system that leverages his unique abilities or resources to an educational need. All eyes stay on the prize, the board limits itself to oversight and advice, and the people who know how to sail steer the ship.

SUPERINTENDENTS

Connected Schools offer great opportunities to a superintendent and even greater responsibilities. It's the superintendent who knows the whole lay of the land, the specific local knowledge and the particular issues that need solving and, even more important, the people in the system and in the community who will add new threads of support. EQ (or Emotional Quotient) matters more here than IQ. It's not a job for a shy, retiring person. There are many, many places in education for that type of person, but not the super's office. If our Connected Schools are to be webs of support, brilliant networks made of what everyone in the community has to offer, then the superintendent is the spider weaving it all together, imagining what can be and then going out and making it happen.

A superintendent isn't a bureaucrat; she's a creator, and the people around her are her material. First, foremost, and always, she's about relationships. The superintendent must be personally connected to the mayor, the local business community, the arts community, the faith community, local and state politicians, universities, all the various linguistic and ethnic communities, teachers, parents, students, you name it—every thread that runs through the community and that can exchange with the schools. She'll be calling on them all, and so she must at all times be aware of where they are so they can play their part in tune and on time.

The super must understand her system's strengths and weaknesses. She has to know the quality and quantity of programs throughout her system: if she needs more arts in the classrooms, if her after-school programs are too thin, whether her teacher training is rich enough, and so much more. But she must also know the value of what her schools can offer, from raising real estate prices to creating Nobel Prize winners. Schools have a living function in every community, and the supers must assess both what they need and what they can give.

The super must understand the strengths and weaknesses of the community. Then she has to start putting the pieces together. This is the very core of Connected Schools—solving school and community problems and fulfilling school and community needs through school and community partnerships. The super is the person who, for all the puzzle pieces scattered around, sees the common image they're all a part of and tries to fit them together to create that image.

The school system is not a one-size-fits-all proposition, so the super must create schools that match her students' broad range of cognitive needs. She has to put together an appropriate menu: Are there single-gender schools and accelerated programs? Are there resources and *real* opportunities for growth available to children with special needs? Are there schools that not only use the arts but create artists? Are there schools that connect to specific industries and businesses in the local community? Are there residential schools, where students committed to a certain field of learning can focus their lives on their passion? A school system is not a static venture; it must constantly grow and change, and it's the superintendent's job to innovate in ways that will help students meet both the expected challenges of adult life and the unknowns of the future.

A good superintendent is a bigger-than-life civic leader. Leadership has many metaphors. You can talk about leading men into battle and leading expeditions and leading a race. But this is a musician's son talking here, so I think of leadership in a different way. To me, elevating children's lives with the four qualities of a mature and conscious contributor to society is a melody we've got to play. We all have to play it in our ways, and that's the point of this book, to give each of us our notes, but if there's not someone standing up in front holding the baton, we're all just gonna be blowing horns. We need someone who can imagine what we should all sound like together, who knows who has to play what, when, and how loud. We need someone to turn us into an orchestra, and that's the superintendent's job. Whether or not she's working within a Connected Schools system, the superintendent has to dream the dream, set the beat, and orchestrate its execution. Be Duke Ellington, Count Basie, Bob Wills, or Georg Solti, but no matter what style you do it in, make sure the people around you play it tight and with energy.

The super must market her schools' value to the community in ways that will let her create partnerships that will bolster the weak points. When that bandleader walks onto the stage, all eyes are on him, and even if there are thirty people behind him, each one an expert at playing his or her instrument, that one man in the tuxedo represents them all to the people in the audience. It's his picture on the posters around town. He's the public face of his band, and he has to sell it. School systems are no different. The super has to go out and draw folks in with a Parent Academy. She has to market the services of her schools throughout her area, providing as much information and as many entry points as possible through relationships, for one, but also by being extremely visible. Supers have to not just be active players in their communities; they must be seen doing it, touching every cultural community and showing how education is a vigorous part of life. A quiet, behind-the-scenes superintendent isn't doing part of her job. As crass as it may sound, a super is the spokesperson for her brand. Sell your people on your schools. Put that menu of educational services, or at least information about it, into everyone's hands. Show us the public school kids who now play in the local symphony, who run laboratories at the local university, who own businesses or go to the local colleges. Give us the human evidence of the value of going to your schools.

The world has some natural leaders who can do these kinds of things instinctively, but we seem short of them in education right now. Over and over, I'm told how the New York City school system, or the Los Angeles school system, or wherever, can't be fixed by one person. "They're just too big," says Mr. Educational Expert. "No single person can oversee the effective distribution of education to a million students a year."

So let me ask, how can FedEx distribute millions of packages around the globe overnight, every night? How does Coca-Cola find its way into every corner of the planet? Each of those companies and thousands of other multinational corporations has a single CEO, but no one wonders whether they're too large to be run by one person. It's assumed that because of efficiencies, effectiveness, accountability, and the need for staying focused on stock price, a CEO can trust the parts and let it grow big. So why can't one person change a major school system? The problem is not so much that public education in America is lacking leadership as that it lacks a heroic vision of what its leadership can and should do. We sense this void, and so what we do nowadays is bring in Leaders with a capital *L*, some up-till-now successful businessman or retired military officer who just lives and breathes the ability to tell everyone what to do, usually in a very loud voice and sometimes with a bat in his hand.

Let's look at the logic of that. I, Rudy Crew, know nothing

about the art of war. I've never been a soldier, haven't been trained for war. I'm unfamiliar with theories of war. But I have watched some John Wayne movies, so put me in charge of the U.S. military. Make sense to you? Same with the retired CEOs. For as much as this book is about applying business practice and accountability to education and how schools need to produce a yield on the investment we as a society make in them, the goal of business is to make a profit while the goal of education is to create rounded young adults, and I don't find much of an intersection there. Forming minds and characters is not interchangeable with stocking Wal-Marts or meeting sales quotas. There's a technical expertise: a knowledge base about how children develop, what they need, what time of day things should be offered, how they should be situated or arranged in a school, and on and on—all of which educators have studied. The arbitrary application of management techniques as if the entire world can be reduced to a production line is silly and destructive. To do her job, a super must have the obvious pedagogical knowledge any educator has to have, a currency on the professional execution of the jobs of teacher and principal. Effective leadership is specific leadership—Gandhi was a brilliant, effective leader, but I don't know that the job of CEO of Exxon would have been a good fit for him.

Beyond the specific knowledge, that greater, higher vision an educational leader needs must be informed by something more than a desire to tell people what to do. To my father, a leader aimed at the highest level of human decency, of human dignity, and gave people a sense of themselves as he did with me. FDR, Adam Clayton Powell, Dr. King—those were his kinds of leaders, men who led with a vision of their whole soul, who pushed people to heights that they didn't even know existed, let alone that they'd have to climb them. Sure, those men could deliver a great speech, but their dashing moments weren't the point; it was the serious day-to-day building, and the people they asked to do it—the poor and pushed aside, those who'd never had a voice, who were now creating the future out of the dust and rubble around their feet. When I finally stepped into leadership positions in the 1970s, I looked around and saw battles over desegregation and delivering quality education to children who'd never had it before. I saw people fighting for classrooms to be painted and windows to be replaced because that's what they needed to make their schools better. I saw teachers and principals doing the steadfast work of elevating lives, and at the very end of the day, when I finally turn off that light next to my bed, that's what I believe my job is. To me, the ultimate reason every great superintendent walks in the door every morning is to elevate the lives of children by instilling the four qualities of a mature and conscious contributor to society. This must be the core value that informs every aspect of educational leadership, no matter where one serves.

But we can't wait for the gods to deliver us an educational FDR or Gandhi or Martin Luther King. We have to train for leadership. Unfortunately, our universities and training systems haven't kept up. Low performance, whether it's in the super's office or behind the teacher's desk in the classroom, can almost always be traced back to low-quality training and little or no ongoing supervision.

On a nuts-and-bolts level, our universities must stop training people just to be good pedagogues. We can't send educators out into the world who don't know how to effectively manage time, money, and people, and to do it within a macroeconomic environment that understands that what happens on Wall Street or in Hong Kong or New Delhi has as much to do with funding for your new reading series as anything else. The health of business directly translates into the kinds of resources that will be available to your local schools. Though our schools are entirely subject to those forces, superintendents and principals as well are rarely trained to identify and deal with such issues on a macro level, and frankly, they're not much better prepared on a micro level, either. There will always be budgets and personnel issues and management; using the taxpayer dollar is the meat of the job, what the phone calls and the meetings and the mounds of paper are about. We need the superintendents and principals of the new century to know spreadsheets and marketing materials as well as they know Jean Piaget and John Dewey.

Unfortunately, people who train in this field tend not to know the business end of this game, because they've been sold the line that education and business are somehow the opposite ends of the stick. I'll say it again—public education is not a form of charity. And yet demanding business experience for school administrators doesn't mean we want a profit-oriented, sink-or-swim, just-the-numbers mind-set. We want the mind-set that values innovation and problem solving, that completes tasks and rewards results more than just effort. Education has spent too much time making kids feel comfortable instead of confident, and that's extended to the educators themselves. Not only do our administrators need to know about management and budgeting; they need productive values, output values, not charity values. At this point, not knowing the realities of business and not knowing the tools and strategies that have been proven effective in dealing with them constitute not knowing how to be an educator.

This leadership training should finish with a rigorous preparatory module, almost on the model of medical school, where residents spend some time on the ground perfecting their skills. We try to do that here in Miami through some of the leadership development programs we've created with Harvard and local universities. In New York we had the Principals Institute, which tried to give people an alternative design by which to build new metaphors for how to do the work in their schools. You can send people to conferences—they're fun and therapeutic—but we need more than fresh ideas. We need to make such ideas technically viable by giving leaders the tools and training to confidently implement them and guide the development of high-quality student-teacher relationships throughout the system.

And most of all, superintendents must dream. Filing reports

and attending meetings are the white-collar version of punching the clock. Everything in this book starts with public school leaders learning to turn everything they know on its side and examine the infinite possibilities that Connected Schools offer. The world isn't just flat, it's tilting, and we need to be out on the edges where it's risky. We can't afford to play it safe in the middle anymore, because pretending nothing's changed is in fact the most dangerous place to be. We have to push to the edges, and even though that's scary and counterintuitive, it's where we have to go. Superintendents no longer have any choice but to innovate and change.

THE SCHOOL: ALL HANDS PULLING

Assuming that Academic Proficiency is already a primary concern, here is a broad outline of how we begin to teach Personal Integrity, Workplace Literacy, and Civic Awareness in our classrooms.

To create Personal Integrity we need to:

- **Teach manners and deportment in school.**

- **Offer service and leadership opportunities.** Kids don't know what they can do before they do it. The more opportunities they have to exercise leadership, the more steps they take toward maturity.

- **Offer ways for children to find and use their talents.**

- **Identify common values.**

- **Provide information on real social norms.** Many parents have all but given in to the idea that peer pressure runs our children's lives, which, aside from excusing oneself from the job of parenting, is simply wrong. More likely, it's the perception of peer pressure, the belief that everyone's doing it, and not any reality. A study published in the *Journal of*

Studies on Alcohol showed that campaigns countering the perception that everyone in college drank to excess had a marked effect on drinking among students. Rather than give in to the horror stories and panic, we have to let kids know that we value their independence and their ability to make good choices for themselves, and that others are making good choices, too.

- **Build an atmosphere of respect for the institution and everyone in it.** This starts all the way at the top, and you can go as high as you like with it. True cultures of caring, high expectations, and diverse approaches to learning, not just mottoes and banners, must infuse our school systems, and that means teachers and parents and principals and superintendents as much as the kids. I guarantee you'll see results.

- **Monitor organization, self-control, and follow-through as deliverable behaviors.**

I recently visited a school in the northern part of Dade County. As usual, I didn't announce that I was coming so I could get a real vision of how the school operated on a day-to-day basis, without a special assembly and the principal running interference. Down one hallway was a whole row of third-grade classrooms, and I decided to see all of them. When I walked into the first one, the children barely noticed me, which was fine; I assumed they were working on something. But their collective response when I introduced myself to their teacher was a roomful of blank stares. A few mumbled, "Good mornin', mister," and that was that. In the second class, the light went on in most of the kids' eyes. They looked up from their work to register that someone different and clearly of some importance had entered, and some said, "Good mornin', Dr. Crew," in a completely appropriate way. But when I entered the third room, the entire class stood up. They pushed their chairs in, and as soon as I greeted the teacher, they all said, "Good morning, Dr. Crew."

Now, if all kids can learn math and all kids can learn how to read, all kids can learn how to react to social situations in an appropriate manner. Clearly the children in these three rooms hadn't been separated out by their innate social abilities; their teachers were teaching them, and only the third one was doing a good job at it. This work doesn't need its own curriculum. It needs moment-by-moment reinforcement.

TO TEACH WORKPLACE LITERACY, WE MUST

- **Teach the practical skills of financial life.** Again, this is a measurable outcome. You can teach how the economy functions. You can teach household budgeting and money skills in a class, along with interview and résumé skills.

- **Create extensive internship opportunities.**

- **Connect vocational programming to the core curriculum.**

- **Teach the value of work and offer positive expectations.**

- **Expose children to positive attitudes toward work.**

- **Help children find their interests.**

- **Present honest and realistic discussions of how things function in the working world and what is valued there.**

TO TEACH CIVIC AWARENESS, WE HAVE TO

- **Teach children how the government works.**

- **Teach and discuss current affairs.** The point is not just to know the names and what's happening but to be able to synthesize the information into an opinion and maybe even action. We need to eliminate passivity, intellectual and otherwise.

- **Teach geography and foreign languages.** How can our children learn how to function globally when they don't even know what state they live in? The biggest reason to worry about competition from China and India is that most of our children can't even find China and India on a map. We have to expose our children to the planet as a whole.

- **Present opportunities for community involvement.**

- **Stress the importance of participation.**

- **Expose children to other cultures and communities.** I am absolutely drawn to the notion of creating ways for young people to be ambassadors to each other, throughout the schools in your district. I love the notion of student governments that come together, talk about and decide upon issues, and then share that information with the school board.

- **Introduce children to the cultural lives of our communities.**

All I'm doing is stretching the canvas and telling you what elements have to be in the picture. The color, the brushstrokes, the style, how the elements are arranged, are all up to each Connected Schools system. Because so much of this lives outside what we've come to think of as "school," we'll rely on the creativity and open solutions that connections to the business, art, science, and service communities will engender for locally specific ideas. With national standards and assessments for Academic Proficiency in place, the other three qualities can be measured locally. But they *must* be measured.

Now, somewhere along the way, we came to believe that the solution to all our problems and the best plan for dealing with the global economy was to get every high school graduate into college. I disagree. Our goal should be to make a high school diploma once again worth the paper it's printed on. As it stands, only about a fifth of our children are ready for truly college-level work when they enter college, which means a huge number of the kids in college are basically covering material that they should have met in high school. Even if we increase the number of college graduates, it won't help them or the economy if millions of them own college diplomas that attest to little other than their attendance, nor should we act surprised when their "credentials" don't land them solid lifetime employment. Ending the spiral of kids learning middle school work in high school, receiving elementary remediation in middle school, and getting the most basic exposure to early-learning material in primary grades begins all the way at the beginning, with universal pre-K. If more children start kindergarten with the right basic hardwiring, we'll eventually graduate all our high school seniors with a level of Academic Proficiency appropriate to the world they'll have to live and work in.

Then, after twelve years of meaningful work, a young person will receive a high school diploma that will attest to his or her general ability to function. And it will be time to make a choice. The PSAT should be a requirement in junior year so that every high school student can look college straight on and know whether or not it's a reasonable option. I'm doing that in Miami; our kids have to take it to graduate. I want them to have to look that test in the eye and determine: Do I want to do this, and is my score on this test telling me that either I'm good enough or I'm not good enough or that I need to work harder but I want some information about this? The children who move on to college will then be prepared for college-level work as soon as they walk in the door. To do that, we have to admit that not everyone wants to, or should, go to college. In the end, the result will be what we truly need—more college graduates, and, even more important, college graduates who can compete on a global basis.

For those who look at college and decide not to take that path, Connected Schools will let them make choices based on interest and to some degree aptitude rather than desperation. We'll be able to say to them, We've given you the tools; now here are the options for you to use that talent and use that skill in the military, in a vocational program or a training program that leads you to a truck-driving school, or whatever it may be. An awful lot of young people, when quality guidance presents them with options, are happy to say, "You know what, I *want* to be a plumber. It's a great job, it's a great career, it matches everything that I'm good at and everything that I want to do with my hands and with my life, and so being a plumber is a noble profession. It's a great job. And it may even be that I want to own my own plumbing firm. So I'm not just a plumber; ultimately I'm going to be an entrepreneur." These kids are going to trade school programs that are the equivalent of more than a few two- or four-year institutions of higher learning. But what they don't get is the same support as college-bound kids. No one gets teary eyed about their kids becoming plumbers, the principal doesn't read off a list of them at graduation, even though they may very well have shown more maturity and planning than someone who's just postponing the necessity of making a living. We've got to stop passing judgment on these programs by where we place them, who we hire to run them and teach in them, what kind of equipment and services we provide for them.

Our Connected Schools succeed when they're able to offer true choices to our children, when they hand out dozens or hundreds or even thousands of diplomas that attest to the fact that every one of those children is leaving that school as a mature and conscious contributor to society. Everyone involved in this process—the principal, the teachers, the parents, and the students—needs to understand and agree to this mission. Your son will only get a quality education out of his school if others do as well, so this is a community effort, and everything that's done must be done with that in mind.

THE PRINCIPAL

A well-run company identifies the unit of production that gives people a reason to buy, and protects it like a mother hen. In education, it's the student-teacher relationship, and because Connected

Schools open onto the world, that relationship isn't limited to a teacher, but can be with another significant adult such as a parent or a corporate mentor or museum curator. Whatever form that relationship takes, though, someone needs to protect it and nurture it and do whatever is necessary on a hands-on level to make sure it works. That, not bus schedules or who gets Spanish II, is the most profound role of the principal. For the strategy of this book to work, to effect a dramatic change in American public education, principals must spend the greatest portion of their time protecting the student-teacher relationships in their schools, thereby improving and maintaining the level of instruction. When principals get that right, everything else goes well: attendance improves, truancy is reduced, crime is reduced, the need for security in a school is reduced. A kind of euphoria infects the school, and you'll immediately see an increased demand for that school's services.

To do that, principals must make connections within their school communities with as much energy and vision and accountability as superintendents bring to their connections with the community at large. They have to know their teachers and administrators on a deeply personal basis, know the specific conditions they face, and help them come up with practical, effective solutions so that caring, high expectations, and diverse approaches to learning exist in each of the classrooms under their watch. They have to know their parents and students as well, communicate with them, form relationships with them, and lead them, always looking toward outcomes in the global context we've established.

TEACHERS

Teaching is a big job, demanding great skill and commitment. In this world there are people who want to make an impression on children's lives, and there are people who want to make an impact. I want to hire the ones who want to make an impact, but unfortunately we've been forced to hire a lot of warm bodies in recent years because there aren't enough good candidates. As an industry, American public education is facing the same situation as American business; we're both putting more money into development than we should have to because the students coming out of school aren't equipped with the requisite skills.

Teachers need a very specific kind of training. They have to be technicians with a heart. They have to know the big picture, such as how the brain works, but a lot of it is ground strokes, knowing the variety of tried-and-true strategies, knowing the breadth of issues that relate to all four qualities of a mature and conscious contributor to society. They have to know the depth and richness of the content that they bring to the classroom and to their individual relationships with each child, and they have to know how to impart all of that content with a sense of passion and clarity. Right now, though, universities prepare our prospective teachers with 80 percent pedagogical theory against 20 percent technical practice, and there's no incentive for universities to change anything about this. What you think, what you believe, what you've read—certainly that's all valuable, but when you're in front of a class full of eleven-year-olds bouncing off the walls, what matters isn't what you've read but that you know how to organize and manage that classroom, that you know how to do an inclusive reading model or how to include children with special needs. I'm assuming you believe that all kids can learn. Now you have to know how many books you'll need at the beginning of the year, what resources are available in the classroom and the school, and how you'll deploy them for the benefit of these children. Those are technical conversations, and too many of our teachers are painfully unprepared for them.

The result is devastating on our schools and our kids. Underqualified teachers split school systems in two. Schools that are in demand usually have Demand Parents and the responsiveness from the system that goes with them; those school communities won't put up with underqualified teachers, which in turn makes them even more desirable. The low-demand schools need to build capacity and change culture before the demand will come, but because they're harder places to work in, they're harder to staff, so they get whoever's left. But whoever's left doesn't build capacity or change the culture, because they know they're the ones who were picked last for the ball game and that infects their attitude. Pretty soon they're not coming to school, and that means not only are they not getting any better, but the children suffer and that sense of failure spreads down to them, too. The smaller the number of capable teachers available, the narrower the school menu gets. Without Demand Parents, the situation continues without protest, and soon the entire school implodes.

Rethinking schools in the form of Connected Schools means we must make teaching a true profession. First, we have to balance teacher training. Yes, prospective teachers absolutely still need rich doses of theory, but they must leave school technically expert at developing cognitive relationships with children. If they can't do the functional work of teaching, then they're not teachers; they can be theorists, philosophers, consultants, whatever, but they're not teachers. If you leave architecture school knowing a lot about the theories of architecture but you can't design a building that will stand, you're not an architect. Young teachers must leave their graduate training armed with defined bodies of knowledge and discrete skills that distinguish them from people who don't know how to do this work. Every major school system, or at least every state, should have a training institution that works hand in hand with universities to create state-of-the-art developmental supports for new teachers. We haven't invested at all in professional development, so teachers start the game without knowing even what the play should look like, let alone how it's adding value to their students' lives. In Miami, I've devoted an entire unit and deputy to training and practice, where we help new teachers integrate theory with the practical results we're asking them to produce in reading and math and science. Now those teachers will be working with live ammunition, not working out of a book. We've gotten further faster than I was able to in New York because we were able to focus 75 percent of the attention on practice and less on the politics.

Second, we must develop career educators. I started out in education totally exhilarated by the challenge. I mean, I was gonna change the world and everyone under five feet tall who lived in it. As I went from Pasadena and then to Boston, teaching social science and business, I wondered how I'd do in my evaluation, whether I'd be retained, how long I'd be a teacher. I had a young family, and as time went by, these questions weren't just about my skills in a theoretical sense but about whether I had a serious career in this field. I was committed, but I knew I'd need help along the way. I remembered interviewing for jobs in business school, meeting people in human resources departments at Filene's and Prudential who were interested in how quickly they could move me into management training programs. But in education there were no particular teaching standards or training paths aside from the occasional conference and the threat of someone coming into my classroom and evaluating me using some criteria that I never really ever knew or saw. My skills and training would stay sharp for two years or so before I needed them retooled and refreshed, but over time I began to feel more and more like a professional. Rigorous training and regular certification create a profession with standards and value.

But if America is going to provide this kind of support, which includes the national minimum salary, then the nine-month teacher must be declared a thing of the past. As I see it, teaching is now an eleven-month job at minimum, and a good month of that should be about professional development. Whether it's a month in the summer or two weeks in the summer and two weeks split somewhere else in the year, I don't care, but professional development isn't simply hanging around the school without the kids there. It must be time spent crafting the fine skills of teaching and building a team of educators that together have the will and ability to raise up every child under their care.

For the good of each school and the development of each teacher, we must create consistent teams of teachers. Quality schools have qualified teachers in place long enough to create a culture of success. In Miami we decided to meet the challenge of those low-performing, low-demand schools, sapped by too many under-qualified teachers. We asked our veteran teachers to be the starter dough, to begin the process of change. That meant transferring to an Improvement Zone school for three or four years. In return for higher pay, they would work longer hours and longer school years, but most important, their mission was to create successful classrooms and provide a model for other, less experienced or less skilled teachers in those schools. Not only do they serve as instructors to their children, but they're an indispensable resource for the educators around them. I did the same in New York with the Chancellor's District. The fact is, no matter its condition, every school needs a core of effective, experienced teachers, but unions have created situations where teachers can transfer in and out of schools with little concern as to their impact on the schools involved. Reasonable clauses about the right to transfer schools have become loopholes to some teachers, who then transfer in the middle of the year so they can slot into a vacancy nearer to their home, or the like. This damages schools, and it undermines the development of children at every level, so part of what we need in return for a national compensation package is a requirement that any teacher must stay in a school for no less than three years before transferring again.

Reducing class sizes so they're small enough for the texture and tone of teaching to happen is another important step toward supporting the career. The issue here isn't really about numbers; it's about the stability and continuity of the student-teacher relationship. An instructor needs to have enough time and space with each child in order to assess him or her personally, which means an optimal range of between fifteen and twenty kids per classroom. No teacher in America should face a classroom with more than twenty kids in it. Ever. Nor should there ever be fewer than ten; below that you lose the natural blending of ideas and thoughts that kids grow from. Smaller class sizes, of course, come with their own problems. As I mentioned in Chapter Five, smaller class sizes put pressure on facilities, and the need to hire more teachers will increase variability in teacher quality, which is already one of our biggest problems. If smaller classes can make teaching doable, winnable work, though, they will help draw the quality candidates we need.

Our ability to reconfigure public schools will be guided by our ability to measure outcomes, and this must now extend to teachers. In the same way that we have to provide each student with enough money for a quality education and then let local schools develop their own Value Adds, I believe it's fair to base a certain percentage of a teacher's compensation, above and beyond the livable base, on merit. Quality of work, not just tenure, needs to be rewarded.

There are three elements that should be included in assessing teacher development:

1. **Student performance.** Like it or not, test scores and student assessments do matter here. If a teacher cannot produce students with the four qualities of a mature and conscious contributor to society on a consistent basis, then she should look for another profession, just as a stockbroker who loses money every quarter would, or a lawyer who loses every case.

2. **Teacher development.** Teaching is a skilled practice. While no one expects a new teacher to know everything she needs to know on her first day in the classroom, over time a good teacher builds a body of skills and consistently improves like anyone else exercising a craft. Therefore, teachers should be able to demonstrate throughout their careers how they have grown, how they have honed their skills and strengthened their ability to offer an engaged product to their chil-

dren. To that end, every teacher should maintain a portfolio of her best practices, in the same way that her students keep a folder of their best work. I've always done this with my teachers, focusing not just on the results but on how they reached them. If you're too set in your ways to do this, then you've turned to stone, and your value is limited in a world that's changing every day.

3. **Parental engagement.** As much as we place a bounty on the student-teacher relationship, we have to extend this to the parent-teacher relationship, to complete the circuit with Demand Parents. More attention must be paid to how well teachers engage their clients. Are phones calls made? Letters or e-mails sent? What was your response to a child with poor attendance? How many opportunities do you offer parents to participate in class activities? As part of the teacher's portfolio, I want to see what she's done to get and keep parents engaged in the educational process.

Those three elements sum up the overall responsibilities of a teacher. The unions have been right to say that merit pay can't just be about numbers, either for the teachers or for their kids, but it's reasonable to pin some of their remuneration on a combination of the three, and school systems should welcome the chance. A teacher who's producing strong outcomes, who's growing in her abilities, and who's engaging her parents has an immediate and tangible impact on her school and should earn in proportion to her contribution, just as people in corporations earn in proportion to the value they add to their companies. If she moderates the French club or coaches soccer, she should be paid for the time and effort, but as a supplement to her work.

And then there are those teachers who, if you've ever been lucky enough to have one, never leave you. They are the ones who have truly mastered their profession, people who have perfected their practice to the point where they are now at the top of their game in all three areas. We need to create a professional tier that recognizes them not just as premier practitioners but as scholars who can in turn pass along their knowledge of this work. Rewarding eminent scholars completes the strategy of enriching the idea of teacher compensation, transforming it from a simple equation of their time for our tax dollars into a relationship that keys income and esteem to growth and outcomes.

In the end, making teaching a true profession expresses a familiar set of goals. With a national compensation package and deeper training and development, we'll be displaying care for our teachers and at the same time establishing high expectations by requiring regular certification and including merit pay as an aspect of their salary. More training and a new set of tools or windows into evaluating teachers beyond test scores will offer a set of diverse approaches to creating high-quality teachers.

There is one more thing teachers must be able to do in Connected Schools. The fine work of caring, high expectations, and diverse approaches to learning is only possible if the teacher listens. As I mentioned in Chapter Three, feedback is how teachers can tell whether they're succeeding or not. Classwork and test scores are two forms of feedback, but usually it's more nuanced. I know this all too well. Back when I was just starting out, teaching freshman English at the Alternative School in Pasadena, I had a young man in my class named Bobby. He was older than most of the kids— bigger, too. He'd been sent away to live with relatives in California for a fresh start after some rough years in the South. Bobby hadn't gone to school much down there, and to be honest, he scared the daylights out of most of the teachers, but he seemed to like me and paid attention to me. So one day, early in the term, I started class by handing out copies of *Jonathan Livingston Seagull*.

"Oh, we're going to have a great time reading this," I said as I went up and down the rows. This was the first book I was ever going to teach, and I was more excited than the kids were; I might as well have had that tiger puppet on my hand. "Can someone give me a sense of what you think this book is about?" I asked, trying to get the conversation going. "Look at the cover. Do you think it takes place in a desert? A city?—"

I looked down, and there was Bobby with his long legs stuck out in front of him, checking out the big seagull on the cover. It seemed to me a perfect opportunity to bring him in right up front, let him put some points up early and get confident, so I called on him.

"So, Bobby, whaddya think? Where are we going to be in this book?"

Bobby mumbled something under his breath. I got closer to him and asked him again. He kept mumbling, though, and I finally had to get in his face to hear what he was saying, which was, "I can't read and I ain't readin' this shit."

What I did next I regret all these years later as much as anything I've ever done in my career. I heard Bobby's words, but I did not listen to them. I ignored every signal he was sending out to me. "Don't worry," I said. "I'll help you." I just bulled ahead and fed my confidence with his problem. "We'll work through the words together. It'll all be great." It was my first year.

Bobby slowly got up out of his chair and came at me until I was against the blackboard. We were about the same height, but at that moment he loomed over me. Leaning into my ear, he whispered, "If you make me do this, I will hurt you."

He was rough, for sure. And he could have hurt me, but what I saw in the eyes of this big young boy were tears. I had exposed him. I'd had my own troubles in my school days, struggled myself with reading, and I knew exactly how he felt. I had sold him out.

Bobby sat back down. He never read the book. In fact, a few days later he simply got up, left the classroom, and never returned. After two weeks with no sign of him, I decided to call his house and see what the story was. I knew what I had done, but maybe there was still a chance of reeling him back in. His aunt seemed surprised that anyone from the school was calling. Bobby, she told me, decided that he couldn't cut it in school, so he'd dropped out. Right away he'd drifted into the edges of all the gangbangers around there, and he'd been shot and killed.

The stakes are high. Teachers must tune in to the heart and mind of every young person in front of them and listen. We want every teacher to reach a margin of productivity where all the kids in her class feel challenged and feel enormous satisfaction because they're stretching for something and, hopefully, meeting it with perseverance, within this rewarding, intimate relationship with an adult.

DEMAND PARENTS AND THE CLASSROOM

Equipping a child with Academic Proficiency, Personal Integrity, Workplace Literacy, and Civic Awareness is a cooperative venture, and the classroom is where school and home come into alignment. Enter the Demand Parents. The classroom, where they deal with issues that directly relate to their own children, is the first arena they must work in. Teachers and parents must establish mutual goals and approaches to those goals, and each side has to agree to support the other in their work toward them. Every instructor who works with that child must be part of an organized approach that takes in all evidence of a child's progress from all possible angles and then tailors the individual strategy in response. When it comes to your son or daughter, teachers very often know a different child from the one you do, so to get a complete sense of his or her development, teacher and parent have to combine what they see in their respective worlds and map out a true, three-dimensional picture of the child. That requires listening on the part of everyone involved.

Along with the four points laid out in Chapter Six—know where your children are in their growing process, do the things that

are proven to add value to a child's education, tell someone when it looks like your child's behaviors are coming off the track, care enough about your children to let them walk in and out the door of reality and not let it smack them in the face—

DEMAND PARENTS MUST

- *Attend all parent-teacher conferences and establish a relationship with their child's teacher.* Right now, beside her parents, your child's teacher is the most important adult in her life. Meet her teacher, and let him meet you. Find out how to contact him if you have a question or information you need to share with him. Tell him that you want a clear channel of communication between the two of you and use it. Trust me, your teacher will welcome it.

- *Monitor their child's attendance.*

- *Attend the open houses, activities, and events at their child's school.*

- *Volunteer at the school.*

- *Join the PTA/PTSA.*

- *Join the Moms' or Dads' clubs.* When children see their parents involved in their school, they invest themselves deeper into the propositions of school and education. The wider and richer the intersection you can create between home and school, the more your children will see a unified, stable world around them, and the benefits of that touch all four qualities of a mature and conscious contributor to society. It's also a vital way for you to create bonds with other Demand Parents and build a community that you then reflect and express through your demands on the school.

- *Keep their conversations with the teacher in the what, not the how.* Parent-teacher conversations at school should be about what things can be added to the menu to help your child, how the school can help him through a rough patch. Teachers don't need you telling them how to do it. Telling a teacher how to teach or a guidance counselor how to guide takes everyone down a nasty path of "how dare you," and that's true throughout any school system. Board members tell supeÂintendents how to do their jobsr and superintendents tell principals how to do their jobs, and on and on down a very slippery slope that leads to bad blood, bad suggestions, and bad performance. Demand Parents know their expertise and respect the expertise of others.

And in return Demand Parents should expect

- *Honest answers to questions.*

- *An invitation to participate in their children's education.*

- *Technical support for their children's educational advancement.*

- *Open channels of communication.*

- *That their children will be treated with dignity and, of course, care.*

- *A knowledge of the differences among the children in the class.* Look around the classroom when you visit, look at the homework. Does the teacher have a way to respond to those differences with diverse approaches to learning? Are there materials or approaches available for assuming the same task at different levels? Are there a variety of activities surrounding the reading of *Macbeth* that will create understanding for the kinesthetic learners as well as the verbal ones?

DEMAND PARENTS AND THE SYSTEM

Public schools are the smallest political unit in America. People who otherwise have little engagement in local government find themselves intimately involved with the public trust when their children go to a public school. While it would be nice if every issue a parent or child might have could be resolved within the realm of the classroom, it's natural and in fact good that some things go beyond. Demand Parents can—and should—organize with each other in order to advocate for changes and causes that have an impact on an agenda broader than their own child's immediate needs; this is the second arena where Demand Parents make a difference.

In dealing with the principal and school administration, Demand Parents

- *Don't come with their hands out; they come with a plan.*

- *Pitch in with more than ideas.*

- *Spread credible, useful information, not gossip.*

- *Work together in organized ways, not in individual crusades.*

- *Achieve with positive actions and words.*

- *Respect the administration and teachers of their school, but aren't afraid of them.*

- *Don't whine, complain, or insult.*

- *Are concerned with getting what they deserve, not taking away what others have.*

- *Ask hard questions, and in return offer quality cooperation.*

- *Look for ways they can provide services the school cannot.*

Some issues go beyond even the walls of the school and require

dealings with higher levels of school bureaucracy and administration. If that's the case, keep the following in mind:

- *Don't try to solve all your problems at once.* Take them in
  steps.

- *Learn about the structure of the system,* who's in charge of
  what and who can make the decision you need made. Don't
  run around making random calls and agitating without a
  purpose when there may very well be a procedure already in
  place to handle your concern.

- *Look at the department of education or school system as a
  business, a culture unto itself.* Like it or not, that's what it is,
  and that's how it functions, no matter how intimate the issues are that you're dealing with.

- *Put yourself in the places of the people you're dealing with.*
  Ask yourself how you can make this situation a win for them.
  How can your goals help them reach their own personal or
  professional goals? Will better scores or a new school with
  better diversity make a decision maker in the system look
  good? As I learned with Giuliani in New York, you can get a
  lot done if you can make other people look good.

- *Value parents who have worked in large corporations or
  professional fields.* People who spend their working days
  navigating the dangerous waters of corporate bureaucracies
  will be useful in navigating the public school ones.

- *Don't look at anyone in the system as your enemy.* You can,
  if it makes you feel better, but it's not an effective strategy.
  Again, presenting solutions that help everyone involved will
  increase your chances for success.

- *Know your local politicians.* They won't solve your problems for you, but they can provide valuable access to decision makers and serve as honest brokers if you reach an impasse.

- *Don't start at the top.* Don't call me in the superintendent's office when you want the sixth graders getting more time in the gym. If I say no, you're finished—plus, that's not my job. There are many thresholds of decision making within any hierarchy like a school system and it's wise to start small. Don't send me a petition about something that someone below me can, and should, decide on. Start a few levels down, where a yes is as good as any yes, but a no lets you retool and repackage and then appeal to the next level.

- *Make sure your strategy mirrors your values.* You can't kick everything and everyone else to the side to get what you want for your child. Look for ways to get what you need without its being at the expense of others. Hard as it may be to believe, there are places and times when you and your child are not the most important people in the world. Finding solutions that take into account ethical considerations helps build an ethical framework in your child.

- *Know that mutual misery is not a solution.* No, we're not all better off if everybody gets less. Self-pity is not a strategy or a solution. The point of this book is for everybody—everybody—to get more in the way of quality education. It is important for people to say that they want the very best in their lives and for their children, and to find appropriate ways for that to happen.

Administrations—the districts, the boards, the superintendent—should all welcome the chance for serious, direct communication with their clientele. Respect the courage and hard work that people have summoned up in what is almost always a very intimidating situation for them. Listen actively and speak honestly; people are smarter than you think, and they can recognize bureaucratic BS in seconds. Demand Parents should be experts in pointing *that* out.

DEMAND PARENTS AT HOME

When Sister Mary Elizabeth told me, "You can't," back in the third grade, I listened to her. I fell into that loop of defeat and embarrassment, and she helped feed it every day. A few weeks later it came to a head. For some reason or another, Sister Mary Elizabeth hit me. I hit her back, and found myself immediately suspended.

At that point my father stepped in. He cared for me, more than words can express, and so right then he began creating expectations for me, expectations that helped me reframe myself, helped me reestablish my inner bona fides as a person, as a colored kid. He took "You can't" and turned it into not just "You can" but "You're going to." He put a piece of cement around my heart so that no matter what happened at school, I knew who I was and what was expected of me. By the time I went back to school and got myself out of trouble, the expectations I brought into that classroom were totally a function of my father.

"I'm interested in building you on the inside," he'd say to me, "not on showing folks the outside." Which I can tell you was most definitely true. He was probably the only black man in America who liked to shop at L. L. Bean. It was a good value, he said, and those god-awful ugly rubber boots did keep me warm while I waited for the bus in the snow. I, of course, would rather have been shivering in some *Superfly* ⅛-inch-thick leather jacket, but I learned the lesson well: build your inside, and the outside will come.

Everything a Demand Parent does, everything discussed in this section, is about building the inside of your child, what we've been calling Personal Integrity. It doesn't cost anything. You don't need a college diploma or even a high school one. You just damn well have to understand the importance of it. Children in the poorest of schools and the poorest of communities especially need to walk in the classroom door believing that *they can*. Demand Parents make that happen with the unconditional love—the care—that lets them establish home expectations, intellectually and emotionally. No matter what happens at school, no matter what happens to the nation's educational policy, no matter who the principal is, if you can send your kids to school ready and rich with themselves, and then meet them at the end of the day with open arms and make it clear to them that they deserve to do well, and that you know that *they can* do well, it will happen.

The first step in building the inside of a child, that Personal Integrity, is to introduce your child to himself. A lot of young people nowadays desperately need their peers because they've spent no time within their own interior landscape. Instead of the inside developing the outside, it's the outside determining who these children are—the labels, who they hang out with and where. You are your child's first teacher, and never more so than when it comes to Personal Integrity. As much as parents and communities must facilitate and complement what happens in school, most of all they have to build that concrete wall around their children's hearts. Start by turning off the television and the PlayStation and pointing them toward things that require them to live and think within themselves. Yeah, it's good to have a computer, and yeah, it's good to be able to Google everything, but there's also something about being able to know the beauty of a sincere thought written in your own hand. Draw a picture, read a book, play with dolls or toy soldiers, anything that involves thinking and pretending and imagining—those are what Personal Integrity and Civic Awareness need to grow. This is hardly just an issue for low-income families. Some of the most underdeveloped, most immature and morally inept children I've ever met have come out of wealthy families. While the Parent Academy is meant primarily to serve the underserved, I would like to see such organizations in middle-class and affluent environments as well, if for no other reason than to help those parents learn how to parent, too. Rich, established parents are in at least as desperate need of lessons in raising their kids as immigrants just making sense of America.

Fathers must step up. Children whose fathers are involved in their schools do significantly better than their peers. Fathers set a tone and create conditions where young men in particular can learn how to become men in a very complex society. Unfortunately, more and more boys come to school without role models, and, as Steve Harvey says, a boy without a male role model is like an explorer without a map. There are many places where young boys need the firm, clear, and soft-textured guidance of a man. I don't mean to denigrate in any way what women can teach and their ability to create good people, but the ability to be soft in the midst of a hard world, to treasure your heart, to cry inside and yet still be okay with crying outside, to become trustworthy—these are things best taught to boys by men. I look at young boys now, how they understand power, their relationship to members of the opposite sex, how they understand and build their own repertoire of skills in being honorable gentlemen in the sense of the Old World gentleman, and I worry. They are so undeveloped inside themselves that they don't know how to do things that young men really should be getting familiar with by the time they're in middle school, things like shaking hands and looking someone in the eye, the ability to hold a respectful conversation, to follow up on work, to extend some modicum of social grace in the appropriate places. And when you talk to those boys about this, it's as though you're asking them to be something less than masculine, when in fact what I'm asking them to be *is* a man.

When I was starting at Babson, my father and I drove up together to Boston from Poughkeepsie so we could have a good, long talk. The whole way up he kept asking me what I wanted as a gift. He didn't have anything now, he said, but he'd send something up later.

"I'm good, Pop," I told him. "This is fine."

But he kept on that all the way until we finally got to the school. It was one of those glorious New England afternoons just before autumn begins, and we looked around the college together. Maybe at the time all colleges simply looked the same to me, but I couldn't help remembering the movie I'd watched with him and my sister all those years before that had made me think about college in the first place.

"Don't make me come up here," he said as we were walking across campus. "Don't do anything that'll let 'em punch you outta here."

Then he helped me unload my bags at the dorm, and he sniffed around there, too, saw the room I'd be in and such, until the inevitable. He clapped his hands and said, "Okay, I think I'm gonna start back now. Gonna go down and stay in a little hotel someplace." By which he meant Howard Johnson. I offered the bed in my dorm room, but I also knew how much he enjoyed staying in a Howard Johnson, so I didn't push it.

We went downstairs together, and as we hugged in front of the car, he whispered in my ear, "I got a little something for you in the back."

He led me around to the trunk, and when I looked inside, there was a huge crate of apples. Literally, a crate of apples. *Man, that is a lot of apples*, I thought. *I'm gonna be eating apples all year. Why the hell is he giving me a crate of apples?*

We hauled it out of the trunk—this thing was heavy—and to my total embarrassment, Dad then grabbed a couple of kids passing by to help us take them upstairs. All I could think was, *I'm a freshman, I'm black, and I'm coming with a crate of apples.*

To my relief, the kids agreed and were actually pretty friendly about carrying a crate of apples to some strange kid's room. Dad and I came back down, and we started a second round of goodbyes.

"Thanks, Dad," I said, "for . . . all those apples. I really appreciate it. It's really sweet of you. I'm really blessed to have . . . you know . . . all those apples."

"They're the last thing I can give you," he said. "It's not as much as I would like for it to be, but it's all I can give you right now. It's gonna last you for a while, and then it's gonna run out. It'll be between you and God then. And everything you get from that point on in your life, you can have the benefit of saying you worked for."

I think of that moment every day. *That* was a man building a man. Fathers must give their sons apples.

Demand Parents take advantage of teaching moments in life and create opportunities where they can talk about moral situations with their child. Being gathered and whole, having Personal Integrity, involves a moral element as well. The blacks and whites of life are easy, but the gray patches are hard, and it's the parents' job to teach their children how to navigate through them. In elementary school we tell kids to keep their hands to themselves, not to hurt other kids' feelings, and the like, but once they're out of the sandbox, we all stop—teachers, parents, everyone. We're too busy teaching them facts, or it's someone else's job. And so just when our kids' lives get more complicated, we stop helping them deal with the moral complexities of life. Right and wrong are day-to-day, moment-to-moment matters.

Keep looking down the road so you can prepare for problems and find clear paths. There's an old saying that one should eat like a king at breakfast, a prince at lunch, and a pauper at dinner. I think good parenting works a little like that. When children are young, parents have to be den mothers. They have to be at every meeting and make sure everything's following the course they set. In middle school they turn into coaches. They have to let the kids play, but they have to watch them while they do it, let them learn through lots of trial and error, and establish purpose. In high school it's about watching and acknowledging and helping them learn to solve problems. They're grown, but they still need you there, just in a different role. At every step a parent is nearby, always ready, always close, but moving out from an embrace to an arm's length. Being a Demand Parent in this way means thinking about parenting, not just reacting to situations. Aim high, my driving teacher told me, and that's true here as well.

Structure and discipline in the home are how Demand Parents mirror the expectations of the classroom. Active parenting requires structure in the home. When I was a kid, my father worked all kinds of jobs at all hours of the day and night, but even in the middle of constant movement from place to place, from job to job, my older sisters coming and going, his work, my school, he had rules. He had structure, and it's how I knew that he really did care and what he cared about. They weren't compulsive or cruel rules, simply things like always shine your shoes, eat at a particular time of day, make your bed, never mumble. If they weren't done for some reason, something was said about it. If my shoes were scuffed, he'd nod over and say, "I noticed your shoes are looking kind of bad." If I didn't speak up, he'd snap at me in a way that made me remember. The consequence was worse than the deed, as far as I was concerned, but no matter where he was or what he was doing, the rules let me know that I still operated in his world, under his care, that I was never alone.

A good home structure, in turn, can create discipline. Having a structured routine of chores, of reading, of practicing an instrument or a sport, setting a routine of things done on a repetitive basis, forms habits of the mind. True creativity, true art, derives from discipline, from nailing the basics, from learning how the tools work. It turns behaviors into ways of being; one who always acts polite *is* polite. And this is right where school and home mesh, along the line of structure and discipline. Though school and home are in many ways very different universes, we've discussed the need for them to share the same set of expectations for children.

That's why homework matters. First, in the context of teaching, homework is essentially an opportunity for your child to practice so he can advance his understanding and build his confidence. If you're a violinist, you practice. If you're a baseball player, you practice. Aside from developing the specific skills involved, homework used well teaches discipline and perseverance. Children come to understand that what they do in school and the perseverance they show in that first-period math, or English, or social studies class is expected elsewhere in their lives. It won't always be pleasant, but there are supports and diverse approaches, and if you think through it and use your mind, not your hands, you'll find a solution. Being present for homework and setting aside a time and place for its completion help children take risks, accept feedback, and build resilience. Even though it's hard, even though it's complicated, because my parents are here, I feel like I can belly up to the task.

The second major purpose of homework is that it lets school communicate with home and helps home align with school. Demand Parents ask what the homework is not because they necessarily understand the work but because they understand that homework is an extension of classroom expectations. They should want to know how long it will take and what other resources or materials their child may need in order to do it, and how their child processes the work forms a way for home and school to signal each other: Your child is doing well, or here is a place your child needs help; let's offer that help together. Parents don't need to be able to speak English to do this, they don't have to know the subject matter, but they do have to run their home in such a way that simply asking about homework becomes an extension of the classroom expectations. In a home, in any home, whether it be a homeless shelter or an affluent family's home, the expectation there is manifested by whether or not there is a place to study. Is there a place to exercise the discipline of putting your mind for a very specific time to a specific task? Demand Parents both know about homework and know how to make homework happen in their homes. Moreover, they know to make sure that it happens routinely. Preparing schools for the twenty-first century means getting home and school aligned, regardless of culture, language, or socioeconomics. Part of the mission for the Parent Academy is to help people learn that balance, to give them a sense of what the range of homework looks like, how discipline works, how they can begin to shape that in their homes.

There *is* such a thing as bad homework. This is a bit of a rarefied point, since our problem in America tends to be not that we have too much of it but that we have too little. Yet it's true that one of the emerging and quite unfortunate hallmarks of prestige schools is a constant piling on of homework of a sometimes make-work nature that seems to test the patience of parents more than the knowledge of children. It's impossible to judge the value of some of these projects, and they do often seem to overreach in demanding parental participation more than parental oversight. Demand Parents who have learned the balance will not be afraid to judge the value of this kind of homework themselves.

DEMAND PARENTS AT HOME MUST

- *Talk with their children about what they're learning in school.*

- *Make sure their child is completing all homework assignments.*

- *Make reading a priority.*

- *Try to schedule at least one family mealtime together every day.*

- *Make sure their child is getting eight to nine hours of sleep every night.*

- *Respect their children.* Being a Demand Parent does not mean belittling, berating, or otherwise subverting your child's developmental process. Beyond treating him with love and respect at all times, it means not abusing or interfering in his relationships with the rest of the world. If you think your son should be starting at third base, don't undermine his relationship with the team and his coaches by throwing your voice or your weight around. Kids gotta get what they get and deal with it. They need to learn how to navigate all different kinds of situations, and while you need to monitor them, you can't be a third wheel trying to force intricate and often intimate relationships in directions you think best.

- *Tell their children they love them every day.*

- *Never give up.* I do not accept personal surrender from a parent. You do not have the right to just simply say, "Okay, I quit. This is too hard." You have the right to say, "I need more information, I need more help, I can't do this right now. I need to gather myself." But you don't have the right to say to your child, "I give up," because you are the protective envelope for that youngster. Once you remove that protective envelope, he knows deep in himself that nothing separates him from the cruel, harsh reality of the world, and he becomes a carnivore. He is exposed to the elements, and that's a very different kind of mind that child now has. That's an emotionally wounded person who is now going to say, "In order for me to not be wounded any further, instead of building confidence, I'm going to exude confidence. Instead of me worrying about being bullied, I'll bully somebody else." Parents do not have the right to give up.

In the end, I want every parent to feel the kind of love and admiration I have for my father. He wasn't a mover and shaker, or a rich man or a star, but he involved himself in my life. He held me up above the waves and taught me how to swim for myself, even though many days I feel that I'm really still just standing on his shoulders.

DEMAND PARENTS IN THE COMMUNITY

When my father laid down the law to me about going to college, I took him very seriously, but I was a normal boy and you know I had that energy. I wanted to go to Scottie's party and the block dances and picnics at Bear Mountain. Trying to get a date with Carol or Angela definitely battled with algebra for the front part of my brain. And so one day I completely lost my mind and cut school to go uptown and hang with some friends. Everywhere I went, I ran into one of the old folks who knew me. "Where you going?" they'd ask me in that stern church voice. "You don't have school? You don't have football practice? Well, you say hello to your father for me." Or worse, "I'll tell your father I ran into you this morning." I never did that again, because the street corners were full of people in my Amen Corner, all the moms and dads and people in my community who stepped in when skipping school seemed like a good idea to me. Those people believed in me as much as they believed in their own children, and when I didn't connect the dots and my father wasn't around to make me do it, they accepted the responsibility to set me right. We have to care about all our children, not just our own. It takes a village to raise a child, but that doesn't just mean everyone else has to be your child's village; you have to do the same for theirs.

Though the primary work of Connected Schools is about education, they can also do the work we need in stitching the communities of this nation back together. Even in big cities, America is truly a series of small towns, and together those small towns build the nation. I remember being in Minnesota once on Memorial Day, driving cross-country with one of my sons, when we came across an enormous parade with what looked like every person in town watching and applauding the local heroes. At that moment I thought to myself, *I could live here. If it just wasn't so cold in the winter.* That parade made me feel good, though, the way it feels for a ninth grader to be included in something on the opening day of school. I belonged. We don't belong anymore. Our communities are becoming more and more simply a matter of geography, and we all suffer for that. Our kids suffer and schooling suffers.

Connected Schools can regenerate our communities. As I've already said, schools are the most basic point of contact we have with the body politic, but this doesn't have to express itself just through power issues. It starts with the involvement of Demand Parents. Parent clubs bring people together with common interests and goals and create an environment where young people see their parents working together on issues, wrestling with them themselves and with others, and modeling what it means to become a persevering adult. When parents see the connection between all the children around them, when they see all children as *their* children, a community begins to re-form. Parent clubs and school committees are just a start; once Demand Parents become involved in school, they're much more likely to engage in the community around them.

DEMAND PARENTS PLAY A ROLE IN THE COMMUNITY BY

- *Volunteering at school*, in after-school programs, at church, as a coach.

- *Speaking out when they see things.*

- *Making friends*, or at least staying in contact, with other parents in their children's classes.

- *Comparing notes with other parents* and laying down a consistent standard of behavior.

- *Being active participants in the places they live.* They go to museums, walk the streets, sign petitions, talk about politics.

- *Voting.* And talking about it with their children. They go to jury duty and talk to their kids about what it is and why citizens have to do it. Schools can teach civic awareness, but

it's up to Demand Parents to show how it fits into the daily
life of all Americans. Our democracy is re-created every
morning, depending on who wakes up and decides to participate that day.

With the parents and the school now blended into one body, now
the other elements of the broader community—the arts community, businesses, institutions of higher education, faith communities, and the like—must rise and be counted. Those groups have a
responsibility to bring themselves to their local schools and school
systems. There's not a public school in this nation that does not
welcome the interest and support of local organizations. For a few
hours a week, a community garden can be a hands-on science lab,
a Civil War–reenacting club a gateway to history, a darkroom a
place where children learn to see the world around them in a new
way. Service organizations can incorporate or create programs that
develop hands-on student leadership. But they can't wait to be
asked; they must step forward to offer themselves and their resources to help children acquire Civic Awareness and the other
three qualities of a mature and conscious contributor to society.

THE ROLE OF THE ARTS COMMUNITY

Orchestras and museums can't continue to moan about falling attendance, the lack of interest in classical music and dance, if they
don't understand that their future is sitting right now in their local
public school. In England the national lottery makes all museums
free. A wealth of family programming and materials creates the
sense that art is not an exclusive world apart but a functional aspect of daily life. In New York, on the other hand, a visit to the
Museum of Modern Art costs an adult $20, and there's much more
attention paid to making tourists feel they've done something sophisticated than there is to integrating a sense of aesthetics into the

lives of a family. We seem to have all but written off ballet as an expensive hobby for little girls and classical music and even jazz as the province of snobs and senior citizens.

If the arts in America want to do better than just survive, they have to throw in with the concept of Connected Schools and aggressively offer themselves to public schools. The American arts community must realign its mission and take ultimate responsibility for driving American arts education. Vast amounts of money go to the arts community, but too little of it is spent on marketing a demand in the generations to come. Don't hand over childhood to video games and the Pussycat Dolls and then scratch your head when young adults don't care about Monet. Paying $50 million for a Jackson Pollock is fine, I guess, but imagine what could happen if a museum invested that $50 million in a citywide art program that pooled the best resources of instruction and material, that brought art to classrooms and, in turn, families of all incomes and classes to the museum. What would the long-term benefit be to not just the institution but the entire city? I'll say it again—the arts are not "extras." They are fundamental to education and to society, and public schools need more help from the arts community to reinvigorate them throughout America. To their credit, many in the arts community are waking up to this reality and creating connective solutions. For example, in 2006 *The New York Times* reported that the Juilliard School and Carnegie Hall had begun a program to send music fellows into the New York public school system to teach music. In return for "high-level musical training, performance opportunities at Carnegie Hall and guidance from city school teachers in how to teach music," the musicians will spend a day and a half each week at an assigned school.

Here are some other ways the arts community can connect with schools:

- *Join forces with institutions like Juilliard and Carnegie Hall to develop curricula for all grade levels*, based on a given discipline's own assets. A large museum such as the Metropolitan Museum of Art or the Art Institute of Chicago could create a template that local art museums could illustrate with their own holdings. One way or another, don't leave it to the schools. You are the ones who know your fields the best; convey your knowledge and your love.

- *Bring art to the students*, not just students to the art. Reintegrating arts into American life and American schools will mean starting a dialogue. Worry less about selling souvenirs of your art in the new, expanded gift shop and consider giving it away in the form of education—that's the long-term investment.

- *Open doors to families.* Art museums must be more child-friendly. There are ways to attract young visitors that aren't patronizing or commercial. Start with letting every child bring a parent in for free. More concerts and performances must be created with children and families in mind. Where is the next Leonard Bernstein?

- *Advocate for arts spending in the schools.* The tax relief you and your major donors enjoy comes out of someone's pocket; let's hope it's not taking the paintbrush out of a child's hand.

- *Encourage artists themselves to participate.* If we make arts = institution, we lose. Children must meet living, breathing painters, actors, writers, dancers, and sculptors who eat food, tell jokes, make money, and in general prove that the arts belong to all humans, not just the ones who can afford them. Visit schools and make the arts live for our children.

- *Offer internships.* Internships and mentorships are valuable to those interested in making a living in the arts community, a field where making a living can be a great challenge.

THE ROLE OF THE BUSINESS COMMUNITY

Transferring school skills to work skills is not an easy or obvious process, and young adults can have a treacherous time with it. How will their skills—academic, but also personal, civic, and work-place—be used in a work setting? Will they really matter? Are there things they're not learning in school that they'll need? What will they need to change about themselves? As currently conceived, nei-ther schools nor businesses answer these kinds of questions. Going forward into a flat world will require greater conversation between institutions that teach and hire young people. Connected Schools look to the business community for ways to create more trans-parency about the transfer process for our students who are soon to be out in the working world.

While the model of Connected Schools is based on having the superintendent identify needs and resources, businesses need to be proactive in looking for ways to partner with the school system. Help create your labor force and consumers and leaders of tomor-row, and do it with more than sponsoring signage opportunities. Support aspects of education that intersect with your own business through mentorships and internships. Bring young people into the workings of your organization, and this doesn't just mean large, faceless corporations. It can mean every level of business, down to the vegetable market on the corner.

THE BUSINESS COMMUNITY MUST

- *Keep score.* Make it necessary for communities to know what's happening with their schools. Even if the politicians aren't interested, the business community must assume lead-ership in this area.

- *Keep the conversation going.* Keep the ball in play, not just from a critical standpoint, but from a positive one as well. Make the news public. Show your support. Call for action.

- *Cause others to weigh in.* When people put their children in public school, it's because other people do it. The more businesspeople who are active parents within a system, the more Demand Parents there will be who can not only advocate from within but train others to do so down the line.

- *Demand performance.* Join the voice of your business community to the voices of parents demanding quality schools. When no one demands, a system goes to sleep. When the business and philanthropic communities show up, it matters.

- *Serve as an intermediary with local and state government.* Those who use the product of the schools—mature and conscious contributors to society—must be the ones who champion the issue of school effectiveness. Announce the fact that you employ graduates of the local school system and make their value to you clearly heard.

- *Offer programs that have an impact on individual students.* Internships, mentorships, and other direct partnership programs are key to Connected Schools.

- *Recognize that the curriculum of the business community and a business environment is not necessarily the details of your specific business.* The point is for young people to learn how business is done, the rules of the road, not the specifics. The details of your patented widget-making process are useful to them only inasmuch as they can teach them about how to work in and create their own processes.

THE ROLE OF INSTITUTIONS OF HIGHER EDUCATION

Education in America is essentially divided into two pieces: K–12, and then secondary education, meaning college and advanced degrees. Historically, college has been an achievement for millions of striving Americans. A young person had to earn passage through the ivy-covered gates to attain the higher status and higher wages offered within, and there remains something healthy about this. As we've discussed, college isn't right for everyone, and the way to meet the challenges of the global economy is not to simply produce millions more undereducated college graduates. But as colleges and universities expand their roles in advancing knowledge in order to generate intellectual, economic, and even moral growth, they must not pull up the bridges behind them, because the future is in those elementary and secondary schools. Institutions of higher learning have a great responsibility to participate in the education and well-being of their coming applicants.

In terms of Connected Schools, there are countless ways colleges and universities can interact with pre-K–12 education that will both provide services to those schools and help advance their own young scholars. They must

- *Expand their platform of services.* Schools of dentistry can match up with local schools to provide checkups and education; schools of ophthalmology can do the same. Any professional program demands practice, and we have thousands upon thousands of children who need services. Making this kind of connection doesn't take an act of Congress; it just takes a phone call and a desire on the part of the secondary school to interact with the community around it.

- *Invest in research that addresses real problems that face schools.* Theories and abstraction are important, but their true value comes when they can be used to solve problems. We need you to apply your brainpower and resources to real life.

- *Support teachers.* Our teachers come from your universities. Find ways to tangibly support the development of teachers within your communities, and not just the ones who graduated from your college. Believe it or not, kindergarten and seventh-grade teachers are just as much educators as your professors, and their impact on the world can be more profound than any number of esoteric pursuits I've seen in academe. Share your knowledge and your expertise. Reward scholar-educators for practical work within school systems as much as if not more than for writing journal articles.

- *Show their schools to our students.* Don't wall yourselves off from the community. Find ways to bring K–12 students in and make higher education a reality in their minds.

THE ROLE OF THE FAITH COMMUNITY

I support the right of individuals to choose where they send their children to school. My goal is to make our public schools so terrific that you'll want to send your children there, not to compel you to do so. In that spirit, then, I ask the faith communities around America to understand the profound importance public education has to everyone in this country. The faith community should

- *Play a role in advocating for children* who do not have Demand Parents or one adult devoted to their individual cause.

- *Vocally support public education* as a matter of social justice.

- *Adopt a school* and create a one-to-one relationship with that school community that includes mentoring young men and women, acting as a neighborhood watch, and so on.

THE ROLE OF THE SERVICE COMMUNITY

Personal Integrity and Civic Awareness are qualities that must be developed through interaction with others. You can tell yourself that you're a contributor to the community at large, but if you don't actually *do* anything, then at best you're a bundle of potential. Our children want to serve; they want to lead; they want to make a difference. We need the service communities—the nonprofits, the food banks, the YMCAs, and the Scouts—to help create opportunities for them to do that. The service community must

- *Bring its programs to our schools.* While enriching our after-school programs, you can spread your message and serve your cause. Kids need clubs to belong to, activities to plan, goals to work toward, and given the realities of today's budgets, schools are hard-pressed to provide them. The hearts of children are like kindling, and a great idea, a good cause, can set them aflame. Bring your fire to us.

- *Not treat our children as charity.* Instead, help us teach them to help others. Finding a way within himself to put others first strengthens a child's self-esteem a thousand times more than self-pity. Caring doesn't just heal the one being cared for; it heals the one doing the caring, too. Children will benefit from learning that giving of themselves is more important than receiving.

- *Understand children's limits.* We are training our children to serve, so it's the process I care most about. Joining a club and participating in its activities teach commitment, follow-through, cooperation, leadership, negotiating skills— I could go on.

- *Introduce children to the world.* For all the talk about diversity in our country, children of different colors and classes still don't know enough about each other. When possible, create activities that don't simply bring together different kinds of children, but that ask them to work together toward a goal. We need your help in teaching our children the diplomacy skills they'll need in a global economy and a pluralistic democracy.

The benefits of all this weaving and webbing go way beyond their impact on the students. These businesses and community groups and arts groups become integrated with the lives of families and, by cooperating on partnerships with the Connected Schools, with each other. The entire community can now speak to one another through its schools. *The light is here*, we say. *This is the garden where we meet as one people to create our future.*

THE ROLE OF THE PHILANTHROPIC COMMUNITY

As we discussed in Chapter Seven, philanthropy can play a major role in the future of American public education.

THE PHILANTHROPIC COMMUNITY MUST

- *Declare the value of public education.*

- *Decry the low standards to which we hold our children's education.*

- *Direct the conversation to education for globalization and democracy.*

And what will our children bring back to us?

I remember one night when I was at Babson. My father called me.

"Son," he said, "I need you to come home. It's an emergency." He had never asked me to do this before, so I immediately thought it was something medical; he had cancer or something. "I'm having a little get-together with some of my old musician friends and I want you to come home."

This, at least, was a relief, though it was still strange. "Yeah, I guess that's okay, Pop. But is there a problem or something?"

"No, but I need you to bring some of your books with you, some of your big books from college."

"Pop, what is it you really need me to come home for?"

"Well, I was talking to them about you being in college, what you studying. A lot of these people never been to college, never seen the inside of a dormitory, things I saw when I brought you there. I thought it'd be a nice thing if you came and talked to them about college."

I said, "I'm more than willing to come home, Pop, but what is it *exactly* you want me to talk to these people about? I mean, I'm studying economics and accounting and . . ."

And right there he got hot. "All right, here's the situation. I need you to come home and talk college to them. Talk like you're talking college. Show 'em all the books, the words and everything, explain all about college to them."

I got tickled on the phone, I'm laughing to myself, but I'd do anything he asked me to do, so I drove back to New York the next weekend with five or six accounting books in the backseat, Samuelson on economics, John Kenneth Galbraith, all that. It was Saturday night, and when I came into the house, there were all his friends sitting in the little room. All of them had their little walking sticks and their little brimmed hats, and I looked around and thought, *What the hell am I supposed to do here?*

Just before I went into the room, I pulled my father aside. "Pop," I said, "I really don't have a lot to say."

He said, "Son, I'm gonna tell you something. There's a lot of people here ain't never seen the inside of a college. And they've lived all their lives hearing about college, thinking about college, hearing other people talk about college, watching the white people go to college. They don't have one stitch of information that attaches to their dream of having been in college. When I was a young man playing music, I wanted to play Carnegie Hall, and truth be known, I lived half my life in New York and I never even got to go in Carnegie Hall. Before I die, I want to go into Carnegie Hall, and before these people die, they want to at least hear somebody who has been in that place called college. Now, your job is to go in there and talk some college to them like I told you when I talked to you on the phone."

And so I went in and sat down, and I explained to them what we did in college, how you registered for classes. I put all my books up on the counter table, and they paged through them and held them, weighed them in their hands.

"Oooh, Lord, there's a lot of information in here," said one old man.

With all my freshman hubris and what my father had said, I'd expected them all to sit there in rapture, hanging on my every word, but the truth was, I might as well have been talking to the wall. They looked sort of interested, mostly bored. What was most strange, though, was the mood. I'd walked in there full of judgment of these old folks, and instead I felt as if I were the one being judged somehow. And yet "judge" isn't the right word. I had the sense that I was somehow paying off a debt, that I was there on approval, that I in some way owed them this dog and pony show.

I looked at the old man hefting Samuelson in his hand, the wrinkles across his face like dry earth cracking in the sun. He'd worked hard.

And then I realized why I was there. I *did* owe them.

Standing there in front of the generation before me, I saw men and women who had suffered, literally suffered in body and soul and mind, so that I would be able to walk the ivy halls of Babson College and rub shoulders with the mighty. They may not have personally contributed to my upbringing—I'd never seen most of them before in my life—but they had plowed the field, planted the seeds of possibility that my father had tended, and now I was merely the harvester. The point of my father's little party was for me to put the fruits of their generations of labor on the table for all of them to see. This was *their* victory as much as mine. I was connected to them. Each one of them was Moses, viewing a promised land ahead they'd led me to in a way, a promised land they would never enter. But one they'd now seen.

We are all Moses, leading our children to the borders of a future that we will not share, just as our parents had before us. There will be new wonders and new horrors, and our grandchildren will dream of things that we will not understand. Globalization is not a far-fetched theory or something to be feared. Our children can either sit back and watch it happen or jump in and help direct its flow. Connected Schools will teach them how to do that. If we grow our children into mature and conscious adults, if we teach them to connect in every way possible with the world around them, they will come back for us.

This is my first book, but the thoughts, feelings, and impressions have lived inside me since childhood. Let me tip my hat to Arthur Sulzberger, Jr., for convincing me that there was something unique to be said about American education. But it is my father who said it exactly right: "Anything worth having is worth working for." And so, I dedicate this book to my father, the man whose character was my first curriculum and whose soul was my first classroom. I am sure that he and his musician friends in heaven are humbly making room in a tidy little corner for a copy of this book. I feel proud to have had a life of walking alongside him as a son and learning with him as my teacher.

My children, Rudy, Ryan, Russell, and Lauren, serve as a constant reminder that growing up is hard, but made slightly easier when you know the rules of the road. In some ways those rules haven't changed from generation to generation. I love my children for the people they are, and the person they've made me be.

Big city school systems mimic small towns in some sense. I am forever grateful for the friendship and loyalty to the cause of many wonderful people I have met throughout my career. They are far too numerous to name here, but I have had the pleasure of serving children alongside them in school systems in Los Angeles County; Boston, Massachusetts; Sacramento, California; Tacoma, Washington; New York City; and now Miami, Florida. Wherever you are, stay strong. You are the best of the best.

R.C.

In New York, thanks to Linda Movish, Ted Brodheim, Donna Smiley, Melinda Moore, and Liz Sostre for their ideas, assistance, and inspiration; to our agents David Kuhn and Lisa Bankoff for always being in our corner. At Farrar, Straus and Giroux, Jonathan Galassi understood this book from the start; Jeff Seroy and Sarita Varma saw the way to spread the word; and Rose Lichter-Marck kept all the trains on time. Most of all, we thank Sarah Crichton. Without her enthusiasm, her encouragement, and her strong, smart editing, this book wouldn't have happened.

F.D.

Rudy Crew, Ed.D., is the superintendent of schools for Miami-
Dade County Public Schools, the fourth-largest school system in
the country. He was formerly the chancellor of the New York City
public school system, the nation's largest. He has been superintendent or deputy superintendent of schools in Tacoma, Sacramento,
and Boston. Dr. Crew has won numerous awards across America
for his work as an educator and administrator.

Rudy Crew, Ed.D., is the superintendent of schools for Miami-Dade County Public Schools, the fourth-largest school system in the country. He was formerly the chancellor of the New York City public school system, the nation's largest. He has been superintendent or deputy superintendent of schools in Tacoma, Sacramento, and Boston. Dr. Crew has won numerous awards across America for his work as an educator and administrator.